THE COMPLETE
KWANZAA

ALSO BY DOROTHY WINBUSH RILEY

MY SOUL LOOKS BACK 'LESS I FORGET: A COLLECTION OF QUOTATIONS BY PEOPLE OF COLOR

THE COMPLETE
KWANZAA
CELEBRATING OUR CULTURAL HARVEST

DOROTHY WINBUSH RILEY

Editor of *My Soul Looks Back 'Less I Forget*

Line drawings by David Calloway appear on the opening pages of the chapters "Umoja," "Kujichagulia," "Ujima," "Ujamaa," "Nia," "Kuumba," and "Imani."

Copyright acknowledgments appear on pages 375-76.

THE COMPLETE KWANZAA. Copyright © 1995 by Dorothy Winbush Riley. All rights reserved. Printed in the United States of America. No part of this book may be used or reproduced in any manner whatsoever without written permission except in the case of brief quotations embodied in critical articles and reviews. For information address HarperCollins Publishers, Inc., 10 East 53rd Street, New York, NY 10022.

HarperCollins books may be purchased for educational, business, or sales promotional use. For information please write: Special Markets Department, HarperCollins Publishers, Inc., 10 East 53rd Street, New York, NY 10022.

FIRST EDITION

Designed by Gloria Adelson/Lulu Graphics
Design Assistant: Nina Gaskin

Library of Congress Cataloging-in-Publication Data

Riley, D. Winbush (Dorothy Winbush)
    The complete Kwanzaa : celebrating our cultural harvest / Dorothy Riley.
       p. cm.
    Includes bibliographical references and index.
    ISBN 0-06-017215-0
    1. Kwanzaa. 2. Afro-Americans—Social life and customs.
  I. Title.
  GT4403.R56   1995
  394.2'61—dc20   95-35963

95 96 97 98 99 ❖/HC 10 9 8 7 6 5 4 3 2 1

Dedicated to my mother, Odessa;
my children, Tiaudra, Robert, Schiavi, and Ted;
to my little helpers, Nandi and Martay;
and to all who come from the
original source: Africa

CONTENTS

SPECIAL THANKS

To my children, Schiavi, Ted, Robert, and Tiaudra, for their unity and self-determination that freed me to work continuously without worry or interruption.

To my editor at HarperCollins, Peternelle van Arsdale, who understands cultural needs and used her keen, probing questions to edit and shape this book from the hundreds of pages I sent her.

To my nephew, Martay, and my granddaughter, Nandi, for their enthusiasm and ears that listened to each story and fable.

To my friends, Rosa Williams, Louise Kirks, Gloria Jones, Shirley Lusby, and Sherlin McNeal, for their faith, support, and encouragement.

To my agent, Marie Brown, for her guidance and understanding.

To each writer, artist, poet, publisher, author, and friend whose Kuumba provided the materials for this book.

To the city and school librarians of Detroit, especially Beverly Mayfield and Gail Gilman.

AN INTRODUCTION TO KWANZAA

HARVEST OF FIRST FRUITS

Time is the boundary of the mind, body, and soul. Before humans captured time in illusory hours and days, they used the cycles of the planets, from sunrise to sunrise, from one new moon to the next, to measure time. All life involves the passage of time—all experiences have a beginning, middle, and end. The awareness of time, past, present, and future, enabled ancient societies to see a continuous cycle in which change takes place. Each event represents the never-ending circle of ending-beginning and beginning-ending, starting at the close of one year and the opening of another.

Time is infinite, all enveloping and eternal. Humankind created rituals or minidramas that engraved order and acceptance of the circular cycle in the minds of the partici-pants. Such rites are common in every society and establish and maintain cultural identity. The rituals of each cycle may not vary, but the individual experiences of the partici-pants cannot be duplicated. For this reason, we can never go back in time and recapture the drama of an ancient harvest celebration, just as no one will ever duplicate the first observance of Kwanzaa.

Stone Age Africans survived by hunting wild animals and gathering berries, seeds, and roots. They were nomadic, following the seasonal changes and the migrations of animals, until the development of agriculture revolutionized their lifestyles. The magical significance of seasonal change grew as the early Africans learned to cultivate crops and tame animals in permanent villages. Need, promise, fulfillment, and harvest were key milestones in the eternal cycle of winter, spring, summer, and fall. The ancestors believed that each season was delicate, crucial, and sacred, so they created specific rites to ensure the completion of the natural order of the universe. Ancient folktales relate how beliefs in prayer rituals, sacrifice, and magic caused fertile spring to return after the death at winter and thus ensured the survival of the tribe.

The calendars of African countries were filled with festivals that celebrated all important events. Harvest festivals usually began in late December and continued for seven or eight days until the first day of the new year, with each day having a special meaning attached to it. The villagers glorified the first fruits of the harvest with dancing and feasting. All were rewarded for their Umoja (unity) in planting the seeds, Kujichagulia (self-determination) for tending the fields, and Ujima (collective work and responsibility) for survival. Welcoming the harvest was a common practice, but each society celebrated its own. The Egyptians' festival was Pert-In-Min (the Coming Forth of Min); the Zulu celebrated Umkhosi; the Sudanese observed the millet festival; the Swazi feted Incwala; the Ashanti, Ibo, and Yoruba commemorated the New Yam Festival, offering the ancestor a fine piece of yam with other gifts of oil or meat; and the Hausas celebrated the "feast of the full stomach," when

RECLAMATION

Honoring the ancestors is one aspect of Kwanzaa that we need to reclaim. American life boxes us in a tiny frame of time removed from the past and the future. We must reclaim our birthright, as the people of Africa, India, South America, and Latin America do, realizing that those who have gone before are ever present, that their spirit is endless and everlasting.

Close your eyes as you slip back in time to reclaim our ancestors. Slip from beneath the quilt pieced together with fragments of grandma's and grandpa's lives. Slip into a dream to spirit you back to your childhood, to your birth, to the time of your parents, to the lap of your grandmother, to the arms of your grandfather, to the faces of generations named and unnamed. Dream, floating past Harlem and Chicago, over the trail of our people migrating from the South, over the wars and the plantations. Linger in South Carolina, watching our people gather indigo, and then hover over the ships from across the oceans that are docked in the harbor with our people chained on board. Catch a cloud, ride to the motherland, and tower over the Pyramids, watching the astronomers chart the stars and medicine men heal magically: Watch our people.

Float on, down the Nile River into the valley, staying with the dream until you see the tribal villages with your image mirrored in the faces around the compounds. Move, until you find the nomadic tribes wandering through the forested paradise over the plains. Join the dance and praise the gods in the harvest festival around the sacred fire lighting your return to Mother Africa, the mother of civilization.

Awake and reclaim the ancestors who gave you the gift of life and the shape of your head, the slant of your eyes, the texture of your hair, the roundness of your buttocks, the rhythm of your feet, the fullness of your lips, the color of

guests ate all the chicken or meat they could hold. Regardless of the location, all first-fruit festivities had five things in common: gathering, reverence, commemoration, recommitment, and celebration.

To open the festival, the ruler or chief said a prayer of gratitude for the richness of the year, good health, strength, and families. The chief poured a portion of the libation, from a special cup, on the ground for any ancestors who might be present and passed the cup around for all to share. Then feasting with music, dancing, and storytelling began. The modern celebration of Kwanzaa, like the ancient rituals, maintains our part in the cosmic rhythm of the universe.

THE ORIGIN OF KWANZAA

Kwanzaa is an African American holiday, which intertwines African traditions with American customs, that is celebrated from December 26 through January 1. It was first celebrated on December 26, 1966, in Los Angeles, by Dr. Maulena Karenga, his family, and friends. Karenga had organized ancient wisdom based on six criteria of a people—history, mythology, creativity, social structure, political organization, and economics—into this African American holiday. The core principles of Kwanzaa, the Nguzo Saba (the Seven Principles), which Karenga expressed in Swahili, a language of East Africa, are Umoja (unity), Kujichagulia (self-determination), Ujima (collective work and responsibility), Ujamaa (cooperative economics), Nia (purpose), Kuumba (creativity), and Imani (faith). The seven symbols associated with Kwanzaa, also expressed in Swahili, are mazao (fruits, vegetables, and nuts), mkeka (place mat), kinara (candleholder), vibunzi (ear of corn), zawadi (gifts), kikombe cha umoja (communal cup of unity), and mishumbaa saba (seven candles).

All ethnic groups seek acceptance in society and their place in the universal order. And each group, through holidays, demonstrates its interpretation of human experience: the purposes of life, the ways to achieve them, and the goals they wish to attain. Holidays are a time to enjoy the laughter of friends and relatives, to eat special food, to remember traditions, and to honor the ancestors. The seven-day observance of Kwanzaa focuses on timeless, universal truths—principles that are pillars of faith, rooted in our traditions, and give us purpose, identity, and direction.

Kwanzaa is an outgrowth of many customs, joined with ancient African tribal practices, that reconstruct our national history and culture. Tribal values of unity and self-determination, along with love, hope, and imagination, arrived in America with the kidnapped African men and women who built this country. Kwanzaa celebrates the survival of these traditions and helps us not only make sense of experiences, both ordinary and extraordinary, but find a deeper purpose to life. Historically, African Americans desperately needed faith, determination, courage, and an abiding hope in the future. Society has changed little in this regard, so we still need the values and philosophies of the ancestors to provide guidance and perspective. Kwanzaa helps African Americans apply the universal principles—grow and change, live and love, create and build, honor and respect— to our everyday lives, using our own creative energy. According to Karenga, "the core principles of Kwanzaa . . . , which I developed and proposed during the Black Cultural Revolution of the sixties [are] a necessary minimum set of principles by which Black people must live in order to begin to rescue and reconstruct our history and lives."

Kwanzaa unites nuclear families and extended families, reaffirming that we must live in reciprocal dependence, while seeking dignity, justice, and equality. It is a system that welcomes change, celebrating the present while planning for tomorrow. This modern holiday allows Africa's children, scattered on every continent, a way to preserve the details of the motherland and to enjoy prosperity, by using ancient wisdom to solve today's problems. The modern harvest is not confined to one season; it is a continuous sowing and reaping of thoughts planted in our minds. We no longer bond in villages, but assemble in sororities, fraternities, churches, schools, and clubs.

During Kwanzaa, we reverently retell the stories of contemporaries and ancestors, or how we "got over." We know that whatever was sown in the preceding seasons has been reaped, and we accept these results. It does not matter whether the fruit is positive or negative; the harvest determines our direction and recommitment for the new year. On the last day of Kwanzaa, the seeds of the future are decided and sown; the celebration ends with a new cycle growth, beginning in freedom or shackled to the pa Thus, Kwanzaa builds on the power of culture and roots plant seeds today for the harvest of tomorrow, gather families to remember success and recommit themselves more purposeful lives under the sacred seven principles

Success is available to everyone, and the principle Kwanzaa present universal beliefs that are found in m other cultures. However, the holiday also presents ur guidelines for Africa's children. Although we cele Kwanzaa the last week of the year, we must live the t ings each moment of every day, physically, morally spiritually. If you wanted to sing like Whitney Ho would you think of your music only once a week? wanted to compose music like Duke Ellington, wou do it once a month? If you wanted to be a champion like Michael Jordan, would you abuse your body, your meals, and skip routine practice? Every da year we must apply and practice the Nguzo Saba and faithfully to harvest success.

your eyes, and the earth tone of your skin. Look into the brown eyes of your child and see the ancestors' eyes peering back at you. Stroke the sun-toasted skin of your daughter; it is the ancestors you are touching. The ancestors speak with your voice, walk with your stride, smile through your mouth, and hear with your ears. Reclaim those who struggled for life and your right to look in a mirror—and see your grandchildren's ancestors.

THE SACRED SEVEN

Children are the heart of Kwanzaa, and we transmit our cultural beliefs and values through them. It was because of children that I first learned about Kwanzaa as a student teacher in the 1960s, when I planned a classroom celebration. My first question then was, "Why are there seven principles? Why aren't there four or twelve or even ten?" I have since learned how fitting it is that Kwanzaa involves seven principles that are celebrated for seven days using seven symbols.

The number seven has always been considered sacred, and with it, humankind has been given all the tools, all the materials, needed to prosper. Metaphysically, the number infuses dreams and the application of practical research that lay the foundation for solving life's problems. The great religions of the world accept seven as a mystical number of the Creator. It represents all things metaphysical, such as the work of priests and monks, prophets, researchers, artists, inventors, composers, and musicians. Seven is a holy digit denoting truth, wisdom, acceptance, perfection, and understanding. The Creator made the world in six stages, or six days, and rested on the seventh, the day of completion, or rest. Our bodies replace cells and completely renew themselves every seven years.

In the Christian and Jewish faiths seven occurs repeatedly: God's instruction to Noah to build an ark and place animals in it "by sevens," the seven days of creation, God blessing the seventh day, the seven kine and seven ears of corn in Pharaoh's dream. For seven days, seven princes with seven trumpets invested Jericho, and on the seventh day they encompassed the city seven times. In addition, the three great Jewish feasts each last for seven days, and between the first and third are seven weeks, and the just fall seven times a day. There were also the seven brothers married to the same woman, the seven loaves that fed four thousand, and the seventy-seven times a person should forgive.

Muslims also view seven as having special significance. Pious Muslims must circle the Kaaba in Mecca seven times and call out "Allah akbar" seven times. They must shower the Devil with three times seven stones at Mina. They speak of seven cardinal sins and seven inner meanings of the Koran. Islamic literature refers to seven candles, seven spiritual robes, seven heavens, seven earths, and seven spiritual leaders.

Seven is sacred to the Cherokee Nation as well, who use it in ceremonies, rituals, art, social activities, and government and consider it the mystical number of rebirth and return. Seven Clans and Seven Clan Districts signify the unity of the Cherokee people and the entire world.

Seven symbolizes the prober who walks unexplored paths, delving beneath the surface to see what is really there, only to discover universal truths. By 1966, when Karenga presented the Nguzo Saba, African Americans had experienced psychic, psychological, physical, and sociological changes. From the fifteenth through the nineteenth century, America gelded Africans into African Americans by destroying their entire historical context, with its inherent goals, purpose, cultural identification, and definition. Yet in the 1960s, African Americans, like those of the 1800s, demonstrated, defending the historical and cultural connection of Africa to her children. The greatest need was the quest for truth to develop cultural acceptance and to revitalize the African past.

So the potter sitting at his work,
And turning the wheel about with his feet,
Who is always anxious about his work,
and maketh all his work by number.

The Apocrypha

UNIVERSAL PRINCIPLES

In *The Science of the Mind*, Ernest Holmes tells us there is a universal mind, spirit, and intelligence that is the origin of everything. The universal mind contains all knowledge and is the potential knowledge of all things. We call the teachings universal laws—divine creative principles that are timeless truths. We live in a universe of law and order, and there are principles by which all our life's experiences, conditions, and events take place. The basic law of life is the law of belief, which, according to Mark 9:23 is, "If you can believe, all things are possible to him that believes."

As an educator, I believe and practice the universal principles by explaining them to my students. At first, my students didn't understand these principles, since they could not see the invisible force ruling their minds or their beliefs. After they researched outstanding African Americans, however, they discovered that success begins when one's mind, free of confusion and doubt, works toward prosperity, health, and success. Consequently, my students learned that success is relative to the distance traveled and the ultimate satisfaction one gains from victory over obstacles and that it does not always mean how much money one has. Some may think of success as material gain (money and comfort), but others may focus on family or children. True wealth and prosperity are as expansive as the heart.

I told my students how thoughts of success entered my mind when I was six years old. One day, while I was playing with a group of children in a vacant field in southwest Detroit, a Hungarian woman planted a seed in my mind. She wore huge gold earrings that were as bright as the sun and a skirt that was long and full. (To this day I love long flowing skirts.) She floated toward the field and asked me, "What is your name?"

"Dorothy," I said.

"Ah, your name means the gift of God, and I see one day that you will be a great teacher," she replied.

Her words meant nothing to me until the sixth grade, when I discovered that Dorothy does mean the gift of God. I remembered the gleaming earrings on the woman and thought that if she was right about my name, maybe she was right about me being a great teacher. From that point on, I controlled my behavior and my grades to make her prediction come true.

My students listened to the story, and during the semester, their self-esteem increased as their grades and achievement soared. Many understood that the first ingredient of success is a positive sense of who and what you are. Success demands that you set and reach goals through a focused vision that includes educational preparation, decision making, and commitments early in life—values celebrated by Kwanzaa.

One year, a seventh grader said to me. "Mrs. Riley, I want to be in your class, but you only teach the smart kids." I told him, "No, I teach all the children to use their minds, and at the end of the year each one is smart." In my classes, we celebrated minisuccesses because life is ongoing and success occurs daily. My students achieved after I applied the cosmic laws to them; they believed, as I believed, that each individual has the ability to succeed against overwhelming obstacles.

About ten years ago, I realized that the Nguzo Saba and universal principles *are* cut from the same great truths. When I started research for *The Complete Kwanzaa*, the connection became even more obvious. If I could create an educational course, it would be based on understanding the universal laws, recognizing our harmony with them, and applying them to life. I would tell about the Kujichagulia of Leola and Renita Banks, who sidestepped poverty once they changed the image of themselves. I would write about Frank Walker, who, with the law of belief, overcame adversity to become a prosperous Houston entrepreneur. I would tell how Horace Sheffield took advantage of the success that surrounded him once he applied the law of faith to his own life. Since it would be impossible to teach every cosmic law, I would start with the basic ones listed next.

LAW OF THE MIND

An idea is the first and foremost part of every action and it moves the world, generating thought currents just as a flame generates heat. Any result—health, success, or wealth—is from the ideas of the mind. They are contagious and no one lives in a climate of creativity without becoming infected. The mind is only potential energy, whereas the thought it creates is the dynamic force that produces reality.

According to Buddha, just as a picture is drawn by an artist, surroundings are created by the activities of the mind. A single picture is capable of an infinite variety of details. So the human mind fills in the surroundings of its life. There is nothing in the world that is not mind created. We must make up our minds and decide what is important to us, then put concentrated thought and energy into getting it. The intent to have abundance and success directs our energy and focuses it on the goals. African Americans are born to win, to conquer, and to rise above all obstacles that confront us. We accomplish this when we create prosperity by concentrating on it with attention and awareness and keeping it in our minds even when we are involved otherwise. Once we are in control, we will be successful in whatever we undertake.

LAW OF FAITH

If ideas and images are the foundations of all work, then faith is the force that makes the ideas real to us and others. Matthew 9:29 states this law simply: According to your faith be it unto you. Whatever your faith puts into substance will become reality in your world. Faith is believing in an invisible presence that responds directly and specifically to you with resources of hope, strength, and peace of soul. It is the inner sense knowing the Creator is working for you, with you, and through you by creating opportunities and expectations to support your purpose. Spiritual beliefs provide comforting help to meet the problems of life and see us through the valleys that inevitably come to each of us. Practicing this law means we are never alone, despite illness, trouble, danger, or sorrow. Faith flows from the mind as a positive mental attitude that provides enduring power, influence, and light for ourselves and others.

LAW OF CAUSE AND EFFECT

The basis of all universal principles is the law of cause and effect, because it is rooted in belief. Our beliefs, actions, and reactions are the cause of every effect or condition that occurs in our lives. We must be careful with what we say, for we are held accountable for the reality that our words create. We have all found, at one time or another, that what we believe about ourselves and our successes, and our very identities, whether it's positive or negative often comes true. This is because life works according to the basic physical principle of cause and effect; cause is a belief or idea and effect is the result. Galatian's 6:7 summarized this law: Whatever you soweth . . . that also shall you reap.

Whether you believe in cause and effect or not, it still operates because our thoughts are more prophetic than we realize. If you constantly think of dangerous, fearful situations, sooner or later they become real. Whatever we plant, we harvest. Businesses do not spring from the earth like a volcano, unless we plant an idea or a seed. The idea may be from an individual, a corporation, or the community, but our desires and needs will direct our actions. You must believe you can have anything you want and you will have it; you are what you believe and feel yourself to be. Successful individuals harvest results from their words because they believe in themselves and faithfully pursue their goals, while others quit. Practicing positive thinking and applying belief account for 85 percent of successes while 15 percent is based on knowledge and expertise. The human mind builds all truths and attitudes—it is not disobeyed and like a circle, what we send out goes around and returns to the source.

LAW OF ATTRACTION

Like thoughts always attract like effects. We attract, through cause and effect, situations that mirror our thoughts. We attract everything that happens to us either consciously or subconsciously so that we can see it and then act. Fright attracts fearful experiences. Confusion attracts chaos. Wealth attracts money. Success attracts success. All water rises or sinks to its own level and wherever you are mentally and emotionally, you will be physically. The subconscious mind proves that our dominant thoughts and beliefs are true by attracting the circumstances that confirm our deepest feelings. We consciously draw forth the wisdom and ideas necessary for the fruition of our ideals, desires, goals, and objectives for success. Similarly, the people we surround ourselves with will either elevate or demote us. It is our choice to attract people who support our goals and endeavors.

As descendants of survivors, we must stop speaking and thinking about limitation and obstacles. We must think of prosperity, speak abundance and expect success. Through this law we learn responsibility to love and care for what we have in order to get what we want. Once we apply the positive power of the mind, we are ready to harvest peace, love, success, and abundance.

LAW OF PROSPERITY

This law works hand in hand with the law of attraction and the law of faith because you are the source of your success. First, you must believe in abundance, and through working with your feelings, thoughts, and intentions, you can create prosperity. Secondly, you must fill your mind with images and expanded thoughts of the Highest Power's unlimited resources for you. Corinthians 3:6 states: I have planted, Apollos watered: but God gave the increase. Finally, increase is what every African American seeks, and to get it, every word that is spoken must express prosperity. Give thanks for whatever you have, no matter the amount, and believe that the power and wisdom of your subconscious will fulfill your purpose and happiness.

Desire to grow and expand, whether it is wealth, business, career, or personal, is a natural part of life. Practicing the law of prosperity brings an increase in friends, travel, luxuries, or whatever you desire. If you expect little, you get little. If you see yourself in prosperous circumstances, the result will correspond to that belief. John H. Johnson visualized a magazine for African Americans before it ever existed, and when he first published the *Negro Digest*, it corresponded to the image in his mind.

When we practice the law of prosperity, we believe in abundance, not only for ourselves, but for others. Therefore, it is easy to help others succeed and applaud them when they do, because we know that the universal resources are unlimited.

LAW OF CIRCULATION

This law of circulation creates many channels for prosperity to flow. It is the basis for giving and receiving and we must learn to *freely give* and *freely receive*. Giving is easy for most of us, but receiving often presents a problem. Learning to freely receive keeps the circle of abundant energy flowing, because if no one received no one could give. For businesses and communities to grow, money and resources, and goods and services must circulate in the community.

We must open ourselves to receive with warmth and sincerity. This empowers the givers and opens the channels for more success. Whatever we receive we should visualize it returning to us a hundredfold. In this way we imagine success for others and automatically increase our blessings. The law of circualtion urges us to receive gratefully from any source that honors our esteem and integrity.

Giving is an important as receiving, and the way you give is the way it will be returned to you. Giving continues a creative circle of energy and attests to our abundance and faith. We activate the law of circulation by giving as much as we receive, and by creating communities using our special skills, talents, and abilities.

We must give to people who can create positive changes in their lives or in the lives of others. We can give to those who are seeking their higher purposes and path. Whatever we receive in life is our reward for what we give to life.

HOW TO USE THIS BOOK

For African Americans to harvest success during the Kwanzaa celebration, we must begin preparations on January 2 of each year. This book is designed for year-round reading, just as preparation for the harvest demands year-round sowing. *The Complete Kwanzaa* contains all the information necessary to celebrate Kwanzaa.

Each chapter of this book is devoted to a particular principle of the Nguzo Saba. It includes poetry, historical and biographical sketches, quotations, folktales, proverbs, and thoughts related to the principle, all of which can be tailored to your individual Kwanzaa celebration.

The fables, parables, and folktales specifically teach lessons in the African oral tradition. They illustrate the role that each person is to play in his or her relations with other people and his or her responsibility to the community. The selections also provide lessons from life—hard lessons that all must face—in such a manner that the listeners are not aware that they are being educated.

Celebrants can select pieces and plan the events for each day. For example, on the second day, when Kujichagulia is observed, a person may select a poem or story to read from that chapter. Others may retell a personal or historical event that highlights self-determination.

Style is a personal expression of our identity, and Chapter Eight is devoted to Kwanzaa's Karamu Festival, which falls on New Year's Eve. During this festival, style, personality, and ambience are expressed by the host or hostess through the menu, music, decorations, and clothing. The Karamu encourages everyone's creativity to blossom. This chapter details three distinct Karamu feasts representing various lifestyles, so you can follow the outlines and easily adapt them to your individual style.

The reader's Kujichagulia shines by reading stories aloud

and adding personal touches. Within the rhythm of the words in the stories and poems are ancient laws, the universal principles passed on to us from our ancestors. Each celebrant interprets and tells the stories according to his or her individual experiences and expectations. We share the stories from the past and realize that we are the stories of the future.

At the end of each chapter guidelines for success are presented that have been gleaned from the words and actions of the persons who are spotlighted. A glossary and pronunciation key are at the end of the book.

THE SEVEN PRINCIPLES OF KWANZAA

Our ancestors' entry into America provided little hope that they would ever be saved or freed from slavery. For more than three hundred years, legendary African Americans followed the spiritual command to seek and act in faith as though they were receiving the promises of this country. Slowly, doors opened and new ways of working and achieving occurred. Frederick Douglass, Harriet Tubman, and others sought freedom using their natural abilities while trusting universal laws. The Nguzo Saba direct us to trust in the promise and to practice these same principles to see successful results from the thoughts that surround us. These principles are as follows.

UMOJA (UNITY)

Umoja is the importance of striving for and maintaining unity in the family, community, nation, and race. "We are one, our cause is one and we must help each other if we are to succeed."—Frederick Douglass

KUJICHAGULIA (SELF-DETERMINATION)

Kujichagulia means knowing who we are and our role in our community as we journey through life—to define our interest, name ourselves, create for ourselves and speak for ourselves, making decisions that benefit the family and the community. "Determination and perseverance move the world; thinking that others will do it for you is a sure way to fail."—Marva Collins

UJIMA (COLLECTIVE WORK AND RESPONSIBILITY)

Ujima means that through unity we must build and maintain our community, to solve problems together the way we bonded to solve problems in the past. "We are responsible for the world in which we find ourselves, if only because we are the sentient force which can change it."—James Baldwin

UJAMAA (COOPERATIVE ECONOMICS)

Ujamaa means to build and maintain businesses using our collective economic strength (Ujamaa) to fill mutually the needs of the community. "Today, we direct our economic and political strength toward winning a more abundant and secure life."—Mary McLeod Bethune

NIA (PURPOSE)

Nia means that we must have pride in ourselves and our ancestry, so we can look within ourselves to build and plan for the total community. "To have a purpose in life offsets all major declines."—Jean Toomer

KUUMBA (CREATIVITY)

Kuumba is using our individual talents, we keep our home and community clean and beautiful by using our creativity (Kuumba) to build and maintain our community. "Potential powers of creativity are within us and we have the duty to work assiduously to discover these powers." —Martin Luther King, Jr.

IMANI (FAITH)

Imani is believing in our people, our parents, our teachers, and our leaders by honoring and remembering the best of our history, the best of ourselves, and the best of our dreams and aspirations for the future. "We live by faith in others. But most of all we must live by faith in ourselves— faith to believe that we can develop into useful men and women."—Benjamin Mays

No successful African American completely envisioned the steps needed to accomplish a goal. Few can pinpoint when success began or which of its effects occurred first. But as time passes, our minds, our bodies, and our affairs change. Today more than 18 million African Americans celebrate Kwanzaa, seeing prosperity and traditions through legacies shaped and preserved from generation to generation. The growing number of businesses, schools, and public groups that are observing this holiday demonstrate its popularity. For example, South Carolina, where slave ships unloaded many of our ancestors, holds a yearly Kuumba Festival in August. In Houston, Texas, Windsor Village Church named its elementary school The Imani School. The Shrines of the Black Madonna bookstores in Detroit, Houston, and Atlanta contain Karamu art galleries. Thirteen years ago, businessmen Jose Ferrer and Malik Ahmed, of New York, started the multi-million-dollar Kwanzaa Holiday

Expo that travels from New York to St. Louis, Philadelphia, and Washington. In their newsletter, *Kwanzaa*, Ferrer and Ahmed estimated that sales from the expo should reach $100 million in 1995 and noted: "All that ails black communities across the nation is addressed through the Nguzo Saba. The beauty of Kwanzaa is its holistic approach encompassing our spiritual, economic and cultural development. We need only to embrace these principles—year round." AT&T, recognizing the significance of the holiday, aired a Kwanzaa message to markets holding the Kwanzaa Holiday Expo. Applying the values of Kwanzaa with our innate spiritual powers produces prosperity. The universal promise is an abundant life harvested by all who seek it and focus their thoughts.

THE SEVEN SYMBOLS OF KWANZAA

1. Mazao   Fruits, nuts, and vegetables
2. Mkeka   Place mat
3. Muhindi   Ears of corn
4. Mishumaa saba   The seven candles
5. Kinara   Candleholder
6. Kikombe cha umoja   Communal cup of unity
7. Zawadi   Gifts

All holidays have symbols that culturally engrave the rituals into the minds of the people. Kwanzaa's harvest celebration of joy, thanksgiving, and praise has practical symbols to strengthen, teach, and guide African Americans in practicing the principles of success daily. The home decor authentically exudes the feeling of the Nguzo Saba, with prominent displays of the seven symbols, and the colors, red, black, and green, that are prominent in the decorative theme. The mkeka may be an African mud cloth or a Kente patterned textile. Statues and other artwork exemplify the principles, as do plants, crafts, and other works that demonstrate Kujichagulia. Selected zawadi may be hand-made to reflect creativity and placed on the mkeka. The focused theme creates an atmosphere that showcases the values and spirit of an African harvest festival. The seven decorative symbols often become family heirlooms that are passed from one generation to another.

MAZAO: FRUITS, NUTS, AND VEGETABLES

Mazao, the crops (fruits, nuts, and vegetables), symbol-izes work and the basis of the holiday. It represents the his-torical foundation for Kwanzaa, the gathering of the people that is patterned after African harvest festivals in which joy, sharing, unity, and thanksgiving are the fruits of collective planning and work. Since the family is the basic social and economic center of every civilization, the celebration bonded family members, reaffirming their commitment and responsibility to each other. In Africa the family may have included several generations of two or more nuclear fami-lies, as well as distant relatives. Ancient Africans didn't care how large the family was, but there was only one leader— the oldest male of the strongest group. For this reason, an entire village may have been composed of one family.

The family was a limb of a tribe that shared common customs, cultural traditions, and political unity and were supposedly descended from common ancestors. The tribe lived by traditions that provided continuity and identity. Tribal laws often determined the value system, laws, and customs encompassing birth, adolescence, marriage, par-enthood, maturity, and death. Through personal sacrifice and hard work, the farmers sowed seeds that brought forth new plant life to feed the people and other animals of the earth. To demonstrate their mazao, celebrants of Kwanzaa place nuts, fruits, and vegetables, representing work, on the mkeka.

MKEKA: PLACE MAT

The mkeka, made from straw or cloth, comes directly from Africa and expresses history, culture, and tradition. It symbolizes the historical and traditional foundation for us to stand on and build our lives because today stands on our yesterdays, just as the other symbols stand on the mkeka. In 1965, James Baldwin wrote: "For history is not merely something to be read. And it does not refer merely, or even principally, to the past. On the contrary, the great force of history comes from the facts that we carry it within us, are consciously controlled by it in many ways, and history is literally present in all that we do. It could scarcely be otherwise, since it is to history that we owe our frames of reference, our identities, and our aspirations." During Kwanzaa, we study, recall, and reflect on our history and the role we are to play as a legacy to the future.

Ancient societies made mats from straw, the dried seams of grains, sowed and reaped collectively. The weavers took the stalks and created household baskets and mats. Today, we buy mkeka that are made from Kente cloth, African mud cloth, and other textiles from various areas of the African continent.

The mishumaa saba, the vibunzi, the mazao, the zawadi, the kikombe cha umoja, and the kinara are placed directly on the mkeka.

VIBUNZI: EAR OF CORN

The stalk of corn represents fertility and symbolizes that through the reproduction of children, the future hopes of the family are brought to life. One ear is called vibunzi, and two or more ears are called mihindi. Each ear symbolizes a child in the family, and thus one ear is placed on the mkeka for each child in the family. If there are no children in the home, two ears are still set on the mkeka because each person is responsible for the children of the community.

During Kwanzaa, we take the love and nurturance that was heaped on us as children and selflessly return it to all children, especially the helpless, homeless, loveless ones in our community. Thus, the Nigerian proverb "It takes a whole village to raise a child" is realized in this symbol (vibunzi), since raising a child in Africa was a community affair, involving the tribal village, as well as the family. Good habits of respect for self and others, discipline, positive thinking, expectations, compassion, empathy, charity, and self-direction are learned in childhood from parents, from peers, and from experiences.

Children are essential to Kwanzaa, for they are the future, the seed bearers that will carry cultural values and practices into the next generation. For this reason, children were cared for communally and individually within a tribal village. The biological family was ultimately responsible for raising its own children, but every person in the village was responsible for the safety and welfare of all the children.

MISHUMAA SABA: THE SEVEN CANDLES

Candles are ceremonial objects with two primary purposes: to re-create symbolically the sun's power and to provide light. The celebration of fire through candle burning is not limited to one particular group or country; it occurs everywhere. Mishumaa saba are the seven candles: three red, three green, and one black. The black candle symbolizes Umoja (unity), the basis of success, and is lit on December 26. The three green candles, representing Kugichagulia, Ujima, and Ujamaa, are placed to the right of the Umoja candle, while the three red candles, representing

Nia, Kuumba, and Imani, are placed to the left of it. During Kwanzaa, one candle, representing one principle, is lit each day. Then the other candles are relit to give off more light and vision. The number of candles burning also indicate the principle that is being celebrated. The illuminating fire of the candles is a basic element of the universe, and every celebration and festival includes fire in some form. Fire's mystique, like the sun, is irresistible and can destroy or create with its mesmerizing, frightening, mystifying power.

Mishumaa saba's symbolic colors are from the red, black, and green flag (bendara) created by Marcus Garvey. The colors also represent African gods. Red is the color of Shango, the Yoruba god of fire, thunder, and lightning, who lives in the clouds and sends down his thunderbolt whenever he is angry or offended. It also represents the struggle for self-determination and freedom by people of color. Black is the people, the earth, the source of life, representing hope, creativity, and faith and denoting messages and the opening and closing of doors. Green represents the earth that sustains our lives and provides hope, divination, employment, and the fruits of the harvest.

KINARA: CANDLEHOLDER

The kinara is the center of the Kwanzaa setting and represents the original stalk from which we came: our ancestry. The kinara can be any shape—straight lines, semicircles, or spirals—as long as the seven candles are separate and distinct, like a candleabra. Kinaras are made from all kinds of materials, and many celebrants create their own from fallen branches, wood, or other natural materials.

The kinara symbolizes the ancestors, who were once earth bound; understand the problems of human life; and are willing to protect their progeny from danger, evil, and mistakes. In African festivals the ancestors are remembered and honored. The mishumaa saba are placed in the kinara.

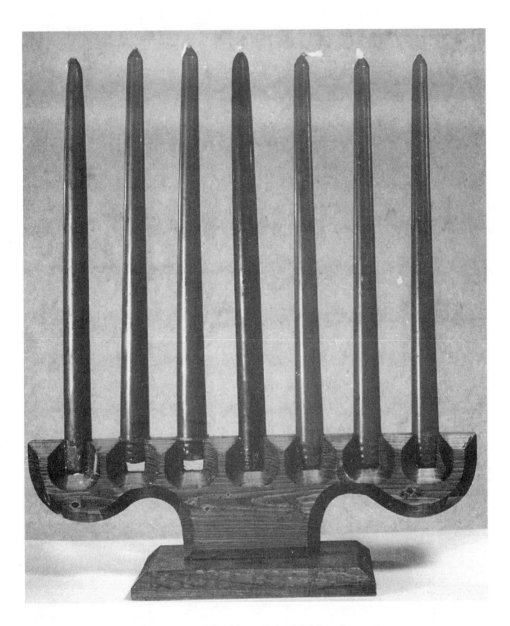

Wooden kinara by John Barnes. Photograph by Bill Sanders.

KIKOMBE CHA UMOJA: THE UNITY CUP

The kikombe cha umoja is a special cup that is used to perform the libation (tambiko) ritual during the Karamu feast on the sixth day of Kwanzaa. In many African societies libations are poured for the living dead whose souls stay with the earth they tilled. The Ibo of Nigeria believe that to drink the last portion of a libation is to invite the wrath of the spirits and the ancestors; consequently, the last part of the libation belongs to the ancestors. During the Karamu feast, the kikombe cha umoja is passed to family members and guests, who drink from it to promote unity. Then the eldest person present pours the libation (tambiko), usually water, juice, or wine, in the direction of the four winds—north, south, east, and west—to honor the ancestors. The eldest asks the gods and ancestors to share in the festivities and, in return, to bless all the people who are present, as well as their families and friends who are not at the gathering. After asking for this blessing, the elder pours the libation on the ground and the group says "Amen."

Large Kwanzaa gatherings may operate just as communion services in most churches, for which it is common for celebrants to have individual cups and to drink the libation together as a sign of unity. Several families may have a cup that is specifically for the ancestors, and everyone else has his or her own. The last few ounces of the libation are poured into the cup of the host or hostess, who sips it and then hands it to the oldest person in the group, who asks for the blessing.

ZAWADI: GIFTS

When we celebrate Imani on the seventh day of Kwanzaa, we give meaningful zawadi (gifts) to encourage growth, self-determination, achievement, and success. We exchange the gifts with members of our immediate family, especially the children, to promote or reward accomplishments and commitments kept, as well as with our guests. Handmade gifts are encouraged to promote self-determination, purpose, and creativity and to avoid the chaos of shopping and conspicuous consumption during the December holiday season. A family may spend the year making kinaras or may create cards, dolls, or mkekas to give to their guests.

Accepting a gift implies a moral obligation to fulfill the promise of the gift; it obliges the recipient to follow the training of the host. The gift cements social relationships, allowing the receiver to share the duties and the rights of a family member. Accepting a gift makes the receiver part of the family and promotes Umoja.

Two-headed Baluba vase, Zaire. Artist unknown. Photograph by Bill Sanders.

SETTING UP
THE SEVEN SYMBOLS

Spread the mkeka on a low table. Place the kinara and the kikombe cha umoja in the center.

Place the muhindi around the kinara.

Set the mishumaa saba to the far right of everything for ease in lighting each day.

Place the zawadi and the mazao on the mkeka.

Before dinner, light one candle representing the principle for that day and explain its meaning. After dinner blow out the mishumaa saba until the next day.

On the second day, light two candles; on the third day, light three; and so on until the seventh day, when all the candles burn together.

GREETINGS FOR THE SEVEN DAYS OF KWANZAA

For the seven days of Kwanzaa, we greet each other with "Habari gani," which means "What's happening?" The answer is the principle of the day.

December 26	Greeting: "Habari gani!"
	Response: "Umoja!"
December 27	Greeting: "Habari gani!"
	Response: "Kujichagulia!"
December 28	Greeting: "Habari gani!"
	Response: "Ujima!"
December 29	Greeting: "Habari gani!"
	Response: "Ujamaa!"
December 30	Greeting: "Habari gani!"
	Response: "Nia!"
December 31	Greeting: "Habari gani!"
	Response: "Kuumba!"
January 1	Greeting: "Habari gani!"
	Response: "Imani!"

A second greeting is "Happy Kwanzaa," and in Swahili we say "Kwanzaa yenu iwe na heri," which according to Karenga means "May y'alls Kwanzaa be with happiness." Since the celebration is a communal act, it is customary to speak of the collective group rather than one person.

DAILY GUIDE FOR OBSERVING KWANZAA

Since Kwanzaa stems from the communal quality of African life, it is recommended that two or more people observe Kwanzaa together. On December 26, the first day of Kwanzaa, a special time is set aside, so family and friends can observe the Nguzo Saba, the seven principles. Many families set aside two days: the first, for quiet meditation of reassessment and recommitment, and the second, to honor and remember the ancestors. Others may plan, as I do, a program that includes reassessment, recommitment, and honoring the ancestors each day. Kwanzaa is a personal holiday, and each family must decide how they want to celebrate it.

The following sample program may be used or modified for all seven principles and for each day of Kwanzaa. It contains the four essential elements of daily observance of the principles: welcome and entertainment, ceremonies and ritual, eating and entertainment, and farewell. Greeters include children as well as adults.

Welcome
- Opening statement by the host or the eldest person present
- Libation to the ancestors
- Harambee—Call to unity
- Statement of the principle and its meaning

Lighting of the Candles
- Historical application of the principle
- Relationship of ancestors and the principle
- Group pledges for the new year

Cultural Expression
- Poem or music
- Song or dance

- Stories of the ancestors
- Historical incidents

Eating and Feasting
- Libation to posterity
- Farewell statement

CHAPTER ONE

PRINCIPLE 1

UMOJA

WITHOUT UNITY NOTHING IS CREATED: THE MEANING OF UMOJA

We never know we are beings till we love. And then it is we know the powers and potentialities of organic, conscious, solar, cosmic matter and force. We, together, vibrate as one in harmony with man and with the cosmos.

—Jean Toomer

Umoja, representing unity, the first principle of Kwanzaa, is celebrated on December 26. During the observance, the family and friends bond as one and light the black candle in the center of the kinara. We describe and talk about unity, so it is meaningful to all who are present, especially the children. Each participant leaves with a clearer understanding that Umoja is the foundation that holds all the other principles. In the ritual each person may reaffirm how he or she can practically apply Umoja daily by contributing to the home, the community, and the nation. My ten-year-old nephew, Martay, contributes to our daily ceremony by making Kwanzaa place cards with the principle of the day printed on the outside. He takes time to hand paint the cards without duplicating a single one.

Moja means one, and *Umoja* means oneness in Swahili, and the greatest success any person achieves is unity with the universal consciousness through oneness with the Creator. From that source we realize that everything in the universe is related—the earth, the sky, oceans, plants, animals, and humans. We are one related family, and whatever happens to one will eventually happen to us all. Frederick Douglass, Sojourner Truth, Carter G. Woodson, Marcus Garvey, and all the other great sages, prophets, and saviors received inspiring direction from the Creator. They taught respect; cooperation through harmony and balance; and continuance of the cycle of life, despite never-ending changes. No human power can limit a person who acts as one with God; only that person can limit himself or herself. Solidarity motivates individuals to share their intellect and originality and fix their attention on specific goals. The law of creation is the strong, authoritative use of the will to direct our future and to create our reality. Martin Luther King, Jr., Booker T. Washington, and Marva Collins are examples of the power of Umoja. African Americans, as the direct descendants of the Highest Source, must use that power to shape our destiny.

The principle of Umoja urges African Americans to live using divine power and to recognize that in our journey on this planet, we should strive to be in unity and harmony with the universal laws that nothing can destroy. Umoja brings about self-reliance, independence, and self-motivation.

Unity occurs when we achieve peace within ourselves and in family relationships. Umoja is the foundation and strength of the family, although there is no set pattern for a typical family. Arthur Ashe's father loved and guided him after his mother died. Surgeon Ben Carson grew up in Detroit with a determined mother who demanded and instilled values in him. Denzel Washington's mother sent him to boarding school after she and his father divorced, but he never forgot the lessons he learned from both his parents.

The structure of the home is not more important than the love and values transmitted to each member of the family. Learning to live harmoniously and to solve conflicts with our parents or guardian and brothers and sisters prepares us for other relationships. The family symbolizes society's basic unit, and when there is peace in the home, the nation enjoys harmony.

The family teaches lifelong values and responsibilities and allows for change within a somewhat restrictive environment. It is the rehearsal stage that teaches us to dream of possibilities and to flow and grow with life. African family patterns emphasized caring for children, yet children were not the responsibility of just the biological parents because everyone in the village united to care for the children. In the village, everyone assumed responsibility for the well-being of others, without selfish regard for what was received in return. Those values built human dignity and pride. Practicing the principles of Kwanzaa is a return to loyalty, trust, friendliness, courtesy, kindness, and honesty found in the caring village of our ancestors.

Love, marriage, parenthood, and family are the basis of happiness—the goal of every human. The joy of life is not found in wealth, in knowledge, or in travel or a career. All these factors contribute to our happiness, but true joy is found in the loving circle of family. Umoja teaches us that there is no permanent happiness without love. We grow through building, struggling, and acting together for the benefit of our homes and communities. Anita Baker reminds us, "You leave home to seek your fortune and when you get it you go home to share it with your family."

The selections in this chapter represent the various meanings of Umoja and how the family reinforces the principle. From Thurgood Marshall and the fight for school desegregation to the poem "My Block," Umoja is illustrated.

FROM THE CORE OF THE UNIVERSE: POETRY FOR UMOJA

HARAMBEE: CALL TO UNITY

DOROTHY WINBUSH RILEY

Harambee! Harambee! Harambee!
Harambee! Harambee!
Harambee! Harambee! Harambee!

Seven times I call you
Seven times I call you to unity.
I call for my mother
I call for my father
I call for my sisters
I call for my brothers
I call for grandfathers
I call for my grandmothers
I call for my family
Come to unity.

Seven times I call you
Seven times I call you to unity.
I call for Umoja
I call for Kujichagulia
I call for Ujima
I call for Ujamaa
I call for Nia
I call for Kuumba
I call for Imani.
Seven times I call you
Seven times I call
Come to unity.

Harambee! Harambee! Harambee!
Harambee! Harambee!
Harambee! Harambee! Harambee!

THE COMING OF EAGLES

HENRY DUMAS

Let us have new wings
among my people!
Let us have bones
among my people!
Let us have visions
among my people!

Let us ride the wind
into the high country
Let us have eagles.

MY BLOCK

Dorothy Winbush Riley

On my block
people weren't afraid to care.
You're a good child was often said,
And this image I locked in my mind.
Your mother told my mother
who told Grandma Ruth,
every word she spoke was always right.
Well, pretty soon
the whole block knew . . .

"Hattie's baby sho' is fine
Miss Fannie Mae is drunk again
Graduation is tomorrow noon,
You, come too!
I checked yo' Mary yesterday;
she was trying to make a car
move out of her way.

Everybody took care of
everybody else's children;
how in the world could
we run wild?
On my block
love filled the air.

CONCEPTUALITY

MARI EVANS

I am a wisp of energy
flung from the core of the Universe
        housed
    in a temple
of flesh and bones and blood

        in the temple
        because it is there
        that I make my home
        Free
    of the temple
    not bound
        by the temple
    but housed
I am everywhere
energy and will of the Universe expressed
    realizing my oneness my
    individuality/I

    I am
the One Force
    I. . . .

LET US HAVE VISIONS:
PEOPLE OF UMOJA

BROWN VS. THE BOARD OF EDUCATION

DOROTHY WINBUSH RILEY

As a model for unity and commitment, we need only look to the efforts of Thurgood Marshall and the NAACP to destroy *Plessy vs. Ferguson,* the 1896 Supreme Court decision to keep all facilities "separate but equal," a mere generation ago. What worked then works today: participation of all classes in a spiritual and cultural movement of change.

Thurgood Marshall joined the National Association for the Advancement of Colored People in 1936, and within two years he was its special counsel. His and other NAACP lawyers' united vision nurtured seedlings of freedom in the hearts of African Americans. During the 1940s and 1950s, struggling parents turned to the NAACP to solve problems collectively. One such problem were laws in the South that prohibited African American children from attending schools with white children and racially segregated neighborhoods in the North that prevented children from attending the same schools.

By 1952 this Umoja reaped five significant cases before the Supreme Court. One case involved thirteen families of Topeka, Kansas, particularly, nine-year-old Linda Brown and her father, Reverend Oliver Brown, who sued the Board of Education when Linda could not attend her neighborhood school because it was reserved for white children. The outcome of this case indicated that America had a date with destiny to end the segregation of public schools that started soon after Abraham Lincoln delivered the Emancipation

Proclamation in 1865. Marshall filed the lawsuit and assembled a team of lawyers and psychologists to show that "separate but equal" schools were harmful to children and a violation of the equal protection clause of the Fourteenth Amendment. This historic case is known as *Brown vs. the Board of Education of Topeka*.

Faith, belief, hope, and determination led Marshall and his team of lawyers to think that they could reverse the tide of segregation in America. Marshall said, "I have to keep believing, because I know our cause is right. Justice and reason are on our side. Everybody knows this but those enslaved to customs." Although they were arguing against the most renowned constitutional lawyers in America, Marshall and his allies altered the legal landscape of America. Throughout the trial, Marshall's training and individual determination enabled him to communicate convincing legal arguments that were based on the Fifth, Fourteenth, and Fifteenth Amendments and other constitutional provisions that guarantee citizenship to every American. Marshall never gave in to the emotional tirades of the opposition, but remained calm and in charge at all times, presenting his case solemnly and rationally.

During the trial, Marshall called on Dr. Kenneth Clark, a prominent psychologist and a key investigator in the case, who had perfect timing when he testified. Clark listened attentively and at the precise moment provided evidence that paved the way for the *world*-changing 1954 Supreme Court decision. Clark testified that in his research with African American children, he had found that when he showed children four identical dolls, two black and two white, the children rejected the black dolls in favor of the white dolls. His presentation of his research, together with the results of twenty years of studies conducted by both African American and white psychologists, proved that when people are isolated or made to feel different or inferior, they suffer severe psychological damage. He used the art of persuasion, coupled with solid research, to change the opinions of individuals, as well as the outcome of the case. Clark did not make fire-and-brimstone speeches, but allowed his innate sense to guide him in handling the uncontrolled monster—institutionalized racism. In so doing, he helped to snatch triumph from the racists and steered the NAACP toward its most significant victory. He was masterful in his presentation, an architect of Umoja and Kujichagulia.

On Monday, May 17, 1954, after almost four months of lawyers and reporters gathering every Monday at the Supreme Court, the Court handed down its decision. "Oyez! Oyez! Oyez!" cried the court marshall. "All persons having business before the Honorable, the Supreme Court of the United States, are admonished to draw near and give their attention, for the court is now sitting. God save the United States and this Honorable Court!" The gavel sounded, permitting the spectators to take their seats.

At precisely twelve noon, the court marshall banged the gavel so hard that everyone jumped to attention as he announced, "The Honorable, the Chief Justice and the Associate Justices at the Supreme Court of the United States!" Dramatically, nine stoical white men, dressed in solemn black robes, mounted the raised marble platform. Shortly thereafter, Chief Justice Earl Warren said, "I have for announcement the judgment and opinion of the Court in No. 1, *Oliver Brown et al. vs. Board of Education of Topeka.*" Near the end of his reading of the decision, the court marshall read:

> Does segregation of children in public schools solely on the basis of race, even though the physical facilities and other "tangible" factors may be equal, deprive the children of the minority group of equal education opportunities? We believe that it does. Thus we conclude that in the field of public education the doctrine of "separate but equal" has no place. Separate educational facilities are inherently unequal. . . . the plaintiffs and others similarly sit-

uated for whom the actions have been brought are, by reason of the segregation complained of, deprived of the equal protection of the laws guaranteed by the Fourteenth Amendment.

African Americans' courageous solidarity in *Brown vs. the Board of Education* transformed our society by influencing the majority to act to overturn the unjust laws of segregation. Their courageous spirit changed the course of American history. The 1954 decision led to the civil rights movement in which the combination of faith, confidence, intensity, and sacrifice propelled people to do the incredible.

Martin Luther King, Jr.'s, actions, after Rosa Parks refused to move from her seat at the front of the bus in Montgomery, Alabama, fueled another fight for self-determination. A year after the *Brown* decision, Daisy Bates and the Little Rock Nine integrated Central High School in Little Rock, Arkansas. That same year, 1955, four students in Greensboro, North Carolina, started a sit-in at a lunch counter, which, like the domino effect, inspired others to action.

EXCERPT FROM
CLIMBING JACOB'S LADDER

ANDREW BILLINGSLEY

This excerpt from Andrew Billingsley's *Climbing Jacob's Ladder*
(1992) demonstrates how Umoja works in the family to achieve
specific goals. Umoja is self-reliance coupled with a practical
attitude, so that the family depends on its own community
resources to solve life's problems instead of waiting and leaning
on others.

My father and mother spent their entire lives within a
one-hundred-mile radius of the sleepy little town of
Marion, Alabama, where they were born. Married to each
other at age nineteen, they would remain so for thirty-
seven years until the death of my father from a coronary at
age fifty-six. During their marriage they would raise three
children to adulthood while caring for numerous extended
relatives and other people's children. But while they never
traveled outside the state of Alabama, they nevertheless
made the enormous transition from the agricultural era to
the industrial era. Moving from the farming community of
Marion in Perry County, to the coal, iron and steel center of
Birmingham, they were able to lift their own family status
from the sharecropper class to the blue collar working
class. In the process they laid a foundation for the movement of their children from working to middle class.

How were they able to accomplish these feats? First by a
remarkable commitment to the value of knowledge, learning and education. They had little formal schooling themselves. My mother went through to the third grade at a
country school and was never taught to read and write. She
wanted the best for her children, however, and she knew
that literacy was imperative. My father went through sixth

grade at the private Lincoln Normal School established by the ex-slaves in Marion just after the Civil War. It was an outstanding school. There my father learned to read and write, figure and think, and speak along with the best of the community.

My mother and father had a reverence for learning second only to their reverence for the spiritual. And they passed this along to their children. They were not isolated. In Birmingham there were still inordinate hardships. But there were also the multitude of wonders that is a city: indoor plumbing, electricity, telephone, radio, newspaper, and above all school and church; there was even a colored branch of the Birmingham Public Library. All were buttressed by other adults in the neighborhood who could read and write. In the next block to the right were two undertakers and a minister, all three literate. And around the corner lived a school teacher. Up the street in the other direction lived the neighborhood physician. And every day there marched proudly through the neighborhood, a black postman. He could not only read and write, which he demonstrated often, but also regaled the children with tales of the far away places he had seen letters from, sometimes even in foreign languages.

There were other values too by which my parents lived that helped to prepare their children for upward mobility. Indeed, for my father, his family, his church, his work, and his Masonic lodge were his life. And for the first time in his life, living in the shadow of the biggest employer in Birmingham, the steel mills, he could get a union job that paid him almost enough to support his family unaided. As for my mother, long before we would discover the ancient African code embodied in the seven cardinal principles of virtue, and long before Spike Lee would encapsulate these principles in the title of his movie, my mother was the living embodiment of the moral code, "Do the Right Thing."

Birmingham after World War II, the civil rights revolution, and the technological revolution would continue to present enormous opportunities. Yet progress is seldom simple. For in the midst of such expanding opportunity lurked a hidden consequence. In the wake of the postwar, postindustrial era, the steel mills were closed. The new downtown high-tech medical center and the expanding financial and communications institutions which replaced the steel mills as the city's major employer, while not restricted by race, had no place for the men who lost their jobs in the steel mills.

BILL AND CAMILLE COSBY: UNIFIED

DOROTHY WINBUSH RILEY

Through humor, Bill Cosby helps us find pleasure in everyday chores and allows us to look beyond our perceived limitations. Laughter improves our perspective on life by creating a new attitude. We can cope with difficult situations if we are able to laugh at the ridiculousness of our own mistakes. Laughter makes the risk of trying again easier by increasing our creative flexibility when we reexamine our views or feelings.

Laughter involves almost every part of the body. The face moves, the body rocks, and the arms and legs flail. In this sense, laughter is like a physical exercise; it speeds up the heart rate, raises the blood pressure, accelerates breathing, and works on the muscles of the stomach and face. Researchers and healers know the benefit of laughter in fighting serious illnesses; laughter helps the body create natural medicine by manufacturing more fighting immune cells. Laughter is also a healer of the soul, and no one understands this fact better than Bill Cosby. Through his humorous anecdotes and monologues, he has empowered his family while clarifying life's mazes and helping us to find a purpose.

Bill and Camille Cosby understand that wealth beyond a certain amount cannot be used and if dormant becomes a hindering curse that blesses no one. Booker T. Washington left a legacy of success, and the Cosbys follow his teachings. They are creating a living monument by circulating money to enrich the lives of others, thereby continuously renewing themselves. More important, the Cosbys weave a living tradition of responsibility and philanthropy for their family. This already glamorous couple grows more beautiful as they practice the art of benevolent giving to the world and especially to each other. Cosby says, "There is a moment when you get a feeling that this person does to you, for you, what nobody else can do. It's not a sexual or sensual feeling. It does not have anything to do with the sound that comes from them or the curl of the hair. It's not a feeling that we are one. It's even stronger than that. It is the feeling that this person has more for you than anyone else on the face of the earth."

It is as important to pick the right mate as it is to be the right mate. The Cosbys reap the harvest of thirty years of rooting, growing, nurturing, and blossoming future seeds. Since 1964, when they met on a blind date, their lives have been linked through a shared vision and commitment to each other. Camille says, "My husband and I function as partners, not only in marriage, but in terms of business. It should be that way. There are a lot of discussions and a lot of respect. We are a team." Both recognize the interdependence of life that demands a balance of the spiritual, the material, the social, and the mental to maintain family unity. Their lives reflect the principles of Kwanzaa.

Cosby's career opportunities were infinite once he combined his creative leadership abilities and his desire for independence to make comedy his life's work. In 1962, his career blasted off when he created laughter about himself in Greenwich Village. For three years Cosby worked the nightclub circuit until a producer saw him on the *Tonight Show*. He became the first African American actor to star in an American television series, *I Spy*, for which he received three Emmys for his portrayal of a globe-trotting, spying tennis pro. After his success on *I Spy*, the world wanted more great acts from him. Within five years the young couple were multimillionaires, living the dreams and fantasies of all people. Through hard work, dedication, and a unique vision of the value of laugher and what is humorous, Cosby inspires us. He jokes about the joys of life, rather than playing on negatives and fears. He never tells racial, sexual, or profane jokes; he draws laughter by describing his life with Camille and their five children.

The couple learned early in their marriage to put first things first, so that every job Cosby took was for the family. Soon after his success in *I Spy*, Camille became his manager; they united on all fronts. She reminds all that "in this kind of business, you have to protect each other. It is difficult for a performer to totally immerse himself or herself in creativity and watch everything else, too. You need someone who really cares about you, someone who is dependable and honest, and that is difficult to find." Cosby knows that any man's greatest achievements are successful relationships with his wife, his children, and his friends; without these relationships, fame is an albatross. With Camille at his side and five children as their center, the couple's personal stability allows Umoja, Kujichagulia, Ujima, Ujamaa, Nia, Kuumba, and Imani to bring forth the gifts of the universe. Cosby's cheerful, yet commanding personality creates a home of love and loyalty. He has the knack of seeing a humorous way out of every situation and allowing others to share his vision.

Both Bill and Camille are driven by excellence and the desire to change the image of African Americans. They applied the same harmonious spirits in creating *The Cosby Show,* whose characters mirrored Camille and the children. The series portrayed the trials and joys of a typical family in raising children. The realistic humor reached all people, regardless of their race, but after nine years Cosby ended the show. *The Cosby Show* paved the way for more cooperative ventures where others found barriers. The Cosbys are a catalyst for love as philanthropists, arts' patrons, filmmakers, and business magnates.

Bill and Camille's family unity and self-determination reflect the dreams of Malcolm X, the plans of W. E. B. Du Bois, and the feelings of Mary McLeod Bethune. Through their actions, we are made aware of the power of Umoja; their behavior exemplifies the Nguzo Saba, with the family as the foundation of success.

"Whether you have a Ph.D., a D.D., or no D, we're in this together. Whether you're from Morehouse or No house, we're in this bag together."—Fannie Lou Hamer

"The ultimate destiny and aspiration of the African people and twenty million American Negroes are magnificently bound up together forever."—Lorraine Hansberry

"I belong to this race, and when it is down I belong to a down race; when it is up I belong to a risen race."—Frances E. W. Harper

"Let nothing and nobody break your spirit. Let the unity in the community remain intact."—Jesse Jackson

"The artist must draw out of his soul the correct image of the world. He must use this image to band his brothers and sisters together."—Leroi Jones

"For if one lost, all lost—the chain that held them would save all or none."—Toni Morrison

"We cannot think of uniting with others, until we have first united among ourselves. We cannot think of being acceptable to others until we have first proven acceptable to ourselves. One can't unite bananas with scattered leaves."—Malcolm X

"You don't fight racism with racism, the best way to fight racism is with solidarity."—Bobby Seale

"Do you ask what we can do? Unite and build a store of your own ... do you ask where is the money? We have spent more than enough for nonsense."—Maria Stewart

"I am nostalgic for the solidarity and sharing a modest existence can sometimes bring."—Alice Walker

"When the son of an African noble house goes defiantly to prison to continue his struggle for freedom, part of us goes with him. And when we get reports of his growth, stubborn dignity, calm, commanding presence, and wisdom, we swell again and think of our ancient heritage and bonds of blood."—Roger Wilkins

TREADING ON THE SINGING DRUM: FOLKTALES FOR UMOJA

THE THREE SISTERS

TIAUDRA RILEY

There is much talent within the African American family just as there is in this story, in which unity is the source of strength, power, and love. "The Three Sisters" demonstrates that communication is necessary for understanding and unity when everyone has the same goal but a different plan for achieving it. Communication is necessary to share our talents, so we achieve Umoja, although the means differ.

Three sisters once lived in a small town near Dallas. As each graduated from college, she set off to climb the ladder of success to take her place in the world. Anissa, the oldest girl, had honey-hued skin and the perfectly chiseled face of a Zulu queen. She became the buyer for a designer. She had a discriminating eye for the beauty and rhythm found in exotic materials, people, and places. One day, while showing a Kente cloth she had purchased in Kenya, Anissa found herself in front of a camera. Her cherry lips and dusk-colored skin enchanted the photographer, who began to focus on her, not on the beautiful geometric patterns in the Kente. Within months Anissa's smile, as inviting as night brightened by the harvest moon, was plastered across the country in magazines, television commercials, and even a cameo in an Eddie Murphy movie. Anissa's two younger sisters supported her success in modeling and bragged bodaciously about her.

Schiavi, the middle sister, became a physical therapist and trainer and developed an exercise program to help young models to stay physically fit. She was as beautiful as Anissa, with a caramel complexion and almond-shaped eyes, but she had no desire to parade before the camera in a daily grind. Nevertheless, she joined the world of aerobic videos when her clients informed her that they could not find any video featuring women of color. Schiavi went one step further and developed a series of videos to help women build a life of prosperity with health and esteem. Her business soon spread, and she opened one of the first African American health spas. Schiavi franchised her methods, and soon her name was as common as McDonald's across America.

The youngest sister, Nandi, benefited from the love and support of her sisters and parents and became an extroverted risk taker, confident of her ability to tackle any obstacles. Her family showed her that barriers were simply hurdles to go over, under, around, or through. Nandi wanted to be a journalist until she worked on Anissa's videos and then decided to become a member of the electronic highway. She changed her major to computer science, visualizing a future with technology as easy to use as a telephone. Nandi worked for one of the major computer companies, where she saw a need in the African community for electronic-related services. The most obvious entry level was through cable television, and the city in which she was living was seeking bids to wire it. She developed a business proposal and asked her sisters for advice. They not only advised her but provided start-up capital, contacts, and investors for her entry into the cable industry.

Anissa, Schiavi, and Nandi prospered, tackling all problems as a united front—that is, until their father, Jack, died. Immediately after the funeral, Anissa announced, "Mother will move to New York to live with me. She can travel with my family, enjoy our cottage in Martha's Vineyard, and then live quietly on our farm in Connecticut." Schiavi's eyes glimmered angrily as she disagreed, "No way, life in

New York is detrimental to anyone's psyche, especially *my mother's.* Mom can move with me to San Diego. She'll love the climate and she can travel with my family to our ranch in Oregon. I am a trained physical therapist and the only one qualified to look after her." Nandi stared and glowered at her sisters. She said quietly but forcefully, her eyes glistening fire, "You are both out of your minds, I am the youngest. I have the most energy and time to give to *my mother.* I am not broke; she can live in my house in Charleston. As a matter of fact, she and daddy always wanted to return to the South."

Without asking their mother what she wanted to do, they argued for three days about where she would live. Schiavi finally said, "You know, we are so selfish and thoughtless; we never asked mom about her plans. Anissa, you should see your face; all this shouting and arguing is showing. You can't model for anyone with worry lines around your mouth and eyes. Your skin looks like cracked china."

Nandi answered, "You are absolutely right, my nerves are shot. I am not used to screaming and hollering at my big sisters. I can't concentrate on my company until we resolve this problem."

Anissa agreed, "I don't know what came over me. I guess I was throwing my weight around as the oldest sister in the family. I thought you would do what I wanted like you did when we were kids. Sometimes I forget you two are as old as Methuselah."

Later that evening, Anissa said, "Mama, now that daddy is gone, we were wondering what your plans are. I want you to live with me, but so do Schiavi and Nandi. We can't divide you into three parts, so will you please decide?"

Odessa smiled proudly at her three daughters. "I heard you for the past three days, but I knew you would find a solution. Anissa, you have your father's forehead, and you think I need protection. Schiavi, you have your father's serious eyes, and you see things like him. Nandi, you have your father's chin, and you are just as determined. As a family we must stay united and supportive of each other. We can't do that if you quarrel over me and begin to resent each other. You are all correct. I would like to live with each of you, but I will live right here in our home for six months of the year. The remaining six months I will divide between my three daughters because united we stand, divided we fall."

THE KING OF BIRDS

RETOLD BY DOROTHY WINBUSH RILEY

I heard this Tunisian folktale in the early 1970s and retold it to my children and students for the lessons it teaches. After hearing this story, the listeners know that despite the size of a problem or the strength of an adversary, unity makes strength.

Once the lion and the kinglet, the tiniest of birds, argued about their strength and courage. "I can destroy you with one swat of my paw."

"No way," taunted the tiny bird, I will knock your teeth into your eyes first." Before the sun moved beneath the horizon, they dared each other to test their strength in battle. "All right, every animal that walks on two legs or four legs will join me; I will lead them to victory," growled the lion.

"I will be the winner and lead every insect and bird that travels through the air on wings. We may be smaller, but we will triumph," promised the kinglet.

The armies gathered, and both generals gave orders to their troops.

The kinglet said, "First, I want the mosquitoes and gnats by the legions to attack the lion about his ears, his eyes, his nose, his mouth—all over his head." So many of the tiny insects buzzed around the lion's head that he could not see or give orders. He ran, stumbling and falling, trying to escape their stings and bites. The lion bumped into the hyenas and the zebras and screeched, "Run, for your lives!" The kinglet regrouped her legions and ordered, "Attack the rhinoceros and donkeys and horses." Before the sun moved one degree in the sky, the confused animals panicked and ran helter-skelter into each other.

Then to make matters even more disastrous, the kinglet

gathered embers and dropped them on the other frightened four- and two-legged animals. She cried, "Fire! Fire! Put out the fire!" In a matter of minutes the lion surrendered.

Even now the kinglet still cries, "Fire! Fire! Put out the fire!" as she flits from place to place. And all the animals know that despite her small size, she is the *king* of birds.

In unity there is strength.

I MUST SING! I MUST SING!

DOROTHY WINBUSH RILEY

The main lesson that this folktale teaches is the we must maintain unity under all circumstances. The group stays unified, despite one member's behavior that puts everyone in danger. Although the donkey places his selfish desires above the safety of the other animals, once threatened, he retreats to the safety of the united front. Instead of angrily turning him away, the other animals welcome and protect him as if he had not brought danger on everyone. When telling this story, it is important to remind the listeners that if the other animals fight the selfish member, all are vulnerable to attack and ultimate destruction.

To the south of the Senufo, in the center of the Ivory Coast, a wandering tribe moved their village to a new site. They left behind a sway-backed donkey, a mange-eaten dog, a rooster with one leg longer than the other, and a ram with one broken horn. The castaways swore unity and brotherhood and determined to live together.

It happened that one day, as the rooster flew from tree to tree, he saw an abandoned silo full of barley. He immediately called his four companions, and from then on, they daily feasted on the grain. Soon, the rooster's feathers shone apple red, and his comb shot off embers like gleaming topaz. He began to walk in such a way that no one could detect his limp. The donkey also saw a healthy improvement, growing so fat that his back looked as if it were straight, and soon, the ram and the dog looked like the leaders of the pack.

Everyone lived in harmony. One day, though, the donkey was feeling so satisfied that he left the silo braying, "I must sing! I must rejoice!"

The other animals rushed to quiet him, "What if a tiger hears you singing and rejoicing so loudly? Then we'll all be in danger," warned the dog.

"The tiger will rip us to shreds; my horns are no match for his teeth," cried the ram. The donkey stubbornly sashayed off and began to bray as if he were at Carnegie Hall. During his final solo, he realized that something was breathing quietly at his back. He turned, and sure enough, a tiger stood grinning confidently at him. The donkey said, with great bravado, "I see destiny that does not like my singing and I won't be able to finish my song. But if I can have one last wish before you devour me, I will go without a fight."

"What is your wish?" whispered the tiger through clenched teeth.

"My friends would be heartbroken if we were separated. We are a brotherhood, and we promised to live together, to prosper together, and to die together. My wish is that you devour us all."

"That is a good oath, and I will be happy to send each of you to paradise," replied the tiger. "Now, take me to them quickly; I have waited much too long."

When the animals saw the donkey leading a tiger to their compound, they didn't panic or try to hide. "Not one of us can beat a tiger alone, but together we can win," said the ram. They thought of an action plan instantly. When the donkey and the tiger came near, the other animals said in unison, "Welcome brother donkey; thank you for bringing a guest. Welcome tiger!"

Before the tiger had a chance to respond to the friendly greeting, the ram ran straight at him, butting him in the middle of his forehead and knocking him into the air. The tiger somersaulted back to earth and was knocked out when his body reached the ground. That ended the tiger. Within days, nothing remained of him except his skin, which the donkey tanned.

For a few months, the compound was a peaceful, quiet oasis. Nevertheless, the donkey proclaimed one day, "I must sing again! I must express myself! I cannot help it; I am a donkey! I must bray!"

The rooster crowed, "Be quiet, you tuneless beast; remember what happened the last time you tried to sing. You are not Isaac Hayes, Paul Robeson, or Marian Anderson."

"Yes," added the ram, "please be quiet! I am in no mood to deal with any visitor that wants to eat me. Your singing is a bad sign."

The dog said nothing because he had received the lion's share of the tiger and was eager for another visitor.

A donkey must bray, and bray he did. Soon his off-key singing was heard above all else, and a second tiger prowling nearby came to see what was butchering the eight musical notes. The donkey expected this visitor and said, with great courage, "I see destiny does not like my singing and I won't be able to finish my song. But if I can have one last wish before you devour me, I will go without a fight."

He made the same request as with the first tiger, and the second tiger agreed. The other animals knew the outcome of the donkey's singing and were prepared. When the two entered the compound, the ram said, "Welcome! Brother donkey, thank you for bringing a guest. Welcome tiger!"

The rooster crowed, "Make our guest comfortable; bring something for him to sit on." The dog went and dragged out the tanned tiger hide by the tail.

"Oh, no!" cried the ram. "Our guest deserves a much better rug than this. His honor deserves a newer carpet than this old one. Go, get another."

The dog then left with the tiger hide and soon returned, dragging the same hide by the neck. "No, no!" cried the ram impatiently. "We have a very important guest with us. He is more noble than his brothers who visited us before. Go, get another rug; this time select the best from our supply of carpets."

The dog left, but the tiger quickly jumped to his feet and ran away as fast as he could, thinking, "I must warn the others; these four are much too strong."

The donkey continued to express himself by singing, but no tigers ever came to sit in his audience again.

ROW TOGETHER:
PROVERBS FOR UMOJA

To be united is to be strong.—Africa

Horn blowers! Blow in unison.—Buganda

Many fishers together will catch even the small fishes.
—Buganda

Teeth without gaps chew the meat.—Buganda

One finger cannot wash your face.—Congo

A single bracelet does not jingle.—Congo

When spiders unite, they can tie up a lion.
—Ethiopia

Two ears but they do not hear two stories.—Ghana

If one finger tries to pick up something from the ground,
it cannot.—Ghana

The roof shelters the whole family.—Hausa

Sticks in a bundle are unbreakable.—Kenya

If the fingers of one hand quarrel, they cannot pick up
the food.—Kenya

Children are the wisdom of the nation.—Liberia

Hold a true friend with both hands.—Nigeria

Home is a warm bed for the family.—South Africa

If you are in one boat, you have to row together.—South Africa

A home of your own is worth wagons of gold.—South Africa

One man cannot launch a ship.—Swahili

United jaws crush the bone.—Uganda

We join together to make wise decisions, not foolish ones.—Yoruba

Paddle all together, left, right, left, right.—Zaire

One arm cannot work.—Zambia

Let the singers sing in unison; then the job can be done.—Zulu

You need your friend to help put the firewood on your back.—Zulu

THOUGHTS FOR UMOJA

❖ Make your family the center of your life.

❖ Maintain balance in your life: laughter with tears, tears with laughter.

❖ All life is interdependent; no one accomplishes anything without the help of others.

❖ Knowledge pays lifelong dividends. Continue to learn; educating yourself takes a lifetime.

❖ Respect and care for the elders, for they have knowledge and experience to guide you.

❖ Live for a cause higher than yourself to enjoy a prosperous life's journey.

❖ Give to society to make other lives more meaningful.

❖ Think success, and it will follow.

❖ Thought rules the world. Your condition and circumstances are the reflection of your habitual thinking.

❖ Become a creative center, giving love, wisdom, and understanding. As you sow, you will reap wonders in your life.

CHAPTER TWO

PRINCIPLE 2

KUJICHAGULIA

DEFINITIONS BELONG TO THE DEFINER: THE MEANING OF KUJICHAGULIA

The Creator gave me the will to create my destiny. I will name. I will control. I will preserve. I will define. I will create the image best for me. My history, my posterity, and my life are for me to shape. Kujichagulia is loyalty to my race, my people, as I stride into the future demanding a place.

—Tiaudra Riley

Africa's children celebrate Kujichagulia, the second principle of Kwanzaa, on December 27, when families and friends gather to light the first green candle and to relight the black candle. The activities and discussions are centered on how self-determination and persistence help African Americans acquire and maintain our identity. The creation of Kwanzaa is an example of self-determination, since African Americans shape a holiday in our own image and interest. Several poems and stories in *The Complete Kwanzaa* resulted from the Umoja and Kujichagulia of my family.

All principles reinforce each other; however, we cannot achieve Kujichagulia without first uniting with each other. Self-determination is having a purpose and working to fulfill it quietly and efficiently without allowing the negative doubts of others to mislead. It is listening to our own voice, trusting our own thoughts, and spreading our own light. Aimé Cesairé says, "Every human word, idea and name, once spoken, becomes real. The word has the power to decide the course of events, change and transform them.... Every name spoken is a thought believed with consequences that alters the environment." As a result, the most important acts of this principle are to name, control, and command ourselves, expecting a prosperous future.

Names are not mere words; they are a link to all the ancestors who came before and all the descendants who will follow. Naming the new life was a creative act and much too serious to be left to the whims of the moment. The ancestors believed that the name contained secrets of the child's existence and defined the challenges to be overcome in the future. In ancient African societies, parents gave names to their newborns that honored the ancestors, appealed to the spirits, evoked the status of the family, or told of the circumstances of the birth. Often the child's name told a story of when the birth occurred—during the day or night, on a special day, or even on a specific day of the week. I have a friend who named her daughter Kikiwa Adjoa, meaning that she was the first girl born on a Monday.

The seriousness of the parents' ritual of naming their child is illustrated in Alex Haley's *Roots:* "By ancient customs, for the next seven days, there was but a single task with which Omoro would seriously occupy himself, the selection of a name for his first born son. It would have to be a name rich with history and with promise for the people of his tribe—the Mandinkan believed that a child would develop seven of the characteristics of whomever or whatever he was named for." Once the child was named, he was identified and accepted as a member of the village.

One's name expressed a great deal: identity, heritage, and value. The last name indicated a person's ethnic and geographic origins. For this reason, it was all the more devastating when ships' captains and planters renamed kidnapped Africans with English names, effectively stripping them of their identities as members of a tribe. From the 1600s to the present, Africans in America have been called many names—names that not only altered our destiny, but severed our roots and the context of security within kinship groups. Without these connections, African Americans faced challenge after challenge in confronting the narrow image forced on us by others. Belonging to a kinship group and participating in its beliefs, ceremonies, rituals, and festivals are a large part of what it means to be human, what it means to have a name. African Americans are one of the only ethnic groups whose surnames do not reflect their African ancestry and their belonging to a kinship group; we still carry first and last names of the dominant culture. As Brazilian revolutionary Paulo Freire stated in *Pedagogy of the Oppressed:* "To exist, humanly, is to name the world, to change it. Once named, the world in its turn reappears to the namers as a problem and requires of them a new naming."

Kwanzaa reaffirms that the quest for and maintenance of significant traditions are necessary for our identity and ultimately for our existence. During the 1960s, when the holiday was first developed, self-determination meant words of action and reflection, words to change and denounce repressive aspects of American society with a commitment to transform ourselves. As African American historian Chancellor Williams said in *The Destruction of Black Civilization,* through Kwanzaa, "We can determine what our heritage really is and, instead of just talking about 'identity,' we shall know at last precisely what purely African body of principles, values systems or philosophy of life—slowly evolved by our own forefathers over countless ages. There can be no real identity with our heritage until we know what our heritage really is. We have been floating along, blissfully basking in the sunny heritage of other people."

Kujichagulia charges all African Americans with designing ourselves. Each of us is born unfinished and must accept the responsibility of shaping his or her identity. Through self-determination we can and do change who we are and how we live. We do not waste time blaming others for the world our thoughts have created. Self-determining people look within to change the causes of their predicament, so that the entire situation changes.

Our destiny does not lie in what we are, but in what we can successfully become once our minds are truly free. Successful African Americans control their fate by living the universal laws of prosperity, belief, faith, and attraction. Kujichagulia is an essential part of the psyche of successful people who create a personal vision with change as a stimulus to growth and prosperity and intuitively accept the laws of cause and effect, taking risks to create their own opportunities. Again, the words of Freire remind us that self-determination means freedom and that "freedom is acquired by conquest, not by gift. It must be pursued constantly and responsibly. Freedom is not an ideal located outside of man; nor is it an idea which becomes myth. It is rather the indispensable condition for the quest for human completion."

The poetry, biographical pieces, folktales, and proverbs in this chapter represent Kujichagulia as it relates to African Americans' image, self-esteem, change, control, growth, and ultimate self-determination. Oprah Winfrey learned how to handle frustrations, mistakes, failure, and rejection. She took a risk when she quit her successful Baltimore talk show for the one in Chicago. Booker T. Washington always gave more than he expected to receive as he created opportunities for legions of African Americans when he dared to build Tuskegee Institute on swampland. Malcolm X risked his life by forging his own identity and system of beliefs, rather then relying on the dictates of others. Michael Jordan's family practiced the principles of Kwanzaa from his youth. From their cocoon of loving support, Jordan developed the skill to strengthen himself and his community economically. He showed how teamwork with the Chicago Bulls led to championships and applied the same principles to his personal life. All the selections focus on hope that strengthens the will to live with determination and to work to make life possible.

"Twin Images in Black." Wood carving, artist unknown. Photograph by Bill Sanders.

STRETCH FORTH YOUR MIND: POETRY FOR KUJICHAGULIA

I'M SPECIAL

DOROTHY WINBUSH RILEY

In all the world there's nobody like me. Since the beginning of time there has never been another person like me. Nobody has my smile. Nobody has my eyes, my nose, my hair, my hands, my body, my voice—I'm special. No one can be found who has my handwriting. Nobody anywhere has my tastes for food, clothing, music, or art. No one sees things exactly as I do. In all of time there has been no one who laughs like me or cries like me. And what makes me laugh or cry will not create identical laughter and tears in anybody else, ever.

I am the only one in all creation who has
   my set of abilities.
I am the only one in all creation who has
   my imagination.
I am the only one in all creation who has
   my determination.
I am the only one in all creation who has
   my mind.
I am the only one in all creation who is
   responsible for my actions, my behavior,
   my words, my success, my failures. I am
   special and I accept me.

Oh, there will always be somebody who is better at one of the things I can do, but no one in the universe will reach the quality of my combination of talents, ideas, personality, and feelings. Like a room full of musical instruments, some may excel alone, but none can match the sound created when all are played together. I am a symphony. Through all eternity, no one will ever look, talk, walk, think, or act exactly like me. I am special. I am rare. And in rarity, there is value.

Because of my value I need not attempt to imitate others—I will be myself. I will accept and celebrate my differences. I am special and I am beginning to see that this is no accident. The Creator made me for a special work. I have a purpose that no one else can fulfill. There is a job for me that no one else can do as well as I. Out of the billions of applicants, only one is qualified, only one has the right combination of what it takes. That one is me—because *I am special.*

CHOICES

Nikki Giovanni

If I can't do
what I want to do
then my job is to not
do what I don't want
to do
It's not the same thing
but it's the best I can
do
If I can't have
what I want then
my job is to want
what I've got
and be satisfied
that at least there
is something more
to want
since I can't go
where I need
to go then I must go
where the signs point
though always understanding
parallel movement
isn't lateral

when I can't express
what I really feel
I practice feeling
what I can express
and none of it is equal
I know
but that's why mankind
alone among the mammals
learns to cry

INTO THE LIGHT

Serena Gordon

I've passed through the tunnel, into the light.
I'm standing on a hill with the world spread
before me—field, deserts, rivers, and
mountains all the cities of the world laid out
at my feet. The choice is mine. I've fought
and struggled to reach this choice, and now
it's arrived it daunts me.

As I look behind, I see the chains discarded
on the ground, and an empty black void. The
demons have been replaced and can be seen
no more. I've held on to myself and my soul
and have reached the light intact. Now I
have to justify that struggle and keep the
demons away forever.

I need to find the right way through the
world, the way that is right for me, the way
that will keep the spark inside me glowing
brightly. Nothing must ever extinguish the
spark, because then the true heart and soul
die. So far I've kept alive and now I can walk
slowly into the light.

NAMING THEMSELVES: PEOPLE OF KUJICHAGULIA

OPRAH WINFREY: ACCEPTANCE, ESTEEM, LOVE

DOROTHY WINBUSH RILEY

Kujichagulia starts with positive self-esteem, a sense that you have value and worth. It is the beginning of freedom and responsibility, forecasting how you succeed or fail, whether you live on the brink, in the dumps, or in the money. Wally "Famous" Amos, the African American entrepreneur and businessman, says, "Self-esteem is like learning how to walk. You take a few steps, fall down. But you build on each step and finally learn how to run." From the moment you emerge into the world, your self-concept is created step by step through experiences filtered from your surroundings. The learned belief that you are uniquely valuable is vital to your development from the time of your birth and is the basis of self-esteem.

Beliefs and attitudes create a mental photograph that determines who you are, what you think you are, how and when you act, and what you become. Most people have two mental snapshots: the first, the person they wish to change because of perceived imperfections, and the second, the perfect person they dream of being. Creating the pictures is a process that never stops, but grows and changes with each thought and act. Life's odyssey is to merge the two images into one of security, love, respect, and appreciation.

The positive thoughts you harbor can open doors you have closed on yourself: how you see your body, your physical abilities, your sex appeal, your intelligence, your actions, your heart, your feelings, your freedom. Once you control your thinking, forgiveness, acceptance, and healing come naturally. As Oprah Winfrey, states, "What is the bigger issue here? Self-esteem. For me, it is getting control of my life."

Oprah Winfrey is a success by any standard. She is a powerful woman in control of her life, who exudes self-acceptance, self-reliance, self-respect, self-confidence, and self-sufficiency. Yet, before she reached this stage, Oprah had to take an eye-opening journey. At the end of that trip, she discovered a loving person—herself. By looking at herself with honesty and self-acceptance, Oprah merged her many images into one of love, poise, strength, and confidence.

Oprah's primary self-worth springs from living in the cocoon of her grandmother's love until she was five years old. Her grandmother Hattie imprinted her with spiritual values, discipline, the ability to take risks, and theatrical flair. Oprah often says, "I am what I am because of my grandmother. My strength, my sense of reasoning . . . all of that was set by the time I was six years old." Grandmother valued precocious Oprah and taught her to read and write before she was three years old. On their Mississippi farm with no television, they read or went to Kosciusko Baptist Church, where as a toddler, Oprah recited Easter and Christmas speeches. To live is to take risks, and Oprah's church speeches were her first chance for praise or ridicule, her first public appearances. Fortunately, the congregation's awe instilled a "can-do attitude" in the young Oprah. Grandmother Hattie's pride was not lost on Oprah's impressionable young mind, and Oprah's healthy self-esteem sparkled.

Life is balanced with pain and happiness. Pain cannot be avoided, but our reaction to sorrow, change, or other hurts depends on our self-concept. Oprah's surroundings suddenly changed after her mother, Vernita, settled in Milwaukee, Wisconsin, and wanted Oprah to live with her and new baby daughter, Patricia. After three years, however, Vernita felt that she could not raise her two children alone and sent eight-year-old Oprah to live with Oprah's father, Vernon, in Nashville, Tennessee. Before a year passed, Vernita decided that she wanted Oprah back in Milwaukee with her new baby brother, Jeffrey. This roller-coaster existence caused Oprah's self-esteem to sink, allowing negatives to shadow her for many years to come.

Teachers shape lives, and one, in particular, noticed that Oprah was an exceptional student who deserved a more challenging environment. Oprah enrolled in the Upward Bound program that helped low-income students prepare for college. "Books showed me there were possibilities in life, that there were actually people like me living in a world I could not only aspire to but attain." Oprah received a scholarship to private lily-white Nicolet High School in suburban Milwaukee. The transfer did more than showcase her poverty, her differences, and her loneliness; it also distanced her from her family and neighborhood friends. At her new school she was like a raisin on a layer of meringue; she fit in academically but nowhere else. "I was feeling a sense of anguish, because living with my mother in Milwaukee I was in a situation where I was the only black kid in a school of 2,000 upper-middle-class suburban Jewish kids. I would take the bus in the morning to school with the maids who worked in their homes."

Adolescent anxiety and little family structure pushed Oprah into delinquency. Overwhelmed, Vernita tried to put her into a detention home. Instead Vernon sent for his exuberant daughter and immediately took control of the teenager, directed her behavior, restored her values, and set expectations for her. He required her to read five books every two weeks, learn five new words per day, write book reports, and keep a journal to nurture her intelligence and channel her energy. "My father turned my life around by insisting I be more than I was and believing I could be more. His love of learning showed me the way."

Four years later, Oprah was a changed young woman, publicly recognized for her achievements: honor student, White House Conference representative, president of the student council, and beauty queen. In her senior year, the future peeked in when Oprah worked after school at the local radio station.

Vernon's demanding parenting paid off, once again, when Oprah won a partial scholarship to Tennessee State University. Destiny had other plans, though, and during her senior year, ABC in Baltimore offered her a job as a reporter. Twenty-two-year-old Oprah left college to become a street reporter, but returned in 1986 to complete the courses and receive her diploma.

During her odyssey, success and failure meandered in and out of her life, and her self-esteem grew with each risk she took and each goal she achieved. Like a mountain, every life has an up and a down side, and Baltimore was a mountain for Oprah. Oprah was hired as a "token" to satisfy civil rights demands and received little time to fine-tune her reporting skills. As a result, the producers criticized her communicative style as being too emotional. Although many mirrors reflect the face, only self-reflection reveals the spirit. Thus, the magnifying glare of television cameras caused Oprah to look in a flawed mirror, not one that emphasized her God-given gifts. Oprah allowed others to define her outer image, and when the producers sent her for a makeover, she lost all her hair. During this period, she lived far below her potential because she surrendered her individuality to others. After three months, Oprah was removed from the air.

The rush-rush, helter-skelter pace stretched her inner beliefs, and her self-esteem vanished like butter on a hot biscuit. "Overeating became my way of coping with a life that was out of control . . . and the extra weight became a shield that I could hide behind as well as an excuse I could fall back on." Negative self-concepts are experienced by more than 90 percent of the world's population, and Oprah joined the crowd.

Soon, another window of opportunity opened for Oprah;

a talk show, *People Are Talking,* needed an expressive, emotional, informal hostess. "They put me on the show to get rid of me, but it was really my saving grace. The first day I did it I thought, this is what I really should have been doing all along. It was like breathing to me." In 1984 Oprah left Baltimore for a job with the poorly rated *A.M. Chicago,* and within seven months, popular demand increased the show from thirty minutes to sixty minutes. Twelve months later, the show was renamed *The Oprah Winfrey Show* and was soon watched by more viewers across America than any other talk show. Oprah says, "Your belief combined with your willingness to fulfill your dreams is what makes success possible."

Chicago provided a platform for unlimited success and self-determination. Two years after she arrived in the city, Oprah formed HARPO Productions to produce her talk show, television specials, and movies. She unlearned negative thinking and surrounded herself with positive, intelligent friends and workers. In her visualizations she faced her difficulties, overcame them, and went on to gain victory. "I was addicted to food. . . . I didn't need the crutch anymore. I had cleared away all the negative aspects of my life and I was ready to fly."

Oprah represents every person's struggles to survive and triumph as she transmits her grandmother's self-determination and faith. She says, "I was born for greatness in my life. I have always felt it. I don't regret all of the past confusion at all. It has made me exactly who I am. And without all those elements, I would be somebody else. I probably would not, without my past . . . be able to handle what is happening to me as well as I think I am."

Oprah preserves her individuality wisely, wielding her creative power as head of a production studio and owner of a television- and film-production complex, a restaurant, and a media company. "Ultimately it's a question—of understanding who I am, and of you understanding who you are and what we're each here to do. We will falter unless we know our purpose clearly."

Oprah understands that creating herself is an endless process that will last as long as breath oozes from her soul. She knows that success means to be Oprah: first, last, and always. Yet, without an understanding and acceptance of herself, Oprah's life would not be the continuous growth of prosperity that it is.

EXCERPT FROM *UP FROM SLAVERY*

BOOKER T. WASHINGTON

The period immediately following the Civil War changed the destiny of African Americans economically, politically, socially, and ideologically. A key player in those changes was Booker T. Washington, a man who had no power to change his birth as property without a name or a heritage. Yet, he did control his determination to learn. His commitment to himself and his community moved African Americans from hovels to homes. Booker T. Washington knew instinctively that the mind is everything—that whatever you think you are, you become. His life experience taught him that the best way to help a person harvest success is to help the person understand himself or herself. He also believed that the environment should not be allowed to make the person, but that the person can and should change his or her surroundings.

By his presence, Booker T. Washington so affected the times that a new way of believing evolved. This excerpt from his book, *Up from Slavery*, illustrates the successful application of Umoja, Kujichagulia, Imani, Ujima, Kuumba, Ujamaa, and Imani.

After the coming of freedom there were two points upon which practically all the people on our place agreed, and I find this was generally true throughout the South: that they must change their names, and that they must leave the old plantation for at least a few days or weeks in order that they might really feel sure that they were free.

In some way a feeling got among the coloured people that it was far from proper for them to bear the surname of their former owners, and a great many of them took other surnames. This was one of the first signs of freedom. When they were slaves, a coloured person was simply called "John" or "Susan." There was seldom occasion for more than the use of one name. If "John" or "Susan" belonged to a white man by the name of "Hatcher," sometimes he was called "John Hatcher," or as often "Hatcher's John." That was not the proper title to denote a freeman; and so in many cases "John Hatcher" was changed to "John S. Lincoln" or "John L. Sherman," the initial "S" standing for no name, it being simply a part of what the coloured man proudly called his "entitles."

As I have stated, most of the coloured people left the plantation for a short while at least, so as to be sure, it seemed, that they could leave and try their freedom on to see how it felt. After they had remained away for a time, many of the older slaves, especially, returned to their old homes and made some kind of contact with their former owners by which they remained on the estate.

My mother's husband, who was the stepfather of my brother John and myself, did not belong to the same owner as did my mother. In fact, he seldom came to our plantation. I remember seeing him there perhaps once a year about Christmas time. In some way, during the war, by running away and following the Federal soldiers, it seems, he found his way into the new state of West Virginia. As soon as freedom was declared, he sent for my mother to come to Kanawha Valley, in West Virginia. At that time a journey from Virginia over the mountains to West Virginia was rather a tedious, and in some cases a painful undertaking. What little clothing and few household goods we had were placed in a cart, but the children walked the greater portion of the distance, which was several hundred miles.

I do not think any of us had been very far from the plantation, and the taking of a long journey into another state was quite an event. The parting from our former owners and the members of our own race on the plantation was a serious occasion. From the time of our parting till their death we kept up a correspondence with the older members of the family, and in later years we have kept in touch with those who were the younger members. We were several weeks making the trip, and, most of the time we slept in the open air and did our cooking over a log fire out of doors. . . . Finally we reached our destination—a little town called Malden, which is about five miles from Charleston, the present capital of the state.

At that time, salt-mining was the great industry in that part of West Virginia, and the little town of Malden was right in the middle of the salt-furnaces. My stepfather had already secured a job at a salt-furnace, and he had also a little cabin for us to live in. Our new house was no better than the one we had left on the plantation in Virginia. In fact, in one respect it was worse. Notwithstanding the poor condition of our plantation cabin, we were at all times sure of pure air. Our new home was in the midst of a cluster of cabins crowded closely together, and as there were no sanitary regulations, the filth about the cabins was often intolerable. Some of the neighbors were coloured people, and some were the poorest and most degraded white people. It was a motley mixture. Drinking, gambling, quarrels, fights, and shockingly immoral practices were frequent. All who lived in the little town were in one way or another connected with the salt business. Though I was a mere child, my stepfather put me and my brother at work in one of the furnaces. Often I began work as early as four o'clock in the morning.

The first thing I ever learned in the way of book knowledge was while working at this salt-furnace. Each salt-packer had his barrel marked with a certain number. The number allotted to my stepfather was "18." At the close of day's work the boss of the packers would come around and put "18" on each of our barrels, and I soon learned to recognize that figure wherever I saw it, and after a while got to the point where I could make that figure, though I knew nothing about any other figures or letters.

From the time that I can remember having any thoughts about anything, I recall that I had an intense longing to learn to read. I determined, when quite a small child, that, if I accomplished nothing else in life, I would in some way get enough education to enable me to read common books and newspapers. Soon after we got settled in some manner in our new cabin in West Virginia, I induced my mother to get hold of a book for me. How or where she got it I do not know, but in some way she procured an old copy of Webster's "blue-back" spelling-book, which contained the alphabet, followed by such meaningless words as "ab," or "ba," "ca," "da." I began at once to devour this book, and I think that it was the first one I ever had in my hands. I had learned from somebody that the way to begin to read was to learn the alphabet, so I tried in all ways I could think of to learn it—all of course without a teacher, for I could find no one to teach me. At that time there was not a single member of my race anywhere near us who could read, and I was too timid to approach any of the white people. In some way, within a week, I mastered the greater portion of the alphabet. In all my efforts to learn to read my mother shared fully in my ambition, and sympathized with me and aided me in every way that she could. Though she was totally ignorant, so far as mere book knowledge was concerned, she had high ambitions for her children, and a large fund of good, hard common sense which seemed to enable her to meet and master every situation. If I had done anything in life worth attention, I feel sure I inherited the disposition from my mother.

In the midst of my struggles and longing for an education, a young coloured boy who had learned to read in Ohio came to Malden. As soon as the coloured people found out that he could read, a newspaper was secured, and at the close of nearly every day's work this young man would be surrounded by a group of men and women who were anxious to hear him read the news contained in the papers. How I used to envy this man! He seemed to me to be the one young man in all the world who ought to be satisfied with his attainments.

About this time the question of having some kind of a school opened for the colored children in the village began to be discussed by members of the race. As it would be the first school for Negro children that had ever been opened in that part of Virginia, it was, of course, to be a great event, and the discussion excited the widest interest. The most perplexing question was where to find a teacher. The young man from Ohio who had learned to read the papers was considered, but his age was against him. In the midst of the discussion about a teacher, another young coloured man from Ohio, who had been a soldier, found his way into town. It was soon learned that he possessed considerable education, and he was engaged by the coloured people to teach their first school. As yet no free schools had been started for coloured people in that section, hence each family agreed to pay a certain amount each month, with the understanding that the teacher was to "board 'round"— that is, spend a day with each family. This was not bad for the teacher, for each family tried to provide the very best on the day the teacher was to be its guest. I recall that I looked forward with anxious appetite to the "teacher's day" at our little cabin.

This experience of a whole race beginning to go to school for the first time, presents one of the most interesting studies that has ever occurred in connection with the development of any race. Few people who were not right in the midst of the scene can form any exact ideas of the intense desire which the people of my race showed for an education. As I have stated, it was a whole race trying to go to school. Few were too young, and none too old, to make the attempt to learn. As fast as any kind of teacher could be secured, not only were day-schools filled, but night-schools as well. The great ambition of the older people was to try to learn to read the Bible before they died. With this end in view, men and women who were fifty or seventy-five years old would often be found in the night-school. Sunday schools were formed soon after freedom, but the principal book studied in the Sunday school was the spelling-book. Day-school, night-school, Sunday school, were always crowded, and often many had to be turned away for want of room.

The opening of the school in Kanawha Valley, however, brought one of the keenest disappointments that I ever experienced. I had been working in a salt-furnace for several months, and my stepfather had discovered that I had a financial value, and so, when the school opened, he decided he could not spare me from my work. This decision seemed to cloud my every ambition. The disappointment was made all the more severe by reason of the fact that my place of work was where I could see the happy children passing to and from school, mornings and afternoons. Despite this disappointment, however, I determined that I would learn something, anyway. I applied myself with greater earnestness than ever to the mastering of what was in the "blue-back" speller.

My mother sympathized with me in my disappointment, and sought to comfort me in all the ways she could, and to help me find a way to learn. After a while I succeeded in making arrangements with the teacher to give me some lessons at night, after the day's work was done. These night lessons were so welcome that I think I learned more at night than the other children did during the day. My own experiences in the night-school gave me faith in the night-school idea, with which, in after years, I had to do both at Hampton and Tuskegee. But my boyish heart was still set upon going to day school, and I let no opportunity slip to push my case. Finally I won, and was permitted to go to school in the day for a few months, with the understanding that I was to rise early in the morning and work in the furnace till nine o'clock, and return immediately after school closed in the afternoon for at least two more hours of work. . . .

When . . . I found myself at the school for the first time, I found myself confronted with two other difficulties. In the first place, I found that all the children wore hats or caps on their heads, and I had neither hat nor cap. . . . When I saw how all the other boys were dressed, I began to feel quite uncomfortable. As usual, I put the case before my mother, and she explained to me that she had no money with which to buy a "store hat," which was rather a new institution among members of my race and was considered quite the thing for young and old, but that she would find some way to help me. . . . She accordingly got two pieces of "home-spun" (jeans) and sewed them together, and I was soon the proud possessor of my first cap.

The lesson my mother taught me has always remained with me, and I have tried as best I could to teach it to others. I have always felt proud that my mother had strength of character enough not to be led into the temptation of seeming to be that which she was not—of trying to impress my schoolmates and others that she was able to buy me a "store hat" when she was not. I have always felt proud that she refused to go into debt for that which she did not have the money to pay for. . . . several of the boys who began their careers with "store hats" . . . used to join in the sport that was made of me because I had only a "homespun" cap, have ended in penitentiary, while others are not able to buy any kind of hat.

My second difficulty was with regard to my name, or rather *a* name. From the time I could remember anything, I had been called simply "Booker." Before going to school it had never occurred to me that it was needful or appropriate to have an additional name. When I first heard the school-roll called, I noticed that all of the children had at least two names, and some of them indulged in what seemed to me the extravagance of having three. I was in deep perplexity because I knew that the teacher would demand of me at least two names, and I had only one. By the time the occasion came for the enrolling of my name, an idea occurred to me which I thought would make me equal to the situation; and so, when the teacher asked me what my full name was, I calmly told him "Booker Washington," [his stepfather's surname] as if I had been called by that name all my life; and by that name I have since been known. Later in life I found that my mother had given me the name of "Booker Taliaferro" soon after I was born, but in some way that part of my name seemed to disappear, and for a long while after was forgotten, but as soon as I found out about it I revived it, and made my full name "Booker Taliaferro Washington." I think there are not many men in our country who have had the privilege of naming themselves in the way that I have.

More than once I have tried to picture myself in the position of a boy or man with an honoured and distinguished ancestry which I could trace back through a period of hundreds of years, and who had not only inherited a name, but fortune and a proud family homestead; and yet I have sometimes had the feeling that if I had inherited these, and had been a member of a more popular race, I should have been inclined to yield to the temptation of depending upon my ancestry and my colour to do that for me which I should do for myself. Years ago I resolved that because I had no ancestry myself I would leave a record of which my children would be proud, and which might encourage them to still higher effort.

SELF-DETERMINED CHANGE OF MALCOLM X

DOROTHY WINBUSH RILEY

Anything I do today, I regard as urgent. No man is given but so much time to accomplish whatever is his life's work. My particular life never has stayed fixed in one position for very long. You have seen how throughout my life, I have known unexpected drastic changes.

—*Autobiography of Malcolm X*

One of the keys to success is how information for change and growth is perceived, interpreted, and applied. Kujichagulia is gathering information that is necessary to change ourselves, the opinions of others, and the outcome of situations. All matter, both living and inanimate, constantly changes, yet only humankind has the capacity for conscious decisions. The life cycle from birth to death touches all; no person is immune to aging, growth, and maturity because our bodies, ideas, and attitudes constantly change. Nevertheless, we try to hold on to the status quo. If change was less frightening, if the risks did not seem so great, opposition would melt like ice cream on a Santa Monica beach. Kujichagulia means accepting and risking change.

Self-determining change occurs naturally when you probe deep inside, accepting what you find and taking responsibility for your existence so growth can begin. Real change occurs when the mind accepts the reality that a new way is desirable and possible. In the words of writer John O. Killens, those, like Malcolm, who strive for self-determination with a greater mission than simple personal changes must remember: "World-changing is a hazardous pursuit. The lives of men who would dare to change the world and challenge the Gods of Power and the Status Quo are never smooth, indeed are always fraught with danger."

Malcolm X's life sustained explosive change from his birth in 1925 to his assassination forty years later. His father, Earl Little, a Baptist minister and disciple of Marcus Garvey, was the perfect target for the Ku Klux Klan's ferocious terror tactics. The family lived a precarious existence, bombarded with prejudice, fear, ignorance, and hatred. The children listened to their father's preaching that commanded them to be self-determined, self-respectful, and self-sufficient. Malcolm was barely four years old when his family escaped a bloodthirsty mob that torched their home in Kansas.

Kansas had been terror filled, but the move to Lansing, Michigan, added even more horror to their lives. At age six, Malcolm's life center again changed drastically after his father was bludgeoned to death, then placed across the rails of a streetcar to be crushed. Despite the evidence of homicide, the police ruled the death an accident without bothering to search for his murderers. The insurance company labeled it a suicide and refused to pay the life insurance policy, so the family was left destitute.

After the violent murder of her husband, Louise Little raised eight children without emotional support; without money; and, many days, without food. Inevitably, without basic self-respect, community support, and kinship groups, her psyche crumbled, prompting the state of Michigan to commit her to a mental hospital.

Malcolm was twelve when he and his brothers were parceled to foster homes as if they were Care packages. Before he entered puberty, Malcolm had watched the slow, disintegration of his mother and experienced the racist hatred of American society when his father was murdered. He coped by mischievously placing a thumbtack on a teacher's chair; the school expelled him, and the juvenile home became his home. From the moment a junior high school teacher discouraged him from thinking of becoming a lawyer because of his color, Malcolm erased thoughts of achievement from his mind. Since he could not find his place in society or feel that education was beneficial, he mentally dropped out of school.

American society judges an ethnic group, a nation, or any diverse population by its least worthy members. As an adolescent, Malcolm represented a seemingly expendable group: He had no parents, no money, and no name, and it was simple for society to discard him like a crushed beer can. Without a family center, he left school, gradually losing his way in a country that treated him like an invisible man. At age fourteen, Malcolm went to Boston to live with his older sister, Ella.

Three months before his twenty-first birthday in 1946, Malcolm, convicted of burglary, entered prison, socially maladjusted and full of rage. Fortunately, the discarded oppressed are often the raw material of a nation's future. Some inmates wither like a cut rose and die, many explode like nitroglycerin that is touched one time too often, while still others make positive adjustments and grow.

The teachings of Elijah Muhammad hit Malcolm like a guided missile, transforming his mental attitude and giving him the motivation to survive prison. As he reflected on his past actions, fears, hopes, prejudices, wants, and beliefs, he began to control what he allowed into his mind.

After he discovered the Nation of Islam, Malcolm X understood that education was necessary to alter his destiny. He copied the entire unabridged dictionary, studied every word to increase his vocabulary, and practiced speaking and writing. Once his understanding grew, his reading increased to include history; philosophy; African history; and biographies of Hannibal, Karl Marx, Mahatma Gandhi, John Brown, Vladimir Lenin, Joseph Stalin, Adolf Hitler, Erwin Rommel, H. G. Wells, and Will Durant. For the next six and a half years, he devoured the prison library as a cobra devours a cow, slowly and completely.

At age twenty-seven, Malcolm walked out of prison a changed man, a minister of the Nation of Islam and in charge of his attitude. When circumstances demanded changes in behavior, Malcolm responded. Flexibility enabled him to grow, despite the label of "criminal." Kujichagulia means that whatever our past, whatever our habits and behaviors, each person can change to meet the demands of the time. At age thirty-five, Malcolm left the Nation of Islam and formed the Organization of Afro-American Unity for people of color worldwide. He began to preach self-improvement and encouraged his followers to stop blaming others for the plight of African Americans. He urged African Americans to take charge of their destiny and vote, and he traveled to Alabama to speak on behalf of Dr. King. In 1964 he organized a Harlem voter registration drive, urging people to vote as Independents, not Democrats or Republicans.

Any man or woman who would successfully transform the attitudes of a nation or the world cannot do so by sowing hatred, fear, discontent, or force. These poisons offer no benefits except anger, frustration, division, and resentment. Malcolm's Kujichagulia transcended his personal history when he responsibly corrected his past behavior and escaped the time warp of despair. Malcolm said, "It would be impossible to find anywhere in America a black man who has lived further down in the mud of human society than I have; or a black man who has been any more ignorant than I have been; or a black man who has suffered more anguish during his life than I have. But it is only after the deepest darkness that the greatest joy can come; it is only after slavery and prison that the sweetest appreciation of freedom can come."

EXCERPT FROM *RARE AIR*

MICHAEL JORDAN

Michael Jordan is undoubtedly the greatest basketball player America has ever seen. As the king of the courts, he crossed all lines—age and race—as smoothly as he scored points in a game. Michael epitomizes self-determination in his passionate and singleminded desire to become a basketball player. He practiced and worked hard from his days in high school to the pro leagues, where he realized his goal. In this excerpt from *Rare Air*, Michael tells how his spectacular career and self-determination began—with growing confidence in himself.

I always felt I could shoot. When I came out of college everyone said, "He can't shoot the jumper." I never had to. I could penetrate zones in college. And teams played me one on one at North Carolina. They never double-teamed me. I always had a quick enough first step to get to the hole. I never looked to be aggressive offensively in college because I was playing in a system and I was learning the game.

That was the education I got from Dean Smith. Coming out of high school, I had all the ability in the world but I didn't know the game. Dean taught me the game, when to apply speed, how to use your quickness, when to use that first step, or how to apply certain skills in certain situations. I gained all that knowledge so that when I got to the pros, it was just a matter of applying the information.

A lot of people say Dean Smith held me to under 20 points a game. Dean Smith gave me the knowledge to score 37 points a game and that's something people don't understand.

I was the kind of guy in school that if I had a term paper to do I'd wait until the very last minute. The first time you are able to come through in that situation then you think you can do it all the time. Now relate that to basketball. The first time you hit a jump shot with no time on the clock, you can always go back to the moment. You have the confidence because you've done it before.

I wasn't afraid to take big shots in the professional ranks because I had made one when I was a snotty nosed kid in 1982 to beat Georgetown. That's why I say that my career really started when I made that shot. I was fearless after that. I had gone through every test there was and I had come out on top. What can be any more pressure than hitting the game-winning shot for your team in an NCAA title game as a freshman?

That started my career. Why? Because I had that confidence. No one could take that away from me. I was in the situation and I came through. Now when I get in that situation, I don't weigh the negatives and positives and hope the positives win. I just go back to my past successes, step forward and respond. That's why your great players make great plays in clutch situations consistently. They have something to compare it to whenever the situation presents itself. They can accept the consequences because they have done it before. It takes talent, but it takes guts. Not everybody has them. Where does it come from? I don't know. But I think it must come from your work ethic.

You do it on smaller scales until you build up to an NBA championship game. You do it in Little League when your team needs a home run and pow, you knock it out of the park. Then in high school you need a basket to win the Christmas championship and pow, there it is. Then you move up to college. Each level, the confidence grows stronger and stronger until you get to the highest level, where I am now, and you're thinking, "Give me the ball. I'll shoot it. No problem." If you make the shot, then everybody will be shaking your hand. If you miss, you've done it before, so what? You've got room for error. But your expectation is success because you've had that success in the past.

DECLARE THE TRUTH TO THE PEOPLE: QUOTATIONS TO INSPIRE KUJICHAGULIA

"He belongs someplace. The day he was given a name he was also given a place which no one but he himself can fill."—Maya Angelou

"You must begin to define for yourself; you must begin to define your Black heritage."—H. Rap Brown

"Strive to make something of yourself; then strive to make the most of yourself."—Alexander Crummell

"These are my plans: to make a name in science, to make a name in literature and thus to raise my race."—W. E. B. Du Bois

"It is through our names that we first place ourselves in the world."—Ralph Ellison

"Africa is the land of our origin, and since she is by fact of history and archaeology, the mother of the oldest civilization, the oldest science, the oldest art, she is by eminent fitness placed first in the compound title, Afro-American."—J. C. Embry

"We can't rely on anyone but ourselves to define our existence, to shape the image of ourselves."—Spike Lee

"The name of Deadwood Dick was given to me by the people of Deadwood, South Dakota, July 4, 1876, after I had proven myself worthy to carry it, and after I had defeated all comers in riding, roping, and shooting, and I have always carried the name with honor since that time."—Nat Love

"All people have a major task, from cradle to grave, of defining who they are."—William Lyles

"The kinship that the ANC feels for the people of Harlem goes deeper than skin color. It is the kinship of our shared historical experience and the kinship of the solidarity of the victims of blind prejudice and hatred. To our people Harlem symbolizes the strength and beauty in resistance, and you have taught us that out of resistance to injustice comes renaissance, renewal and rebirth."—Nelson Mandela

"Definitions belong to the definer—not the defined."
—Toni Morrison

"J. C. Beman says that when his father was presented with manumission papers, he was asked what name he had selected, he replied that he had always loathed slavery, and wanted to be a man; hence he adopted the name, *Beman*."—William Nell

"We wish to plead our own cause. Too long have others spoken for us."—John Russwurm

"I told Jesus it would be all right if he changed my name."—Spiritual

"When I left the house of bondage I left everything behind. I wasn't going to keep nothing of Egypt on me, an' so I went to the Lord an' asked him to give me a new name. And he gave me Sojourner because I was to travel up and down the land showing the people their sins and bein' a sign unto them. I told the Lord I wanted two names 'cause everybody else had two, and the Lord gave me Truth, because I was to declare the truth to the people."
—Sojourner Truth

"My great-great-grandmother walked as a slave from Virginia to Eatenton, Georgia—which passes for the Walker ancestral home—with two babies on her hips. She lived to be a hundred and twenty-five years old and my own father knew her as a boy. It is in memory of this walk that I chose to keep and to embrace my maiden name, Walker."—Alice Walker

"Every person comes into this world seeking his name. This is the centrality of life. By one's name is not meant the name upon a birth certificate nor the name by which one's parents call him. Rather, what is the name by which God calls you?"—Herman Watts

"My good name is all that I have in the world and I was bound to protect it from attack by those who felt that they could do so with impunity because I had no brother or father to protect it for me."—Ida B. Wells

"We are going to have to be more self-sufficient, almost the way black communities were when they were segregated. We need to buy the theaters in our communities; we need to buy television stations. We need to have more money in our own banks if we want to purchase and be competitive."—Camille Cosby

POWER OF THE WORD: FOLKTALES FOR KUJICHAGULIA

OLAGOUSSA: A MAN OF CHARACTER

RETOLD BY DOROTHY WINBUSH RILEY

Each person has the ability to shape his or her character by controlling the words spoken and the actions taken. In this African folktale, Olagoussa proves that if a man is determined, honest, and wise, he never has to lie.

In the city of Accra on the Gulf of Guinea in Ghana, there lived an honest woodcarver, named Olagoussa, a brave and strong man who was both willow and rock to the people. He was not very rich and not very poor; he had everything he needed and was content to live a quiet, simple life. Olagoussa did not have a quick tongue with easy words; he talked slowly and never made hasty promises. He had more work than he could finish, since the people trusted, honored, and respected him because he completed all work as promised. Not once in the memory of the griot had Olagoussa told a lie, not a big lie and certainly not a small lie.

Soon, word of his character reached the ears of Bahumbe, chief of the Soninkas. After listening to his councillors speak of the greatness of Olagoussa, the chief said, "I do not believe such a man exists. No one is filled with such goodness and honesty that he never tells a lie. Bring him to me."

The eldest councillor said, "You can believe me, this man is known from ocean to ocean for his honesty."

The chief replied, "I don't believe a man can live his

entire life without telling a lie, unless he is alone in the desert with only the sand as a companion."

Within days a messenger brought Olagoussa to the chief.

"Is it true that you have never told a lie or uttered a false statement?" the chief asked.

"Yes, I believe it is true," replied Olagoussa.

"This is very hard for my ears to believe. How can you be certain you have never told even a small lie, and who's to say you won't find yourself in a future situation when you will have to lie?" asked the chief.

"That is true, but the situation or circumstances are not important, for I cannot tell the future and cannot predict what is false," Olagoussa answered.

"You are truly an amazing, virtuous man. I hope you keep your virtue and never lie because the people have made you almost into a god. And the day you tell a lie will be the most horrible for you because I will destroy you," the chief said.

Olagoussa said farewell to Bahumbe and went back to his village. Nevertheless, it irritated the chief to think that such an honest man lived. He thought that Olagoussa was arrogant, but not clever enough to remain virtuous and decided to test him.

Seven days later, Bahumbe sent for Olagoussa. When Olagoussa arrived, he found the chief and his hunters gathered in front of the compound. They had their weapons in front of them and appeared to be going on a hunt. "Olagoussa, you must go to my wife in the next village and give her a message. As you can see, we are going hunting and plan to catch a gazelle. Tell my wife we will arrive in the afternoon of the day after next and that she is to have food prepared for us. Wait with her, and you shall share the food."

The chief and his men went one way, and Olagoussa quickly went the other way toward the next village. As soon as Olagoussa was out of sight, Bahumbe returned to his house and told his men. "We will not hunt today; in fact, I shall fast for the next two days in my house. We shall see if this man does not utter a falsehood."

Meanwhile Olagoussa arrived at the next village, went to Bahumbe's wife, and told her, "I have an important message from your husband."

"Well, what is it? Tell me!" she demanded.

"Let me see," Olagoussa said, "it seems, or it is likely, or maybe perhaps, but, on the other hand, it is not with any certainty, that Bahumbe went hunting."

"What do you mean, it's not very clear or you are not certain? What is the message? Did my husband go hunting?" Bahumbe's wife asked angrily.

Olagoussa said, "Looks are illusions, and when I left it appeared they were going hunting or had just returned from a hunt. Of course, I saw no meat; however, that was the impression I received, more or less; nonetheless, the opposite can also be true."

"What are you saying? I still don't know whether he went hunting or not. Did he tell you anything else?" Bahumbe's wife asked.

"Yes, you are to be prepared to cook a gazelle, in the event they went hunting, or cook a gazelle if they have none because they'll be hungry when they arrive. And, oh yes, I am to wait here for them," Olagoussa said.

"When is he coming? Or should I ask, is he coming at all? I have learned absolutely nothing from your gibberish. Why did my husband send one such as you with a message?" Bahumbe's wife cried.

"As I said before, more or less as clearly as I could see, it seems, though not conclusively, that your husband will be here sooner or later, today, tomorrow, or the next day."

The puzzled woman looked at Olagoussa and said, "Go in the other room; there is a mat for you." Two nights passed, and the chief did not appear. Finally, on the morning of the third day, Bahumbe and his men came laughing into his house.

"Where is this honest man who has allowed himself to speak a falsehood? I promised him I would destroy him if he ever told a lie, arrogant braggart!" Bahumbe said.

"What do you mean, told a lie! This man told me nothing!" said his wife.

"Didn't he tell you I was going hunting to catch a gazelle and would be here yesterday?" screamed Bahumbe.

"No, he did not! He said you might do this or you might do that, that it was likely, then again it was unlikely, as well as it was certain and uncertain. I got absolutely no sense from his message," his wife answered.

The chief was embarrassed and shamed. He apologized. "I am wrong Olagoussa. You are an honest, wise man. Now, I believe, as all others already believe, that you will never, never, tell a lie. Take these gifts to your family for your honesty."

Olagoussa replied, "Thank you, and that is perhaps true as long as it is probably a certainty, we shall presume."

PARABLE OF THE EAGLE

JAMES AGGREY

There are many versions of this African tale, and I have heard it preached as a sermon, taught in university classes, and told at storytelling events. This tale teaches that if you don't know who you are, you will be anything anyone chooses you to be. To achieve Kujichagulia, an individual must belong to a group and possess freedom or remain at the mercy of controllers.

A man went through a forest seeking any bird of interest he might find. He caught a young eagle; brought it home; put it among his chickens, ducks, and turkeys; and gave it chicken food to eat, even though it was an eagle, the king of birds.

Five years later, a naturalist came to see him and, after passing through his garden, said: "That bird is an eagle, not a chicken."

"Yes," said its owner, "but I have trained it to be a chicken. It is no longer an eagle; it is a chicken even though it measures fifteen feet from tip to tip of its wings."

"No," said the naturalist, "it is an eagle still; it has the heart of an eagle, and I will make it soar high up to the heavens."

"No," said the owner, "it is a chicken, and it will never fly."

They agreed to test the eagle. The naturalist picked it up, held it up, and said with great intensity: "Eagle, thou art an eagle. Thou dost belong to the sky and not to this earth; stretch forth thy wings and fly."

The eagle turned this way and that, and then, looking down, saw the chickens eating their food and jumped down to join them.

The owner said, "I told you it was a chicken."

"No," said the naturalist, "it is an eagle. Give it another chance tomorrow."

So the next day, the naturalist took the eagle to the top of the house and said, "Eagle, thou art an eagle; thou dost belong to the sky, not to this earth. Stretch forth thy wings and fly!" But again the eagle, seeing the chickens feeding, jumped down and fed with them.

Then the owner said, "I told you it was a chicken."

"No," asserted the naturalist, "it is an eagle, and it still has the heart of an eagle. Give me one more chance, and I will make it fly tomorrow."

The next morning, the naturalist rose early and took the eagle outside the city, away from the houses, to the foot of a high mountain. The sun was just rising, gilding the top of the mountain with gold, and every craw was glistening in the joy of that beautiful morning.

He picked up the eagle and said to it, "Eagle, thou art an eagle. Thou dost belong to the sky and not to this earth; stretch forth thy wings and fly!"

The majestic king of the birds looked around trembling as if new life were entering its body, but it did not fly. The naturalist then turned the eagle's head and made it look straight to the sun. Suddenly, the eagle stretched out its wings and, with the screech of an eagle, mounted higher and higher and never returned. It was an eagle, though it had been kept and tamed as a chicken.

My people of Africa, we were created in the image of God. Men have made us think we were chickens, but we are eagles. Men and women of Africa, you are descended from kings. So stretch forth your wings and fly! Don't be content with the lives of chickens.

WAVE YOUR FINGERS IN THE AIR

RETOLD BY DOROTHY WINBUSH RILEY

The next folktale is based on a story in Abraham's *Afro-American Folktales*. All stories are written to be retold, and I have used this story many times to teach my children the value of sharing. Self-determination is the ability to choose where your food, money, and other resources will go. You can choose to hoard everything you have or share it with your community.

In earlier times, after Abraham Lincoln signed the Emancipation Proclamation, families would share food. A man named Nathan had two daughters: Ida Mae, who lived in Istabula, and Harriet Ann, who lived down the road a piece in Wallebega. Whenever Nathan could, he would bring them food and say, "Wave your fingers when you eat. Don't forget, daughter, wave your fingers."

Ida Mae didn't understand what he meant, but Harriet Ann understood completely. She knew her daddy meant that whenever he brought her food, she was never to eat it alone. She was to share the food with her neighbors; sharing made the food taste better, and she always had company.

One day Nathan gave each of his daughters twelve ears of corn. Ida Mae went outside, like she usually did, and waved her fingers in the air as if she was making signs to the clouds. Then she went inside and cooked the twelve ears of corn and ate every kernel. Harriet Ann went to the front yard and waved her fingers in the air, calling, "Paul, Eula Mae, come over for dinner; my daddy bought a passel of corn today." When Eula Mae and Paul arrived, they brought black-eyed peas and fresh fish to add to the corn.

Each time Nathan brought food to his daughters, that is what they did: One ate alone, and the other shared with her neighbors. Time catches up with every man, and soon Nathan joined his wife in paradise. Word passed through the towns, and people immediately rushed to Harriet Ann's house. One man brought her a cow, and another brought her a goat. The women brought everything, from sugar to coffee to flour. Harriet Ann's house flowed with people bringing gifts to remember Nathan. No one bothered to visit Ida Mae.

After a week passed, Ida Mae visited her younger sister and said, "No one brings gifts for our father in my village. No one brings me any food. I don't understand why you are getting everything and I am getting nothing!"

"Remember when father brought us food, what did you do with yours? Did you wave your fingers to the air like he said?" Harriet Ann asked.

"Well I went outside and waved my fingers to the air, just like he said," Ida Mae answered.

"No wonder, no one visits or shares with you. The air must bring you whatever you need because you waved your fingers to it. Father meant for us never to eat alone, and the same people who shared my food bring me food everyday," Harriet Ann said.

STORMEE AND CHARLES

TIAUDRA RILEY

The theme of this modern fable is commonplace in African American society, and Stormee and Charles resemble many students who venture into the corporate world. Kujichagulia means that we have choices in clothing, hairstyle, and activities. Since our identities are so closely related to the work we do, it is important to decide how much we allow work to shape our identities and self-determination.

"I can do it myself!" the toddler screamed. Aisha, her mother, was accustomed to these fits and thought, "I guess I knew she would be as willful as a thunderstorm, which is why I named her Stormee." As her daughter grew from a temperamental willful toddler into a headstrong self-determined young adult, Aisha watched amazed, knowing one day that Stormee would meet her match. She had taught Stormee to create her own destiny and to stand up for her beliefs; these two things would guarantee success.

At Cass Technical High School Stormee took advance placement and college preparatory classes, was a member of the National Honor Society, and won a National Merit Scholarship. As a high school senior, Stormee had a 3.88 grade-point average, a SAT score of 1490 out of 1600 points, and a score of 32 on the ACT; college recruiters were hot on her trail with scholarships. Aisha wished that Stormee would select a local school, since two had offered Stormee full four-year scholarships, yet she knew intuitively that she had to allow Stormee to make her own choices. She looked at her wall of awards and trophies and thought that her daughter had never performed poorly.

By the end of April, Stormee had received more than three large shopping bags full of college brochures and propaganda letters. She even received phone calls from alumnae urging her to attend their colleges.

"Ma, they keep sending me all these applications, and I have told them I am not interested in their schools," Stormee said.

"Be, happy," responded Aisha, "You're a hot, young, gifted, and black commodity; every college wants you. By the way, what college have you chosen?"

"Ma, I know you want me to stay near home, but I went on college tours with our church three times, and I want to go to a black college. You taught me to think for myself and make my own decisions. You always said that if I stand up for what I believe, my success will be guaranteed."

Stormee chose prestigious all-female Spelman College in Atlanta, and during freshmen orientation she met a young man, Charles, who attended the all-male school across the street. From the moment they met, Stormee and Charles argued over everything—the weather, politics, prestige, words, definitions, and even music—yet they held tight to their friendship.

"Charles, it is not cold outside," Stormee said.

"You are from Detroit, I'm from Florida and I'm cold," Charles answered.

"A woman has the right to do whatever she wants with her body," Stormee asserted.

"Not with my child she doesn't!" Charles responded. "Abortion is wrong. They teach you all that junk at that feminist school you go to, Storm."

"It is not a feminist school, and if it was, what would be wrong with that since it is also the top liberal arts school in the South," Stormee replied.

Their battle of words continued. As the year ended, Stormee, a political science major, applied for an internship at a law firm in Atlanta that had one woman on a staff of thirty-two. This fact didn't faze Stormee, who knew that the firm would see her brilliant academic record and offer her one of its ten internships. Charles, also a political science major, applied for an internship at the same firm. Even though his academic record and school activities were not as dazzling as Stormee's, he received the internship. Stormee did not even receive a courtesy call or a form rejection letter.

On his first day, Charles had an orientation meeting with Percival, the office manager. "The first thing you must do is dress properly," Percival told him. "We provide a salary advance, so you can purchase a suit from Sayms and Sayms. Our interns all wear dark green suits with plain green ties that are exactly two inches wide. We have a rule here that no matter how hot Atlanta is, our staff is in uniform."

Charles was surprised because he prided himself on his preppy shirts and creased pants. He was so meticulous that the guys teased him about his clothes.

"And one other point I want to cover is your availability," continued Percival. "You are on call twenty-four hours a day, seven days a week. Stop in the security office and pick up an electronic pager, so we will have no problems locating you when you are not here."

"You mean I won't even be free on weekends?" Charles asked.

"It depends. However, don't worry; it'll be good training for you," Percival said as he rose from his chair. "We selected you because we like you; we can mold you. You are just the kind of young man we are seeking."

Charles pondered and pondered that statement. "What did the office manager mean by they could mold me? Mold me into what?" He looked around and saw only one other African American, a secretary; he decided to ask her what the statement meant, although he had an idea that he would not like her answer.

He walked to the secretary's desk and asked, "Mrs. Lucille, the supervisor said they can mold me because I am the kind of man they are seeking. What did he mean?"

She peered over her eyeglasses at him and replied, "Why don't you ask him? You know the answer; your mama didn't raise a fool."

On the third day, Charles saw Percival and asked, "What did you mean when you said you could mold me?"

The supervisor looked puzzled and then pleased as a peacock. He said, "Well, Charles, you don't look like a troublemaker, and we can train you to think like us and represent the firm. When you graduate, you will have a place with us."

At the end of the day, Charles called Stormee and told her every detail. For once she didn't argue; she was as silent as a heart that has stopped beating.

Charles said, "Storm, I know it's an opportunity, but I feel chained and stripped of my identity. This electronic pager is like a dog collar; I can't do anything without it. I might get a call from the office."

Stormee finally said, "Everything has a price, Charles. Right now I have work to do; I will talk to you later."

Charles then called the dean of his college. At the end of that conversation, he had a plan to enact.

After the first month, Charles met with his supervisor to discuss his performance. Percival smiled like the Cheshire cat and said, "Charles, we here at Wite, Whyter & Whitese are extremely pleased with your performance. We knew when we selected you over all the other young men with names like Malik and Sundiata that you were almost perfect. The only other person we even considered after we gave Ralph and the rest of the guys their internships was a girl named Thunder or something, and she sounded like a troublemaker. We would like you to stay on here, so what do you say?"

Charles grinned back and in his nicest voice responded, "I say no!"

Percival exclaimed "No! what do you mean? No! We

have given you an opportunity, young man, that few ever receive. You're making a big mistake, but I expected it from an arrogant person like you."

Charles smiled, "Furthermore, I am resigning. You cannot mold me into the kind of man you want; my self-determination will mold me into the kind of man *I* want to be. God created me, and He made me a man; the rest is up to me." Charles's response left Percival looking like a four-eyed fish gasping for water.

Percival was even more surprised when he had to testify against the firm in a lawsuit filed by Stormee.

The moral of the story is that whoever allows his identity to be shaped by others will have no identity in the end.

WISDOM OF THE NATION: PROVERBS FOR KUJICHAGULIA

Chance comes to those who know what they want.
—Ashanti

Ancient things remain in the ears.—Ghana

The slave does not choose his master.—Ghana

The man who goes ahead stumbles, so that the man who follows may have his wits about him.—Kenya

The fruit must have a stem before it grows.—Liberia

Children are the wisdom of the nation.—Liberia

A beggar has no dignity.—Liberia

Endurance pierces marble.—Libya

A man's deeds are his life.—Nigeria

If you know the beginning, the end will not trouble you.—Senegal

If you don't grab for yourself, then nothing is going to help you.—Traditional

The frogs say, "Although I have nothing, I always have my hop."—Vai of West Africa

Perseverance is everything.—Yoruba

THOUGHTS FOR KUJICHAGULIA

❖ Learn to think for yourself. Do not allow others to control your thinking. Be open to positive ideas, positive experiences, and positive ways of thinking.

❖ Accept your history; know your roots, the contribution and the sacrifices made by our people to civilization. Recapture your heritage and ideals to liberate yourself.

❖ Control the politics and politicians of your community. Organize to create the kind of community you desire.

❖ Cast down your buckets where you are. Look around your neighborhood. See what needs to done. Then do it.

❖ Resolve to leave a legacy that inspires your children to greater effort and achievement.

❖ Take a chance and create opportunities from all situations, no matter how negative or discouraging.

❖ Lose yourself in a great cause.

❖ To be successful, grow to the point where you completely forget yourself.

❖ Maintain good character; it, not the circumstances of your life, is the key to success.

❖ Use your brains and skills to satisfy the common needs of the community. All labor has dignity.

❖ Be determined to get an education no matter what your circumstances are.

❖ Solve problems with patience, hard work, and wisdom to bring order out of chaos.

❖ Find a mentor. Educate yourself by associating with great men and women.

CHAPTER THREE

PRINCIPLE 3

UJIMA

WE ARE EACH OTHER'S HARVEST: THE MEANING OF UJIMA

Ujima, the third principle of Kwanzaa, is observed on December 28. After the second green candle is lit and the black candle and the first green candle are relit, the program focuses on collective work and struggle to benefit the community. Ujima is clearly expressed in the words of Malcolm X, who said, "The American black man should be focusing his every effort toward building his own businesses, and decent homes for himself. As other ethnic groups have done, let the black people, whenever possible, however possible, patronize their own kind, hire their own kind, and start in some ways to build up the race's ability to do for itself by starting his own programs to lift up his own sense of values." Ujima is a return to traditional values of kindness, generosity, patience, tolerance, cooperation, and compassion. It is a sense of truth and justice, right and wrong, and doing things for and taking care of others through services that build and maintain a community.

Mayor Dennis Archer of Detroit immediately applied the principles of Kwanzaa after President Bill Clinton announced that several cities could write a proposal to receive $100 million for an empowerment zone. The mayor appointed a strategic planning committee to measure, describe, and assess resources that were available to bring about change, those that could be made available, and those the committee would like to have. The committee's major responsibility was to focus attention on the needs of all families, children, and businesses in a twenty-mile stretch of Detroit. The members' imagination stimulated problem solving and the creation of a winning proposal for $100 million. Ujima is putting each other to work solving problems so that all benefit and have mutual pride in the harvest.

Ujima is a way of rebuilding the African American community by succeeding individually and sharing our success with others. Today African Americans are better educated and have greater economic resources and more political power than ever before. That power elected Congresswoman Maxine Waters of California, who says, "I can never believe that nothing can be done. I can never believe that there can't be change. I have to believe that not only can we change things, but that I can contribute to that."

The selections in this chapter demonstrate how Ujima solves problems through businesses that draw on individual experiences not only to support one family but to give employment to others. Economic problems that are so closely tied to discrimination can sometimes be solved when we recognize that if we cannot get a job working for somebody else, perhaps we should start working for ourselves, as Joe Dudley, founder of Dudley Products of Greensboro, North Carolina, did.

GUIDED BY A DREAM:
POETRY OF UJIMA

PAUL ROBESON

GWENDOLYN BROOKS

That time
we all heard it,
cool and clear,
cutting across the hot grit of the day.
The major Voice.
The adult Voice
forgoing Rolling River
forgoing tearful tale of bale and barge
and other symptoms of an old despond.
Warning, in music-words
devout and large,
that we are each other's
harvest:
we are each other's
business:
we are each other's
magnitude and bond.

KEEP A DREAM

Dorothy Winbush Riley

Keep a dream tucked in your heart
to lead you through this life.
Do not allow it to depart through
turmoil, pain, or strife.
At peak of day or late at night
your dream will shed prophetic light.

Keep a dream tucked in your mind
to help you to achieve.
When true success is hard to find,
your dream you can retrieve.
For locked deep within your brain
are fond desires you must attain.

Keep a dream tucked in your soul
where no one else will know
the pathway leading to the goal
where only you will go.
For life when guided by a dream
will travel past the moon's far beam.

IT TAKES A WHOLE VILLAGE

JUDY BOSWELL GRIFFIE

It takes a whole village to raise a child
and I am a village raised child.

I am mothered by village mothers
and fathered by village fathers
fed by the village cooks
and clothed by the village weavers.
I am protected by village keepers
and taught by village teachers.

I challenge the village warriors
and charm the village maids.
I dance to the village drum
and chant the village song.
I worship at village altars
and weep at village pain.

I hear stories from the village griots
and honor the village elders.
I am loved by the village,
loved by the village—All
And every breath and heartbeat
echoes praise to my village God.

I am a valued African gift
made so by village love.

CLOSED DOORS

Margaret Adelaide Shaw

You who find
closed doors before you
Turn not bitter
while you wait;
Work and grow, for
nothing shrivels the soul
like burning hate.
Work and lift the things
you fashion higher with
each passing sun;
Take no thought of
bolted doors; They shall
open every one.

THE VILLAGERS: PEOPLE OF UJIMA

MAN BECOMES HIS DREAMS

HOWARD THURMAN

Dr. Howard Thurman was a husband, father, teacher, theologian, scholar, mystic, and pacifist. He was part of a group that traveled to India in 1935 to learn about nonviolent passive resistance from Mohandas Gandhi. He returned to America and applied the philosophy to all aspects of his life. As a teacher at Boston University, his views inspired Dr. Martin Luther King, Jr. Another student, Jesse Jackson, said, "Dr. Thurman always challenged me and mine to move to what he called the 'irreducible essence'— and I searched for that irreducible essence. . . . His point was that if you ever developed a cultivated will, with spiritual discipline, the flame of freedom would never perish. . . . He sowed the seeds that bred generations of activists who tore down ancient walls of oppression. Howard Thurman was our gallant leader."

In the following essay, Dr. Thurman speaks about dreams as prophecy. Each individual can become his dream when he no longer wishes, but *knows;* no longer hopes, but *accepts;* no longer prays, but *announces;* no longer expects, but *believes that it has already happened* and finds his irreducible essence.

It is always miraculous to see a dream take shape and form. Dreams in themselves are made of the chiffon of men's hopes, desires, and aspirings. There may be no limit to their fabulous unfolding, rich in all the magic of the fantastic. A dream may be held at the focal point of one's mind and heart until it takes over the total process of one's thinking and planning, until at last a man becomes the living embodiment of what he dreams. This is the first miracle: a man becomes the dream; then it is that the line between what he does and is and his dream melts away. A new accent appears in how he thinks, the signature of the dream must guarantee the every act. In some ways he seems to be one possessed; and perhaps this is true. The second miracle appears when the outline of the dream begins to take objective shape, when it begins to become concrete and to take its place among the particular facts of life. This means that something more than the man becomes the embodiment of the dream. Others begin to see the manifestation and to feel the pull of its challenge. In turn, through sheer contagion, they relate themselves to it and its demands. If the embodiment takes the form of an institution it means that at the center of the institution there is a living, pulsing core which guarantees not only flexibility but also a continuous unfolding in an increasing dimension of creativity. It is the very nature of such a dream that it continues to grow, to develop, to find ever more creative dimensions. Hence, the dream is always receding; it can never be contained in life, however perfect. So it is with the institution which is its embodiment. It must always contain its dynamic character, and its greatest significance must ever be found in the new heights to which it calls all who share its contagion.

"The Whole Village" by John Muafangejo. Photograph by Bill Sanders.

MAE JEMISON: TRANSCENDING EARTHLY BARRIERS

DOROTHY WINBUSH RILEY

Mae Jemison created a self-fulfilling prophecy with beliefs that propelled her beyond Earth into the stars. The moment she began to think, plan, and work, her thoughts were propelled into reality, fulfilling her childhood dream. While she worked toward her accomplishments, Mae applied Ujima by returning to work in her community.

Mae Jemison, chemical engineer, physician, and mission specialist on the 1991 shuttle *Discovery* flight, succeeded despite the odds. She recalled that in her childhood, "We couldn't afford a telescope, but the family would venture outside as avid star watchers to ponder and discuss the seemingly infinite magnitude of space." Those nighttime adventures propelled Mae Jemison to dream and eventually to live the life she visualized. Mae skyrocketed beyond earthly restrictions with determination, education, and a belief in herself. By holding fast to her principles and beliefs, she successfully became the first African American female astronaut to travel in space.

Like most youngsters, Mae asked questions about the stars twinkling in the heavens and precociously probed for answers to satisfy her curiosity. "When I was about five or six years old I used to look at the stars with my uncle and he would tell me they were just like the sun except they were millions of miles away. That was why they were so small. I have always been interested in astronomy and what goes on in the world. So I guess you could say I've been interested in space travel ever since I can remember." She watched television spellbound as *Apollo 11* successfully landed on the moon in 1969. Her dreams were limitless as she read books while planning to be an astronaut. "I read lots of books about space. I had an encyclopedia about the different phases of *Apollo*. I don't remember the time I said, 'I want to be an astronaut'; it's just always been there."

Dreams are fueled by action. Mae prepared herself, even though the space program was the playground of white men. At Morgan High School in Chicago, her passion became more strategic. "I went through a phase when I was probably from ten to fourteen years old, where I read lots and lots of astronomy books, not science fiction, but actual astronomy books." She credits her success to nurturing teachers and parents who "let me go off and do things, explore on my own." By 1973, Mae, a sixteen-year-old high school graduate, knew she wanted to be a biomedical engineer and entered Stanford University in California on a National Achievement Scholarship.

Four years later the opportunity to live her dream of space travel occurred when the National Aeronautics and Space Administration announced that it was seeking candidates for the space-shuttle program and encouraged scientists from the private sector, especially minority women, to apply. Mae was overjoyed but decided to wait and apply when she had received her B.S. degree in chemical engineering. "Being an astronaut isn't something you can plan for because there is such a small chance of success. I knew I had to have other options. But I knew I would pursue it when the right moment came in my career."

Her time was not wasted because the young achiever went to Cornell Medical College to earn a medical degree. While at Cornell, the multifaceted Mae was president of the Cornell Medical Student Council. She also studied in Cuba, Kenya, and Thailand with the American Medical Student Association.

After receiving her medical degree, Mae joined the Peace Corps and was sent to Sierra Leone and Liberia as a medical officer. "At twenty-six, I was one of the youngest doctors over there, and I had to learn to deal with how people reacted to my age while asserting myself as a physician."

In 1985, with a world of experience under her hat, still taking evening engineering classes and working as a general practitioner, Mae felt that the time was right for her to apply to NASA. In 1986 she applied, as did more than 2,000 others who wanted to travel in space.

Mae continued to work as a general practitioner while waiting for her dream of being an astronaut to materialize. She passed the first scrutiny by NASA, and in June 1987 received the news that she had been accepted for training.

For the next five years, Mae worked in Houston designing the experiments to be conducted during her flight with scientists from America and Japan. "It was what I wanted to do for a very long time.... It was the realization of many, many dreams of many people." On September 12, 1992, Mae fulfilled her childhood dream when she and six other astronauts boarded the space shuttle *Endeavor* at Kennedy Space Center in Florida.

The space-shuttle landing on September 20, 1992, established Mae Jemison as the first female African American space traveler who could speak eloquently and forcefully on the subject of space exploration. As she said, "Very clearly, I was sure I would be an astronaut, even if there had never been any astronauts, period."

THE POLICY OF SELF-RELIANCE

JULIUS NYERERE (FROM *FREEDOM AND SOCIALISM: A SELECTION FROM WRITINGS AND SPEECHES 1965–1967*)

Julius Nyerere became the president of Tanzania in 1961, and for almost twenty-five years he ruled the country peacefully. Under his leadership, he united Tanganyika and Zanzibar and instilled national pride within the diverse tribal groups. His chief goal was the promotion of Ujamaa through economic cooperation, racial and tribal unity, and self-sacrifice. The following excerpt from *Freedom and Socialism: A Selection from Writings and Speeches 1965–1967* stresses the power of words and the value of hard work.

But it is obvious that in the past we have chosen the wrong weapon for our struggle, because we chose money as our weapon. We are trying to overcome our economic weakness by using the weapons of the economically strong—weapons which in fact we do not possess. By our thoughts, words and actions it appears as if we have come to the conclusion that without money we cannot bring about the revolution we are aiming at. . . .

Everybody wants development: but not everybody understands and accepts the basic requirements . . . hard work. Let us go to the village and see whether or not it is possible to work harder. . . .

Between MONEY and PEOPLE it is obvious that the PEOPLE and their HARD WORK are the foundation of development, and money is one of the fruits of that hard work.

From now on we shall stand upright and walk forward on our feet rather than look at the problem upside down. Industries will come and MONEY will come, but the foundation is the PEOPLE and their HARD WORK. . . . This is the meaning of self-reliance.

JEFFREY HOWARD: "THINK YOU CAN! WORK HARD! GET SMART!"

DOROTHY WINBUSH RILEY

> This generation of black Americans and all who follow us are beneficiaries of two of the most successful social movements in history, movements that gave many of us unprecedented access to education, jobs and the best that America has to offer. The first movement, conceived and led by Charles Hamilton Houston (and brought to its conclusion by Thurgood Marshall after Hamilton's death), was the legal struggle to end segregation, which, after nearly a quarter century of battle, did just that. The *Brown vs. the Board of Education* decision of 1954 removed the protective cover of laws that had lent respectability to racist exclusion since 1896. The Civil Rights Movement finished the job with boycotts, marches and voter registration campaigns that rendered the remaining traditional practice of segregation too expensive to maintain. The "Two Movements" were brilliant in their planning and execution. Both has compelling objectives—clearly articulated missions with which people strongly identified. Each mobilized a broad base of support among black folk, too, by defining clear operational approaches that generated beliefs in our capacity to achieve our objectives.
>
> —JEFFREY HOWARD

Since the Emancipation Proclamation, each generation of Americans descended from the enslaved Africans who were brought to this country have been more educated than the previous ones. The application of knowledge is vital to the advancement of our children, our culture, our community, and ourselves. Education traditionally empowered families to claim a place in society, and once they had staked their claim, they duplicated it by educating their children. Harvard-trained psychologist, Jeffrey Howard, practices Ujima by charging individuals and communities to confront and surmount modern psychological barriers to success through the collaboration of foundations, agencies, and schools. For Howard, intellectual development is a long process stemming from confidence to struggle and determination to work hard, combined with expectations of success from parents and teachers.

Looking at the past two decades illustrates that waiting for grand initiatives from the outside to save the African American community is futile. We will have to rely on our ingenuity and resources. Howard knows that the community must be responsible for teaching and training its children. To that end, he proposes a third movement, patterned on the unified purposefulness shown during the fight for desegregation—a movement to help students understand themselves and their intrinsic motivation and to help them gain independence.

In 1985, Howard created the Efficacy Institute outside Boston, with four volunteer staff members; now the institute has twenty-five paid staff and trainers instructing ten thousand teachers to apply his ideas about intellectual development. The Efficacy Program encourages students to identify and then avoid any influences that undermine self-confidence, effective efforts, motivation, and intent to achieve. Students learn to focus on skills that can help them work more efficiently and view failure like Susan Taylor, "as missteps to greater achievement." Instead of finding external causes for the missteps, students analyze their situations and, with self-determination, decide to work harder to achieve or to change their strategies completely.

We have been affected by what our people have endured. Becoming the most developed people in this society should be understood as the proper response to what has been done to us. We must create unity and exercise self-determination, collective economics, creativity, and faith to provide solutions and make better use of our resources. Howard believes that "problems are going to get solved by a mobilized black community. For the Equal Opportunity Generation, success in mobilizing our people and our resources to give our children what they deserve is the minimum requirement for self-respect. We will never be able to hold our heads high until we create the conditions they need to move into the light."

Howard's interest in intellectual development stemmed from his attendance at Chicago's high-achieving Tilden High School and continued at Harvard. He noticed that the most successful African American high school students in the country were not continuing the legacy of educational excellence they had brought with them.

His beliefs caused him to switch his major from law to pursue a doctorate in clinical and social psychology. In 1972 he conducted his first efficacy training for twenty African American undergraduates. The results inspired him to start a consulting firm for diversity issues and to conduct efficacy workshops for African American professionals. In Detroit, Howard trained employees of Dayton Hudson's Department Store, who then asked him to use his theories with high school students in the public schools. From their need to build the community using networking, the non-profit Efficacy Institute went to work. "We have much more to work with than previous generations did, more money, more know-how, more position power. We know more about how this society works, and there are many more of us who are well-positioned to use that knowledge." The principles of Kwanzaa challenge us to marshal those resources to change our beliefs and ideas about success and what is possible, to give the next generation a more prosperous educational harvest than the present one has reaped.

THE STORY OF JOE DUDLEY:
"I AM, I CAN, I WILL"

DOROTHY WINBUSH RILEY

Imagine that you are labeled a failure from the moment you enter school—retained and doomed to repeat first grade, then identified as mentally retarded. And to make matters worse, you have a speech problem that prevents you from expressing yourself. How could you hope to achieve and succeed in life? This is what happened to Joe Dudley, but the love and faith of his mother made a lie of everything the educators said. Joe's mother had faith in the force of the word of God and visualized her son as a role model for others. Joe could see her vision and worked to make it a reality.

Today, Joe Dudley is CEO at Dudley Products, a multi-million-dollar cosmetics and hair care company. He and his wife, Eunice, practice the values of Kwanzaa: unity, self-determination, purpose, and cooperative economics, so others will not suffer as he did in school. Using Kujichagulia, he graduated from college and became an empire builder. With a ten-dollar investment in a Fuller Brush Kit, he started selling the products door to door and finally came to own his own distributorship, store, and beauty salon. Joe saw potential and opportunity that escape others, and in 1969, he and Eunice began making their own cosmetics line in their kitchen. Their children packaged the products while he and his salesmen sold them door to door. Successful people have strong beliefs, and what they believe in, they make real. Their beliefs have a boomerang effect, leading to increased self-confidence, high expectations, and goal setting. Joe believed that he would eventually head his own company, and he worked to make his belief a reality.

His success gives him the power to practice the Nguzo

Saba in his community, with the philosophy, "I am, I can, and I will!" And he tells youngsters, "As young people growing up in America today, it is important that you understand that no one has the power to control your destiny but you. With the right attitude and the will to succeed, nothing can hold you back but you. You must learn to set goals and be persistent in working toward those goals."

Visionary leaders are spirit driven. Joe recalled his achievements in school, despite his teachers' predictions, and in 1976 he developed his plan to sell Dudley professional products directly to beauty salons. Step by step he created a clear, detailed, concrete plan to elicit the commitment of everyone involved. He built on the unified strength of committed people, and two years later, Dudley Products moved into a sparkling brand-new manufacturing plant and corporate headquarters in Greensboro, North Carolina.

To help his children succeed, Joe stated: "Even though my wife and I could afford to give our three children material riches, we chose instead to teach them the value of studying hard, working hard, saving money and having strong moral values. We could give our children money, but we couldn't give them initiative, courage, loyalty, integrity, or insight in the needs of mankind. These are the things they must learn for themselves as they go through life. Those are the values we must instill in all of our young people." Joe and Eunice model this behavior for the young and their employees by practicing Ujima. The workers voluntarily donate money weekly to service projects, including a $250,000 Adopt-a-School Program with a high school and a middle school. They also sponsor four-year renewable scholarships to North Carolina A&T or Bennett College.

Success is determined not only by the goals that are achieved, but by the peace of mind that accompanies it. Joe had a mental picture of what he would be in the future. Our dreams push visions forward. Thoughts provide creative methods of how to accomplish the ideas of the mind. Vision means looking toward the unseen, not the seen. Now, Joe Dudley's business leads in revitalizing the community as his company responsibly provides money for services and direction to raise the standard of living of others.

WE HAVE VISIONS:
QUOTATIONS TO INSPIRE UJIMA

"To struggle and battle and overcome, absolutely defeat, every force designed against us is the only way to achieve."—Nannie Burroughs

"A role model takes responsibility not only for her own life but for the lives of others."—Johnnetta Cole

"A stream cannot rise higher than its source. The home is no rarer, purer and sweeter than the mothers in those homes. A race is but a total of families. The nation is the aggregate of its homes."—Anna J. Cooper

"Excellence should no longer mean for your personal achievement. Excellence should mean when you achieve personally, you reinvest that personal achievement back into the community to improve the human condition."—George Fraser

"No matter what accomplishments you make, somebody helps you."—Althea Gibson

"Change does not roll in on the wheels of inevitability, but comes through continuous struggle. And so we must straighten our backs and work for our freedom. A man can't ride you unless your back is bent."—Martin Luther King, Jr.

"Our road to that glorious future lies through collective hard work to accomplish the objectives of creating a people centered society."—Nelson Mandela

"The many of us who attain what we may and forget those who help us along the line—we've got to remember that there are so many others to pull along the way. The further they go, the further we all go."—Jackie Robinson

"We had a vision. We had a commitment and we had an undeniable will collectively to succeed."—Isaiah Thomas

"We have been worked, now let us learn to work."
—Booker T. Washington

"No one among us has a monopoly on wisdom. By sharing collectively from our background of actual experience we can take a major step toward unity in objectives—even methods."—Whitney Young, Jr.

"Together we must learn to live as brothers or together we will be forced to perish as fools."—Martin Luther King, Jr.

"There is never time in the future in which we will work out our salvation. The challenge is in the moment, the time is always now."—James Baldwin

"Our children must never lose their zeal for building a better world."—Mary McLeod Bethune

"I am here, and my breath/our breaths/must thunder across this land/arousing new breaths, new life/new people, who will live in peace and honor."—Sonia Sanchez

FROM THE GRIOTS: FOLKTALES FOR UJIMA

EVERYBODY'S BUSINESS

DOROTHY WINBUSH RILEY

This story is based on a folktale told in the Upper Volta of West Africa. Like all folktales, this one includes a moral lesson woven into the action. The moral is that we are responsible for what we allow to happen in our communities and our cities and that a dispute can have disastrous effects on everyone in a community.

Once, in times past, there lived a very rich man who was the patriarch of the strongest clan of his village. He filled his house with piles and piles of clay pots, each brimming with every kind of food the mind could imagine. A family of mice, who lived in the wall covered by the pots, were prevented from getting at the food that was right on their doorstep by a ferocious cat. One day a young mouse declared, "We must have our freedom to move and hunt for food. I will fight anyone who tries to force us to stay in this hole. I will not be chased, and I will not be locked up. We must survive, and we must fight!"

His family tried to dissuade him from making idle promises because the young, determined tomcat had kept them in their hole without food for days. The next morning, when everyone had gone to the fields to work, the patriarch ate and fell asleep before his dishes could be removed. The young mouse watched and decided he would sneak some table scraps to feed his family.

As quick as a mosquito's bite, he shot across the room, grabbed the food, and was on his way back when the cat blocked his path. "Well, you are not too smart," the cat said. "I've been waiting for one of you cowards to try to get food. I can finish you off quicker than you can blink, and then I'll wait for the rest of your family."

The young mouse remembered his promise, grabbed a sword hanging nearby, and said, "You cruel, selfish cat, you will not finish me. No! You have a fight on your hands!"

"Oh, you think you can beat me, do you! Well, we'll just see about that!" hissed the cat, who picked up another sword. The battle started, and it was terrible, with swords clashing and sparkling fire as each attacked and counterattacked. It didn't disturb the sleeping man, but it did disturb the dog who was burying a bone in the yard. The dog rushed into the house, placed himself between the two fighters, and said, "Stop this foolishness this very instant! Stop it!" Neither the cat nor the mouse even looked at the dog, but continued to fight more ferociously than before.

The dog ran to the field and called the animals: the rooster, the horse, the goat, and the bull. He said to them, "I need your help this very moment to stop the horrible fight that is going on in the patriarch's house."

"Who is fighting?" asked the rooster. I like a good fight, and I am usually the champion."

"A cat and a mouse," the dog answered.

"You mean you have called us from our work because a cat and a mouse are fighting! Everyone knows they are enemies and love to fight each other. Cats have always attacked mice!" whinnied the horse.

"Yes, but this time the mouse is fighting back, and he is determined to win," replied the dog.

"Why should we get involved?" asked the bull. "It is obvious that this mouse is a fool and must accept full responsibility for his futile battle."

"That is true. And we must assume our responsibility as members of the village," the dog countered.

"I don't understand," said the goat.

The dog said, "Let me explain. The patriarch is asleep in the room that is piled high with walls and walls of pots. If either the cat or the mouse hits a pot, it will cause an avalanche of falling pots that will hurt both fighters and the patriarch. The sparks from their flashing swords can set the roof on fire. The fire will spread and destroy the entire village."

"Dear, dear me!" replied the rooster. "What an imagination you have! Whoever heard of a simple fight between a cat and a mouse causing such damage? I am sorry, but I may get hurt if I try to stop them."

"I have no idea what they are fighting about, and it's none of my business anyway," said the horse, "and I never enter a house or interfere in house fights." "The cat and the mouse have a right to fight. Just leave them alone!" snorted the bull.

"How long have they been fighting," asked the goat? We goats fight for weeks and weeks, and nobody ever stops us. I don't understand how their fighting is going to destroy the community. My friend, dog, you are too funny for even an old goat like me."

"It is perfectly normal for cats to chase mice," the horse declared. "I see nothing wrong with the fight. So what if a man is asleep in the room; isn't that where he sleeps each night? I can't believe one pot falling will hurt anyone. And if it does, the fault would be the cat's and the mouse's." The dog stood speechless as all the animals left. He turned and ran back to the house, where the cat and the mouse were still foolishly fighting. Then the cat raised his sword to hit the mouse, but instead hit a clay pot, which caused the whole wall of pots to crash down on him, the patriarch, and the mouse.

When the patriarch's family returned from the fields, they discovered the disaster. They planned the funeral and sent the children to capture the rooster, the goat, and the bull. All the animals ran to the granary where the dog lay sleeping.

"Help me! Hide me! Protect me!" cried the rooster to the dog. "They want to sacrifice me; please help me!"

"Can you save me?" bleated the goat. "They are going to serve me at a dinner for the memory of the patriarch. My brother, dog, please help me!"

"I am to be killed to feed the hundreds of people who will come to the village," snorted the bull. "Isn't there something you can do to save me? Please do something."

Before the dog could reply, the horse straggled into the compound and cried, "These people are cruel. I have been ridden for hours from one place to another without a minute's rest. When I slow down for a second, they beat me with switches."

"They have to tell other villages of the death of the patriarch, and you are the only horse in this village," the dog replied. "And as for you, rooster, goat, and bull, I can't help you; I am powerless. You should have helped me stop the fight between the cat and the mouse as I asked you to do. That would have saved you this trouble. In a community a fight is everybody's business. It doesn't matter if you are rich or poor, large or small; it is your business whoever you may be."

A PARABLE OF THE CORN

DOROTHY WINBUSH RILEY

Marilou Awiatka, author of *Selu: Seeking the Corn Mother's Wisdom,* writes that "Corn is the fruit of the gods, it was brought to us by the Creator, so that we may remember him. Our lives, we must remember, are holy. The corn is sacred. We are sacred. We hold the seeds of the gods to the future."

Corn is one symbol of Kwanzaa that represents children. The plant is everywhere in the world and where corn grows, hope blossoms with the generations of the living and unborn seeds that continue the ancestral web. "A Parable of the Corn" illustrates that each person has seeds of growth within, and planting and tending the seeds ensures the survival of the people. The seeds of one generation are harvested by the next through determination and work. Thus, to leave seeds of prosperity, we must cooperate and respect the Earth-mother—so like the workers in a cornfield, we plant together, grow together, and reap together.

The clouds, silent as thought, watch the sun rise above the horizon, and the natural cycle of renewal continues. All animals, large and small, from the ant to the elephant, perform specific tasks in nature's perfect balance. Birds carry seeds from place to place, and beavers clear away underbrush, so seeds can grow into plants. One plant, corn, has sustained humankind for centuries. Even though modern botanists cannot find its ancestors, corn thrives. Cosmic balance, harmony, and strength are shown in the plant's leaf, stalk, and ear.

Corn, like people, is everywhere in the world. Despite different soil conditions, temperatures, and wealth or poverty, adaptable corn seeds grow. Collective work and cooperation bring a crop to harvest: The field is cleared and prepared for planting; then farmers plant four to six rows of seeds in shallow fields (many have machines that lay up to twenty-four rows at one time, while others use scientific technology to plant seeds under controlled conditions in laboratories). The kernel begins life as a seedling with three important parts: the embryo, which grows into the new plant; the endosperm, which supplies the energy; and the seed coat, which covers the first two, protecting them from danger during the early stages of development.

The top of the cornstalk has a tassel that grows pollen, and the ears have filaments, called silks, that receive pollen. The invisible pollen drifts from the tassels and sticks to the corn silks. Because the ear is wrapped in the leaf and the silk protrudes only from the top, corn needs a community filled with supportive neighbors to receive the pollen; it thrives surrounded by relatives. After the male tassel and the female nubbins of silk mate, propagation usually occurs. When a tube grows from the pollen into the silk, a single kernel begins to form and swell with milk. The kernel grows, with a long leaf cradling each ear, just as a mother cradles her newborn infant. One cob of corn produces kernels of white, yellow, red, brown, and blue, indicating cosmic unity despite diversity. Each kernel grows harmoniously and respectfully in its own space, sharing the energy source, the protection, and the families.

Seasons come, seasons go; the caterpillar emerges as the owl salutes the moon; rain falls, burying the seedling securely in earth's fertile soil, and within days a new corn plant begins life. Throughout the growing season, the community of corn struggles while the husk cradles each ear of corn. Storms come, as they will, but the neat cornstalks bend with the wind, buffering the young they hold. Their roots intertwine beneath the land, supporting and anchoring each other, giving and receiving strength against weeds, insects, and other predators that feed on the vulnerable. Then, protected by husks, leaves, and a vibrant community, the ears of corn mature to become food for civilization. The corn draws strength from the village of bakers, builders, artists, weavers, designers, teachers, athletes and healers, planners, leaders, writers and singers, all of whom are seeds of the corn. Every part of the plant benefits humankind—the stalk, husk, kernels, cob, and roots—in preparing a harvest for tomorrow.

THE FRUITS OF CIVILIZATION:
PROVERBS FOR UJIMA

One head does not go into council.—Africa

He made you rise to work at dawn. You will thank him at sunset.—Africa

Two small antelopes can beat a big one.—Ashanti

The desires of the lazy are too great for their labors.—Bambara

God gives nothing to those who have their arms crossed.—Bambara

A chattering bird builds no nest.—Cameroon

The stream won't be advised; therefore, its course is crooked.—Cameroon

Little by little the bird makes its nest.—Haiti

Even the milk from our own animals does not belong to us. We must give to those who need it, for a poor man shames us all.—Ivory Coast

Property is the prop of life.—Nigeria

There's no profession without a boss.—Africa

One man cannot launch a ship.—Swahili

Being of use does no harm.—Tanzania

A good thing sells itself; a bad thing advertises itself for sale.—Tanzania

The man who has not carried the loads himself does not know how heavy they are.—Uganda

In a community a dispute is everybody's business, whether they are high born or humble, rich or poor, whoever they may be.—Uganda

Other people's wisdom often prevents a chief from becoming a fool.—Yoruba

Work is the medicine for poverty.—Yoruba

THOUGHTS FOR UJIMA

❖ Let your imagination fly. Don't be limited by others' narrow imaginations.

❖ Follow your dreams by preparing for the opportunities that are awaiting you.

❖ Discipline, hard work, and concentration will determine how well you succeed in life.

❖ Visualize your success; decide on your goal; and, through hard work, you can overcome any obstacle.

❖ Become a daily point of light. In your space, in your time, and with the grace of God, make a difference in the world.

❖ Develop a talent not only for finding money, but for finding high-quality employees for key positions. Money doesn't run businesses; people do.

❖ Prepare yourself through effort, education, business, and interpersonal skills to guarantee success in anything you do.

❖ Look at all tragedies and mistakes as stepping stones to opportunities and growth.

❖ Help others to harvest success, and you automatically benefit.

❖ Make time for youth; use a hands-on approach to give back to the community by working directly with children.

❖ Put your family first in everything. The family that works together, succeeds together.

CHAPTER FOUR

PRINCIPLE 4

UJAMAA

DESTINY IN OUR HANDS: THE MEANING OF UJAMAA

We must still press forward, sensing opportunities that lead toward the empowerment of our people. We must become self-defining women and men who work together harmoniously to build upon the common social, economic and political needs of Black people. And we must fortify ourselves with the spiritual armor that strengthens us and helps us to survive and endure in this world.

—Susan Taylor

Ujamaa, the fourth principle of Kwanzaa, is celebrated on December 29, when families and friends gather to light the last green candle. Once the other candles are relit, the program centers on how African Americans can spot and create opportunities to apply Ujamaa. Both Ujima and Ujamaa deal with economic organization: business, work, and money. On the fourth day of Kwanzaa we assess our circumstances and recommit ourselves to working and building our own shops and other businesses to profit the community.

According to Paul Robeson, to work "is to be free—to walk the good American earth as equal citizens, to live without fear, to enjoy the fruits of our toil, to give our children every opportunity in life—that dream which we have held so long in our hearts is today the destiny that we hold in our hands." Work puts the law of circulation into action and is the reason we have a harvest of success. It is the way we create and develop ourselves and confirm our worth. Once we receive and freely give, dreams materialize. We live on a unified plane, no individual lives entirely alone, and cooperative economics means that we think about others; our thoughts don't center only on ourselves. The law of circulation means to give enthusiastically: to lose ourselves in a cause, in a purpose. Our actions allow Divine power to flow through us and to build order on a secure financial base. Applying Ujamaa means that the home, the family, and the community grow stronger through the laws of circulation, attraction, and prosperity.

We must began to model successful businesses in secure communities. We must create the image of success, and the law of attraction will draw it to us once we specify what we desire. African Americans labored hard and long to be a part of this society, and systematic hard work for ourselves is not a frightening proposition. Ujamaa urges us to use that energy to build a community—brick by brick, house by house, business by business. Practicing the universal principles and Kwanzaa forecast growth from the joy of saying we did it! We mastered it!

The ideas of achievers like Don Barden provide the material things of the world—things that are not part of our natural environment through work and planning. Every job, whether it is baking cookies, developing real estate, or starting a cable company, begins with a single thought that becomes the source of all causes and effects.

Ujamaa is having a fruitful purpose like Berry Gordy who, in *To Be Loved*, tells how working as a songwriter built his self-respect, nourishing and invigorating him to collaborate in creating legends-making Motown. Ancient Africans applied the law of circulation because everyone shared the bounty or the famine; no one gained all the wealth by exploiting others. In the same manner, Berry shared and inspired all members of Motown to work cooperatively for a common goal: the next hit record. Ujamaa stresses production from local resources for local needs, Motown did even more by satisfying the global thirst for African American music. Berry quit a secure job because he felt like W. E. B. Du Bois, who said, "The return from your work must be the satisfaction which that work brings you and the world's need of that work. With this, life is heaven. . . . Without this—with work which you despise, which bores you, and which the world does not need—this life is hell."

Frederick Douglass's belief that "man is worked upon by what he works on. He may carve out his circumstances, but his circumstances will carve him out as well" is manifest in the life of the entrepreneur A. G. Gaston. Gaston understood that every person, rich or poor, is obligated to do something in this world by using his or her imagination, talent, or skills. As a young boy, he discovered that if he supplied the needs of his community, he could design his own world, despite segregation. Gaston knew that what he felt himself to be, he became, and his work contributed to who and what he is. The workplace affected his thinking, his values, and his actions, motivating him to find other needs and to fill them.

Ujamaa is taking responsibility for your future as Gregory Baranco of Atlanta, Georgia, did. In 1969, during a summer internship at Ford Motor Company's Dearborn Stamping Plant, Baranco began his plan to become an automobile dealer. He left the well-paying job at the plant to get hands-on training and experience in a dealership and joined Audubon Ford that year. Nine years later, he opened Baranco Pontiac. And now with Pontiac, Lincoln-Mercury, and Acura dealerships all over Georgia, Baranco grosses over $70 million in sales as president of the Baranco Automotive Group. Baranco epitomizes the principles of Kwanzaa, especially, Ujamaa.

TREASURES OF MY DREAMS: POETRY FOR UJAMAA

SACRED DUTY

SAMI BENTIL

The sound
of an ancient horn echoes
from our past, the call to the
sacred duty
of true nation building.
Arise and unite,
you well minded
able bodied children
of Mother Africa scattered
all over the world,
use the divine gifts of
talent so bountifully bestowed
upon you to help all our people
create communities
where genuine freedom
and justice reign supreme.
Go Forth.
Be fruitful
in every
positive way
to fill each
and every corner
of our beautiful planet
with abundant life,
love,
beauty,
everlasting joy.

THANKSGIVING

William Stanley Braithwaite

My heart gives thanks for many things—
For strength to labor day by day,
For sleep that comes when darkness wings
with evening up the eastern way,
I give deep thanks that I'm at peace
with kith and kin and neighbors too;
Dear Lord, for all last year's increase,
that helped me strive and hope and do.

My heart gives thanks for many things—
I know not how to name them all.
My soul if free from frets and stings,
my mind from creed and doctrine's thrall.
For sun and stars, for flowers and streams,
for work and hope and rest and play,
for empty moments given to dreams—
for these my heart gives thanks today.

THE SEASON OF REMEMBRANCE

HOWARD THURMAN

Again and again it comes:
The Time of Recollection,
The Season of Remembrance.
Empty vessels of hope fill up again;
Forgotten treasures of dreams reclaim
their place;
Long-lost memories come trooping back to
  me
This is the season of remembrance,
My time of recollection.
Into the challenge of my anguish
I throw the strength of all my hope:
I match the darts of my despair
with the treasures of my dreams;
Upon the current of my heart
I float the burdens of the years;
I challenge the mind of death
with my love of life.
Such to me is the Time of Recollection,
The Season of Remembrance.

AFTER THE RECORD IS BROKEN

JAMES A. EMANUEL

My mind slips back to lesser men,
Their how, their when.
Champions then:
Big Stilley, with his bandaged hands,
Broke through the Sidney line, the stands
hysterical, profuse the rival bands,
Poor Ackerman, his spikes undone,
His strap awry, gave way to none,
Not even pride. The mile he won.

Now higher, faster, farther. Star crossed
Recede, and legends twinkle out, far lost,
Far discus-spun and javelin-tossed,
Nor raise again that pull and sweat,
That dig and burn, that crouch-get set
Aglimmer in old trophies yet,
Now smoother, softer, trimmer for speed,
The champion seems a better breed,
His victory a showroom deed.

Oh, what have we to do with men
Like champions, but cry again
How high, how fast, how far? What then?
Remember men when records fall.
Unclap your hands, draw close your shawl:
The lesser men have done it all.

SELF-DEFINING MEN AND WOMEN: PEOPLE OF UJAMAA

MARIE BROWN: AGENT OF CHANGE

DOROTHY WINBUSH RILEY

Being a literary agent is not only about making money; it is a way of establishing an identity, of becoming who you are.

—Marie Brown

A literary agent works on behalf of an author to find a publisher, negotiate the contract, and promote the author's work. Marie Brown is one of four African American women who cracked publishing's glass ceiling to enter the billion-dollar literary agents' field. Brown, self-determined, self-disciplined, and self-directed, sprouted entrepreneurial ideas after twenty-five years of deep immersion in the world of publishing. As an exceptionally successful African American woman, she represents the African American spirit of faith, resiliency, determination, and purpose.

Brown's life demonstrates the principles of Nguzo Saba, from the way she was raised to her current thoughts about success. She learned high esteem from her mother, a school-teacher, and her father, a civil engineer and professor. Marie lived in a cocoon of learning, and she recalls, "Books were my passion. . . . I love books. The campus libraries were my homeroom." She became a junior high school teacher after she graduated from Pennsylvania State University with a bachelor's degree in psychology and education.

In 1967, one year after the first Kwanzaa celebration, Brown began her odyssey in publishing, when the civil rights movement forced corporations to hire minorities and women. Doubleday and Company lured Brown from her job introducing teachers, students, and parents in Philadelphia to African-centered and multicultural books to work as an acquiring editor of such books. For two years Brown immersed herself in publishing and, then, newly wed, moved to Los Angeles when her husband was transferred.

In New York, the hub of the publishing world, editorial jobs were available, but not in Los Angeles. However, problems always camouflage opportunities when they are looked at with imagination. Brown did freelance editing and worked in a bookstore, where she discovered that African Americans spend millions of dollars buying books. She used this knowledge to launch her agency more than a decade later.

Doubleday welcomed her return in 1972, and for nine years, Brown promoted books by writers of color that were usually ignored. In 1984, from her Harlem apartment, she opened a literary agency, to be a bridge for African American writers. It was something she wanted to do in an area she loved; by working with books, she would be practicing Kujichagulia, Ujima, and Ujamaa, as well as Kuumba and Imani. In addition, she understood herself well enough to know what would make her happy.

Being the boss affected every aspect of her life; she couldn't leave her business behind when she left the office; her home was the office. Loneliness was a constant companion because she no longer had the physical and psychological support of a corporate staff. However, her strong sense of self, coupled with her harmonious belief in the universal laws, kept her on course.

Brown's work in California and other stepping-stone jobs made her a resilient achiever who is not afraid to risk failure to succeed. She is more diverse and more adaptable to the needs and desires of individual clients as she analyzes and listens and responds to the marketplace and the writers she represents. And she successfully uses imaginative vision to help others reap their own harvest. As Brown puts it, "I can see what can be published successfully. The difficulty is in trying to match what you know is a good project with the consciousness or awareness of the publisher you approach."

Her generosity, sunny disposition, and ability to work with top people make it possible for Brown to fulfill the dreams of others. She is polite, but not condescending; efficient, but not brusque; direct, but not discourteous—all of which makes influential and powerful people seek her guidance. Brown also develops a relationship with each of the eclectic authors she represents. Her agency not only empowers these writers, but enriches the world.

By practicing the principles of Kwanzaa, Brown makes her dreams come true and then uses her gifts so others can harvest theirs. She is an American success story in a growth market with a great future. And she notes, "I will be an agent ten years from now—but on a different scale—concentrating on commercial marketing. Instead of a group of whites printing what they think blacks want to read, the industry can then learn about this audience, and their needs, and then publish books a larger black audience will buy."

THE CHURCH: FROM CIVIL RIGHTS TO SILVER RIGHTS

Dorothy Winbush Riley

From slavery through the twentieth century, the African American church has applied the principles found in the Nguzo Saba as the salvation of the community. It served all needs: religious, spiritual, emotional, financial, political, and social. Through its collective strength, the church fostered businesses, banks, schools, and colleges while keeping its eye on the schizophrenic nature of American racism. Time is marching into the twenty-first century and the nature of the black church is expanding. It will always work to supply the needs of the people; however, now it is moving toward self-determination through economic strength. African American churches across this country provide strategic planning in finances, business advice, loans, and housing. The institution knows that with a strong economic base, our civil rights are protected.

The African American church movement was born when Richard Allen and his followers organized Bethel African Methodist Episcopal Church in Philadelphia in 1788. From that moment, the church movement has applied the principles of Kwanzaa through economic self-help among its members, political refuge for escapees, and a home during segregation. One example is the 202-year-old Bethel African Methodist Episcopal Church in Baltimore, which provides a broad range of services, including a faith store and employment referrals, to meet the needs of its 6,000-member congregation. Another example is Allen Temple Baptist Church in Oakland, California, which has, since its founding in 1919, given spiritual and physical support to its members. This church collaborates with other religious and local groups to provide services to more than 150,000 people in the city. It also manages a credit union and has built two apartment complexes for 126 senior citizens.

Every church has a purpose, and Rev. Charles Adams, of Hartford Baptist Church in Detroit, believes that "the church needs to concentrate on the business of creating economic institutions and move from fighting for civil rights to creating silver rights." This church's congregation of more than six thousand contains some of the most creative minds in the city. Reverend Adams and a development team, led by presidential and mayoral advisers Nellie Varner and William Pickard, have reclaimed the immediate community. Today, when you drive down Seven Mile Road, McDonald's and Kentucky Fried Chicken franchises are on land leased from the church.

One of the largest hospitals in Detroit closed, vacating 80,000 square feet of land in the heart of the city. Members of Hartford's congregation pooled their resources to buy the land for $500,000 (it's now worth more than $5 million) and will build a $17 million shopping center on it. The church practices and observes the principles of Kwanzaa and applies Ujima and Ujamaa daily.

In Windsor Village Church in Houston, Texas, Rev. Kirbyjon Caldwell applies the principles of Kwanzaa to create a kingdom builder of each member. He knows that any community that allows the greater society to define its character, designate its needs, and plan and implement programs to meet those needs will suffer continual devastation. Before he became a minister, Caldwell earned a master's degree in economics from the Wharton School of Business. His work with stocks and bonds prepared him to build a community church that needs millions of dollars. He says, "I didn't know how to process it, I wasn't looking to do it. I didn't know about the seminary, but I knew somehow I was supposed to pastor a church." Like other giants, Booker T. Washington and Frederick Douglass, Caldwell had a vision of the possible; he accepted his mission and returned to Southern Methodist's Perkins Theological Seminary in 1981.

Nine years later, Caldwell, now an ordained minister, stood in front of Windsor Village Church with twenty-five members on the rolls but only twelve who bothered to attend the services. He believed in the power of collective work and responsibility to develop the family and the community. He had his work cut out for him as he started to build a strong community surrounding a strong church. Now he leads seven thousand self-determining members by applying faith, vision, and economic principles. The church's members actively participate in more than ninety ministries, including choirs, scout troops, sports teams, alcohol and drug rehabilitation counseling, AIDS/HIV outreach, Patrice House (a twenty-four-hour shelter for children), Imani School (preschool through fifth grade), tutoring and mentoring programs, and Okechuku (God's Gift for Boys Training to Be Men).

His contagious vision infected the Houston community and drew people from every level of society—rich, middle class, and the poor. This cross section of people, ranging from professional athletes Warren Moon, Zina Garrison, and Evander Holeyfield to upper-middle-class African Americans, adds to the vibrant purpose of Windsor Village. Caldwell stresses the principles of Kwanzaa: unity and stable families (Umoja), self-determination (Kujichagulia), personal responsibility (Ujimaa), work and self-discipline (Ujimaa), education (Nia), pride in self and ancestry (Kuumba), and faith (Imani).

Fiesta Mart, a Houston grocery chain, noticed the good works and gave Windsor Village twenty-four acres of land with two 100,000-square-feet buildings on it. The gift, valued at $4.4 million, brought Caldwell's vision of a self-determining community closer to reality. Knowing the importance of naming, Caldwell christened it the Power Center; the center's focal point will be a two-story Holeyfield Chapel, to be built with a million-dollar donation from Evander Holeyfield. The Imani School will move to the center, as will a bank to provide accessible and affordable mortgages to the people. Other businesses that are planned include a clinic, an art gallery, a recreational center, and a variety of federal-social agencies to meet the needs of all the people. You can do a lot with twenty-four acres, and wherever Caldwell finds a need, he fills it with kingdom builders from his Windsor Village Church.

A. G. GASTON:
FIND A NEED AND FILL IT

DOROTHY WINBUSH RILEY

Arthur G. Gaston built a million-dollar empire in Alabama, and to ensure that it would exist after his death he created an employee-owned stock company. Gaston's autobiography, *Green Power: The Successful Way of A. G. Gaston,* describes his determination and rise to success. He looked around his community, saw the needs, and created businesses to fill them.

Many begin life with great wealth and resources, but few accomplishments exceed those of Arthur G. Gaston, who can reflect on more than seventy years of service to the community and the nation. Born in 1892, twenty-seven years after the end of the Civil War, A. G., as he is known, was raised by his grandmother in Demopolis, Alabama, while his mother worked as a maid. His father died soon after his birth, and Gaston grew up in a female-headed home. There were no swings, recreational centers, or playgrounds for African American children in the segregated town, but this did not prevent Gaston's grandmother from using self-determination to solve the immediate problem of a playground for her grandson. There was an old swing in the yard, and all the children came to swing. In the African fashion, Gaston bartered admission to the yard for a button, a pin, or candy from the children.

Birmingham provided more work for Gaston's mother, so she and Gaston moved there, but Gaston carried his ideas, values, and beliefs, never forgetting that first successful venture in his grandmother's backyard. One day, Booker T. Washington spoke at the Tuggle School, which Gaston attended, and gave him a lifelong vision: *Build up the community where you live, look around and see what needs to be done, and then do it.* Like Marcus Garvey, Gaston shared Washington's values and business philosophy and decided to make a name for himself, just as the president of Tuskegee Institute had done. Gaston believed that once he had money, he could determine his own social and political future. Later in life, his admiration for Tuskegee's founder prompted him to name many of his businesses after Booker T. Washington.

Gaston left school after completing the eighth grade to sell newspaper subscriptions and to bellhop in Mobile. In 1918, he served with the all–African American army unit stationed in France during World War I, yet before he returned to racially oppressive Birmingham, Tuskegee Institute influenced young Gaston once more. Robert Moton, Tuskegee's president, urged the young men to return to America and accept second-class treatment and not to expect the kind of respect they had received in Europe. Gaston understood, but returned to the city fired with a clear, compelling vision that he would succeed by finding what needed to be done—problems that could be solved in his own community. He had found his place, and he would stay in it until he achieved success.

On his first job with the Tennessee Coal and Iron Factory, Gaston earned $3.10 per day, yet he was able to save most of his weekly salary. He spotted opportunities; for example, many workers didn't bring lunches, so he sold peanuts and box lunches. His second rule of success was always to save part of his earnings; with that nest egg he lent money to those who couldn't manage their money.

All over the South, the community traditionally banded together to bury the dead because individual families could not afford to do so. Gaston immediately recognized a community need and started the Booker T. Washington Burial Society by collecting a sum of money each week from people and guaranteeing them a decent burial.

In 1932, unified support from his family and the needs of

the community then motivated Gaston to start the Booker T. Washington Insurance Company and the Smith and Gaston Funeral Directors. By 1939 Gaston found another opportunity disguised as a problem when he couldn't find enough trained help for his businesses. True to his nature, he and his wife established the Booker T. Washington Business College to train their clerical help.

Because African Americans were not allowed to stay in segregated hotels, Gaston built the A. G. Gaston Motel and Hotel in 1954 to accommodate our people. Similarly, since it was practically impossible for African Americans to obtain loans and mortgages, Gaston created the Citizens Federal Savings and Loan in 1957 to provide mortgages for homes and churches. The same year his creative juices flowed as he founded another resource for the community, The A. G. Gaston Boys and Girls Club, to provide wholesome recreation for children.

The joy of life comes from what we create, what we give to the world. It is better to give than to take because in giving, we are in harmony with our true nature and the order of the universe. Gaston understands that everything in nature and every effort is given to us by the Creator. The brutal conditions of Jim Crow could not stop him from being human or from creating businesses to fill the needs of his community.

In 1987, Gaston created a stock-option program for his businesses and sold all the stock to his employees, leaving a business legacy for his employees to pass onto their descendants. He said, "When the founder of a business dies, the business usually dies." In selling the stock, he is perpetuating the principles of Ujamaa, the philosophy of Booker T. Washington, and his own business genius: to find a need and fill it. This son of a single mother has, throughout his life, empowered African Americans to "build up the community where you live, look around and see what needs to be done, then do it."

BARBARA GARDNER PROCTOR: ADVERTISING WITH VALUE

DOROTHY WINBUSH RILEY

No one ever started at the top. Yet, the idea of a successful life will create success and move you from the lowest rung on the ladder to the seat at the top. Once the seed is planted in your mind and sowed with faith, determination, and preparation, opportunities follow to lead you to prosperity. Barbara Gardner Proctor's life is evidence that all progress and advancement is based on the invisible force of faith. The Highest Power heard and answered the desires of her mind and placed her in situations to prepare her for the next level of success.

Faith and purpose were embedded in the heart and mind of Barbara Gardner Proctor by her grandmother. Like many achievers who were raised by their grandparents, Proctor learned that negative circumstances are temporary and can be changed with faith, determination, and hard work. She recalls, "My grandmother always thought I would do something. She taught me what is important isn't on the outside, but inside. She said it was important to put something inside you, some courage, knowledge, and a skill, things that no one can take from you." Her grandmother's love motivated Proctor to learn and earn an academic scholarship to Talledega College in 1954. Within three years, Proctor graduated with degrees in English and psychology and was on her way to Chicago.

Success was not waiting to be plucked like a rose from the streets of the city. Nevertheless, Proctor found work as a freelance ad writer and even as a disc jockey. One day an advertising agency needed a copywriter. Although Proctor knew little about advertising, she welcomed the opportunity to learn the business. In 1971, she founded Proctor and

Gardner when the agency she was working for fired her because she refused to work on an ad it created that parodied civil rights and sit-ins. Timing leads to success, and Proctor's agency tapped the initially untouched African American consumer market.

Starting Proctor and Gardner was difficult. However, an $80,000 loan from the Small Business Administration helped her to stay afloat for the first six months. Afterward, accounts from the Sears, Roebuck and Jewel companies opened the lucrative doors to the world of advertising. That loan in 1971, coupled with Proctor's imagination, determination, and faith, led to the agency reaping up to $15 million in billing in the 1990s. Proctor had faith in her mission and was brave enough to take risks that tested her level of faith. She says, "Risk is one trademark in business; as a businesswoman, you cannot be afraid to fail and to accept the responsibility for the results."

Proctor believes that she is responsible for her success and has learned the secret of handling disappointments, obstacles, and conflicts. Her agency does not accept accounts from liquor or cigarette companies, which she believes relentlessly target women and minorities, and always portrays African Americans with positive and constructive images. Furthermore, her accounts reflect companies that are tastefully advertised and support family values. Proctor knows that image is the key to self-determination and power. As she put it, "Advertising is the single most important way of reaching everyone in America, and I feel a deep sense of responsibility for my work."

DON BARDEN:
SPRINGBOARD TO SUCCESS

DOROTHY WINBUSH RILEY

Each person has the potential and opportunity for success in his
or her life. Don Barden's accomplishments demonstrate that those
who take time and use discipline to decide on a goal, while at
the same time embrace life changing risks, harvest prosperity.
Everyone rises to the top just like an elevator that makes many
stops on the way up. Not many people go from the basement to
the penthouse in one single ride. Don Barden experienced several stops, using the time to learn and excel as preparation for the
next level of success. He knew that whatever situation he found
himself in, it would be a springboard to greater prosperity.

Don Barden, the CEO of Barden Communications, knew
that one sure way for an African American male to succeed
in the 1960s was to attend college. So, Barden, the ninth of
thirteen children, did just that. However, in 1963, he had to
drop out of Central State University in Ohio because he
could not afford the tuition. He then moved to Lorain,
Ohio, where he did odd jobs until he had saved five hundred dollars and opened his own record store. Soon business was so good that he added a nightclub that attracted
top entertainers. In 1968, Barden sold both businesses and
opened a public relations firm. Next he started a real estate
development company and sold real estate. His hard work
and risk taking paid off when he was elected to the Lorain
City Council. This high-profile position landed him a job as
a talk show host in Cleveland and an opportunity to see the
value of cable television. Each move was a springboard to a
new and more successful venture.

In 1980, Barden bought 2 percent shares in two Ohio
cable franchises for $2,000 each and sold them within two
years for $200,000. Barden's timing was perfect when he

moved to Detroit, which was beginning to select a contractor to wire for cable, and he received the contract in 1983. Barden then sold shares to obtain enough capital to begin his work. Always the risk taker, he diversified his holdings by buying two radio stations and started his own record label.

Today, Barden Cable trucks dot the city as workers install and repair cables in thousands of homes. In 1994, Barden received $100 million from Comcast Company of Philadelphia for his share of the cable company. Since then he has invested $10 million in South Africa and formed the Barden-President Riverboat Casino company to finance a $116 million riverboat gambling project in Indiana. Don Barden's life demonstrates that with planning, hard work, self-determination, economics, faith, confidence, and risk taking, you can be a successful entrepreneur.

BUILD YOUR WORLD: QUOTATIONS TO INSPIRE UJAMAA

"Men must not only know, they must act."—W. E. B. Du Bois

"Wherever you spend your money is where you create a job. If you live in Harlem and spend your money in Chicago, you create jobs for people in Chicago. If you are black and the businesses are run by people who are not black, then those people come in at 9:00 A.M., leave at 5:00 P.M. and take the wealth to the communities in which they live."—Tony Brown

"We have to be accountable for the state of our race. Our bondage and our battle is economic. We're not slaves but servants. We have to spend more time at economic conferences, be producers and provide jobs. The answer is economic self-sufficiency."—Shirley Chisholm

"You have the ability, now apply yourself."—Benjamin Mays

"Determination and perseverance move the world; thinking that others will do it for you is a sure way to fail."—Marva Collins

"Every people should be the originators of their own designs, the projectors of their own schemes and creators of the events that lead to their destiny—the consummation of their own desires."—Martin Delany

"Business? That's very simple—it's other people's money."—Alexander Dumas

"What matters is not to know the world but to change it."—Frantz Fanon

"Life has brought to an end so many things. Evidently it is demanding of me. Start again. Begin new things. Again set to work to build your world."—Jean Toomer

"American society cannot define the role of the individual, or at least not that of the *responsible* individual. For it is our fate as Americans to achieve that sense of self-consciousness through our own efforts."—Ralph Ellison

"According to the commonest principles of human action, no man will do as much for you as you will do for yourself."—Marcus Garvey

"The work of human beings is to watch out for each other."—Whoopi Goldberg

"We will either find a way or make a way."—Hannibal

"Words are nothing but words; power lies in deeds. Be a man of action."—Mali Griot Mamadou Kouyate

"Do not do that which others can do as well."—Booker T. Washington

"Let the Afro-American depend on no party, but on himself, for his salvation. Let him continue toward education, character, and above all, put money in his purse."—Ida B. Wells

GIFTS OF THE CREATOR: FOLKTALES FOR UJAMAA

ECHEKWA LIBERATES FIRE

DOROTHY WINBUSH RILEY

Myths are the ancestors of science and the first attempts to explain why things happened. Storytelling was the cord that held society together and provided identity within the tribe and the nation. The griot shared the ancestral memories and in this myth Echekwa foresees the importance of fire and tempts God by giving fire to the villagers.

In the beginning of forever there was no fire, so the discovery of fire marks a great stage in civilization. According to African legends, the people of the Congo forest brought fire to mankind. One day Echekwa was chasing an elephant and arrived in the village of God, where he saw fire warming God's mother, cooking meat, and shaping iron. He wanted to take the magic light back to his village, so he quickly grabbed a burning coal and ran toward his village. Unfortunately, God caught him and took the fire back.

Echekwa did not surrender his desire for fire. He returned to God's village, where he found a fence of liana surrounding the fire. The athletic Echekwa jumped over the fence, grabbed a leaf of fire, and started running. Again God caught him and made him return the fire.

Finally, the young man visited God wearing a bark cloth so long that it dragged on the ground. He praised God for the gifts that God had given mankind: the beautiful land, birds, fish, the lumbering elephant, and the nosy monkey. As Echekwa talked, he placed his bark cloth near the flame, where in a snap of the finger, it caught on fire. Quick as a panther, he jumped up and raced toward his village with the burning cloth. God was startled, but still tried to catch him even though Echekwa was more than a quarter mile in front. When God arrived in Echekwa's village, fires were burning in front of every home. Because of Echekwa's persistence and determination to share fire with his people, God allowed Echekwa's people to keep the element that would shape civilization.

PELAHATCHEE PEOPLE

RETOLD BY DOROTHY WINBUSH RILEY

Stories have specific meanings as they tell of personal triumph over, around, or through treacherous circumstances. *Pelahatchee People* imparts cultural values found in Kwanzaa, because the well-being of the family resides in sharing the joys and the sorrows, the wealth and the want, the love and the heartbreak. This story is based on incidents that were told to me by Larry Wynn, who instills the values of his grandfather in his children today.

Before the names of things as we understand them in standard English were known to us, our ancestors roamed the hidden valleys, savannas, and plains of Africa. A strange fate brought them out of our diamond-laden, mineral-rich land to Livingstone City, in Sumpter County, Alabama, where our Great-grandfather William was sold into slavery on the Norod Plantation. Soon after, William jumped the broom with Peggy, and their son Albert, our grandfather, started us on a new destiny in America.

Albert, born in 1858, five years before Lincoln signed the Emancipation Proclamation, was physically a slave, but his mind eluded the chains. Like all the African descendants born on the plantation, Albert grew up working; at age seven he handled the plows, the horses, and the crops. His intelligence, even at that young age, convinced him that he would not spend his life working like a mule under the whip of another man.

Emancipation didn't improve the lives of those who were living on the Norod lands because the former slaves became sharecroppers. About that time, Albert took the surname Winn, the beginning of the word *winner*, for record keeping as a free man. The Civil War had devastated the South, and few industries remained after Sherman, Grant, and other generals marched through the towns.

King cotton was in ruins, boll weevils destroyed every crop, and money and food were scarcer than a fresh kettle of fish. No matter how hard the Winns worked, the share-cropping bill rose like yeast cakes.

Life does not stop for sorrow, and when Albert was about nine years old he met his future wife, Julia, while she was being nursed on the Brownridge Plantation. He watched her grow and every time he made a delivery to their mill, he'd comment, "She sho is a fine little gal." As Julia grew, Albert told anyone who'd listen, "I'm gonna marry Julia; she's going to be my wife!" Sure enough, when Julia turned thirteen, she and Albert were married by a traveling preacher.

The more children a couple had, the more help they had with the farmwork. The young couple had eleven chil-dren—Jim, Walter, Charley, Will, Clarence, John, and Nathan, fine strong sons, and daughters, Cora, Ninnie, Janie, and Florence, and the entire family labored. But the hard work didn't dent their sharecroppers' debt because sharecroppers never saw the fruit of their labor and it took every penny to feed eleven children. Albert saw the futility of sharecropping and the strength being sapped from his sons and the beauty being stripped from his daughters. He could take only so much physical and mental abuse before he would break, crushing everything and everyone around him. So, he silently rebelled and became determined to cross the state line, more than a hundred miles away, into lumber-rich Mississippi.

Each time a train passed through, Albert longed to be moving down the line away from Livingstone City. He observed the trains for some time and learned when they stopped and refilled their water at the gristmill. One star-less night, he gathered his family, and they slipped silently as spiders aboard the train while it refilled with water. I want you to get a clear picture of this fifty-two-year-old man leading his wife, their sons and daughters, and sons-

"Ancestors Known and Unknown." Boxwork by Shirley Woodson Reid, 1989. Wood, metal, fibers, clay, and gold leaf. Photograph by Bill Sanders.

in-law and daughters-in-law, plus all the grandchildren. Picture all the family members carrying whatever belongings they owned in quilted bundles on their heads or backs. Think of Moses leading the Hebrew children out of Egypt, and you can see Albert leading his troops to a better life. Under the safety of darkness, the Winns left the sharecroppers' debt, the invisible pay, and a meaningless future on the Norod Plantation.

The entire family stuck together and enjoyed prosperity in the lumber-rich town of Pelahatchee, Mississippi. The two eldest sons followed the chain of command to became generals in Albert's army. God carried the Winns in his arms, until the total devastation that occurred after the Great Pelahatchee Fire. Before the inferno, 3,000 people worked in the lumber mills that supplied wood as far west as Texas and as far north as Ohio. But no one can bank the ashes of a burned-out industry, so more then 1,500 workers left this once-prosperous town for other parts of the South and even for the North.

One of Albert's generals, Walter, migrated to Canton, Mississippi, where other family members soon joined him. Charley moved to Jackson to find work, and Ninnie returned to Alabama, around Birmingham. (Ninnie even traveled to Chicago, but she returned to Alabama after experiencing the fast life of the city.) Janie Bell, beautifully mature, joined her older brother, Walter, in Canton, where Albert would also come to live out his life after Julia's death. These four had been Albert's right hands; thus, he encouraged them, as he did all his children, to seek prosperity and success and never to settle for the empty shell of poverty. He would say that the Pelahatchee fire was out, but the Winns were winners in the race for life.

Grandfather Albert is etched in my mind because my father, John, the youngest child, stayed in Pelahatchee with him to farm after the fire. About 1918, John married Sudia Grant, and true to family tradition, they produced twelve children. I was the youngest, yet I remember Grandfather Albert striding proudly with his grandchildren walking in his shadow. I remember visiting Uncle Charley or Uncle Walter, and just sitting and listening quietly while the grown folk talked about the old times. I remember the love and respect Grandfather Albert received wherever he walked or visited. My childhood memories were deeply engraved by the stories that Aunt Ninny and Uncles Walter and Charley told of how the family survived slavery, share-cropping, prejudice, poverty, and war.

Years before *Roots* made family reunions popular, Charley and Walter, along with Ninny and my mother, began the tradition of meeting once a year to celebrate how the Winns had progressed since they crossed into Mississippi. During these reunions, the family shared fried chicken, baked fish, dumplings, smoked ham, biscuits, rolls, rice, collard greens, clams, shrimps, black-eyed peas, green beans, peach cobbler, banana pudding, and other foods of every kind and taste while they basked in the love that flamed like the rays of the sun. These gatherings continued into the 1960s, when they stopped because the four founders were entering the winter of their lives.

It wasn't until 1971 that I began to feel a void in my life because the younger generation had not maintained the tradition established by the four founders; we were allowing it to be buried with them. If I still remembered, I knew others shared my feeling and knew we had to do something. About that time, I read about Kwanzaa and recognized that the principles of Nguzo Saba were much like those that Albert taught the family: family unity, self-determination, creativity, success, prosperity, and faith. Persistence is part of my nature, so after contacting the Milwaukee Greens; the Atlanta Joneses; and the Louisiana, Mississippi, and Detroit Winns, plus a year of hard work, the fourth generation met in our first Kwanzaa in 1972, celebrating our common ancestry in Jackson, Mississippi. We, the descendants of

Albert and Julia, enslaved on an Alabama plantation, are survivors. We must gather to maintain and ensure the covenant with our ancestors in our pursuit of success, prosperity, and love. Always remember that home is a seed from which the future blooms, and the family is the nursery that tends it day to day. You are my family—the fourth and fifth generations of Albert and Julia Winn.

NJAMBE THE TAILOR

RETOLD BY DOROTHY WINBUSH RILEY

This story is based on a fable from the Congo. I have heard it told with Njambe as a hunter, a carpenter, an artist, and a cook. Each time the person's hard work and skill create a demand that he cannot meet. Two lessons that this story teaches are that every problem has its own solution and that you can't find the solution by running away.

Luba watched Njambe as he stitched busily on his sewing machine. Njambe had a great deal of wisdom and knew how to make pants for the men and dresses for the women. As soon as night melted into day, Njambe measured, cut, or sewed for the great number of people who waited in his house. One day the people argued with each other as they stood waiting for Njambe to finish their clothes.

"When will you finish my pants, Njambe?" asked one man. "You measured and cut them more than three weeks ago, but they still hang on the chair. Now you are beginning a pair of pants for Kwesi. When are you going to finish my pants?"

Before Njambe could answer, a petite woman pushed her way to his sewing machine. She said angrily, "I want my dress! I gave you my cloth more than two months ago, and I have not seen a dress yet. You must stop making those pants and finish my dress."

Suddenly, everyone was demanding that Njambe stop and make his or her pants or shirt or dress. The noise grew so loud that Njambe ran from his house to the village elder for advice.

"I have taken on too much work, and now I can't manage it," he said. "I seem to start making one thing and then someone brings me beautiful material, and I stop to work on it. I never seem to finish anything. What can I do?"

The village elder listened and replied, "You have an easy problem, and I have the perfect solution." After they talked for ten minutes, Njambe returned to his house, which was still filled with angry customers.

He said, "Everyone, listen to me. I have a plan to give all of you your clothes. But, I need to hire three men or women to help me. Is there anyone who would like to work and measure the material to fit the patterns? I need someone to lay the patterns and then cut the material; it is easy work, and I will show you how to do it. I will hire someone else to help sew. I ordered a second Singer machine from America, and it came today."

"I wish to learn to sew using the sewing machine," said Nsangi. "I will work with you."

"And I will work with you," said Njoji. "That way I can learn to make my own pants."

"You make good clothes, and I want to learn from you. I will cut the material for you," said Kwame.

Njambe smiled as he looked at the pile of clothes he had cut out and the pile of material waiting to be cut. "Let's get to work and make everyone in the village happy." This is the way Njambe started his first business, which grew to fifty people who sewed clothes according to his patterns and designs. He accomplished this feat when he learned to finish one project before he started a second and to hire people to help him when he had too much work.

TO CHANGE THE WORLD: PROVERBS FOR UJAMAA

It is the fool whose own tomatoes are sold to him.
—Africa

When you want to sell a cow, you must leave home.
—Angola

The trader keeps more than he pays the porters.—Angola

Ten tailors will sew your garment badly.—Bambara

A coin in cash is better than ten on credit.—Bambara

Foresight spoils nothing.—Cameroon

The sleeping fox: No hare fell into his mouth.—Congo

When cat and mouse make an alliance, shopkeeper watch your wares.—Egypt

Never lend more than you borrow.—Egypt

If farmers do not cultivate their fields, the people in the town will die of hunger.—Guinea

When a needle falls into a deep well, many people will look into the well, but few will be ready to go down after it.—Guinea

If you are not there to work, your share of the harvest will not be there either.—Kenya

With money, no mother.—Kenya

Necessities never end.—Kenya

Treat the world well. . . . It was not given to you by your parents. . . . It was lent to you by your children.—Kenya

The squirrel starts work in the dew.—Kikuyu

When the workers are working, they are serious. —Liberia

Compete, don't envy.—Libya

The trader owes his wealth to his feet.—Mali

Where there are many fields, many farmers have work. Where there are many people, many teachers have work. —Mozambique

He who has goods can sell them.—Nigeria

The field will yield its fruit when you are tired.—Shona

The slowest camel in the caravan sets the pace.—Somali

Where there are fruit trees, there live industrious people.—Swahili

A good tailor will sew even on New Year's Day.—Swahili

Work makes life sweet.—Traditional

A lazy man will wait till easy work comes his way. —Yoruba

We join together to make wise decisions, not foolish ones.—Yoruba

The cure for poverty is work.—Yoruba

You never carved the bark of a palm tree and you expect to drink palm wine? Does the juice come without labor? —Yoruba

The animal without a sickle cried during the harvest. —Zaire

While the sun shines, get firewood for the night. —Zambia

If you sleep, your shop, too, will sleep.—Zambia

THOUGHTS FOR UJAMAA

❖ Find a need and fill it.

❖ Open your mind to the possibility of being somebody in the world by creating your own company.

❖ Never borrow anything that you can't afford to pay back. Many of us borrow above our ability to pay, and at the first minor difficulty we are in serious trouble.

❖ Take risks; they may open the path to opportunities.

❖ Experiment creatively and encourage everyone in your company to experiment.

❖ Establish a reputation at a bank to achieve a productive place in society. A banker is a good person to know, and your reputation at a bank can mean success or failure.

❖ Reflect on your past successes. Use them to aim for greater and greater achievements.

❖ Be an inspiration by setting and maintaining high standards of performance, achievement, and morality.

❖ Keep a part of your income. Every person should pay himself or herself something of whatever he or she earns.

❖ Profit from the success and mistakes of others; you will not live long enough to make all of your own.

❖ Know who you are and compete only with yourself.

❖ Create an atmosphere in which everyone believes that your goals and mission are reachable.

CHAPTER FIVE

PRINCIPLE 5

NIA

DEARER THAN BREATH:
THE MEANING OF NIA

*Daily life presents problems for each individual to
solve. Each test allows the person the opportunity
to be responsive and responsible to life. Purpose is
the essence of life whereby each male and female
has a specific mission in life. A specific purpose
that only he or she can fulfill. No one else can fulfill an individual's destiny, but that person who
has the necessary tools and skills to achieve.*

—Newbill Niles Puckett

We celebrate Nia, the fifth principle of Kwanzaa, on
December 30, when families and friends gather to light the
first red candle. After the black and green candles are relit,
the events for this day center on how we can use our purpose to build and develop our communities. Once we
become self-directed, we can restore our people to their traditional greatness through our work and service.

At our birth, the universe makes space for each of us.
Wealthy or poor; African, Hispanic, or European; intelligent or foolish, we inherit our rightful place. Once we
know who we are, what we are, and where we are going,
we are in harmony, spiritually and physically, with the creative intent of the universe. Then we have a purpose—a
solid rock, an anchor—that prevents us from being pulled
in one hundred directions and from adding to the chaos of
the world. Nia is doing what needs to be done: any creative
or helpful action that glorifies life in our search for happiness. It is preserving and increasing the legacy that the
ancestors left us.

Our purpose indicates which mountains to climb and
which ones to walk around, which oceans to swim and
which ones to cruise, and which dreams to dream and which
ones to live. Although we did not create the world around us,

our behavior shapes and changes it. Positive involvement stimulates our energy flow as we achieve balance in living active, healthy lives. Clearly defined intentions provide guidance in all areas by focusing on what is important. They help us make conscious decisions that are in alignment with our needs and the needs of our community.

When the fulfillment of a purpose is in harmony with our values, life is full of promise, pride, progress, and power. When we have this direction, we make choices with ease. Have you ever pondered an important decision, thinking, "Should I do this or should I do that?" The answer is simply to follow the behavior that is in accord with your purpose. If neither choice agrees with your purpose, then wait for a more harmonious path to follow.

When we believe that our purpose is worthy and that we are the one the Creator has selected for the task, nothing stops our progress. Happiness is being used for a purpose that you recognize as a mighty one. Individuals with a mission are not bionic heroes made of steel and iron; they are ordinary persons performing acts of extraordinary leadership who see a need and respond to it. They believe that it is their responsibility to act and make the world better. They have something to do, and it is to improve conditions for others through service, a gift that helps the helper and the one who is helped. Providing help to anyone less fortunate activates the greatest force of the universe—the determination to love. Despite historic distortions and lies, African Americans have displayed love for centuries.

Clara Hale found completeness and love through Nia. Helping began with her; she did not wait for governmental programs or others to start. Love is giving, love is growth; love finds opportunities where others see despair. Through love, Hale attracted the support of her community, which donated to the women and children of New York. Her sharing relationship transformed the community in that many changed their lifestyles and found a reason for living.

Celebrating Kwanzaa reminds us that we have a proud heritage of helping each other to preserve, appreciate, and pass on to our children. This tradition continues at Spelman College, where all students must perform community service. Several students volunteer at the Atlanta Children's Shelter for homeless children under age five who have no place to go after their mothers leave the shelter early in the morning to try to find work. The mothers do not have to pay for their children's care from 7 A.M. to 5 P.M., unlike a regular day care center. The center needs volunteers, and Spelman students know that helping is the only way our people can survive. In addition, the young women carry away memories of the children's hugs, kisses, and smiles as they return to the security of their own families.

Like the women of Spelman College and Clara Hale, we must never underestimate our power to make a difference. We must stop, look around, and recognize that where we are is where our purpose lies. Where we live is the place for us to strengthen each other and our community. The future will change as rapidly as the past when we measure our lives spiritually and ethically and believe, as does writer June Jordan, who said, "The intrinsic purpose is to reach and to remember, and to declare our commitment to all the living without deceit and without fear and without reservation. We do what we can. And by our doing it, we help ourselves."

THE ESSENCE OF LIFE: POETRY FOR NIA

I SHALL LIGHT A CANDLE OF UNDERSTANDING IN THINE HEART WHICH SHALL NOT BE PUT OUT

ESDRAS

LORNA GOODISON

I shall light
First debts to pay and fences to mend,
lay to rest the wounded past, foes dis-
    guised as friends.

I shall light a candle of understanding.

Cease the training of impossible hedges
    around this life
for as fast as you sow them, serendipity's
    thickets will appear
and outgrow them.

I shall light a candle of understanding in
    thine heart.

All things in their place then, in this many-
    chambered heart.
For each thing a place and for Him a place
    apart.

I shall light a candle of understanding in
   thine heart
which shall not be put out.

By the hand that lit the candle.
By the never to be extinguished flame.
By the candle-wax which wind-worried
   drips
into candle wings luminous and rare.
By the illumination of that candle
exit, death and fear and doubt,
here love and possibility
within a lit heart, shining out.

EXCERPT FROM *DELTA*

MARGARET WALKER ALEXANDER

Then with a longing dearer than breathing
love for the valley arises within us
love to possess and thrive in this valley
love to possess our vineyards and pastures
our orchards and cattle
our harvest of cotton, tobacco and cane.
Love overwhelms our living with longing
strengthening flesh and blood within us
banding the iron of our muscles with anger
making us men in the fields we have tended
standing defended we have rendered
rich and abiding and heavy with plenty.

We with our blood have watered these fields
and they belong to us,
Valleys and dust of our bodies are blood
    brothers
and they belong to us;
the long golden grain for bread
and the ripe purple fruit for wine
the hills beyond for peace
and the grass beneath for rest
the music in the wind for us
the nights for loving
the days for living
and the circling lines in sky for dreams.

FREDERICK DOUGLASS

ROBERT HAYDEN

When it is finally ours, this freedom, this lib-
    erty, this beautiful
and terrible thing, needful to man as air,
usable as earth; when it belongs at last to all,
when it is truly instinct, brain matter,
    diastole, systole,
reflex action; when it is finally won; when it
    is more
than the gaudy mumbo jumbo of politicians:
this man, this Douglass, this former slave,
    this Negro
beaten to his knees, exiled, visioning a world
where none is lonely, none hunted, alien,
this man, superb in love and logic, this man
shall be remembered, O, not with statues'
    rhetoric,
not with legends and poems and wreaths of
    bronze alone,
but with the lives grown out of his life, the
    lives
fleshing his dream of the beautiful, needful
    things.

"Akua Mma." Ashanti wood carving, artist unknown.
Photograph by Bill Sanders.

DESTINED TO MAKE A DIFFERENCE: PEOPLE OF NIA

MARIAN WRIGHT EDELMAN: SERVICE IS THE PURPOSE OF LIFE

DOROTHY WINBUSH RILEY

"The children—my own and other people's—became the passion of my personal and professional life. For it is they who are God's promise and hope for mankind." Marian Wright Edelman is an advocate for children—homeless children, orphaned children, adopted children, runaway children, abused children, loved children, unhealthy children, hungry children, illiterate children, dying children—all of America's children. Early in life, she discovered her purpose, the unreserved commitment to changing the way children are treated and mistreated in our world.

Each human is born into the world to do something uniquely distinctive to preserve our cultural heritage with meaningfulness. Marian was the youngest child in a family in which both parents nurtured action, achievement, and leadership despite their living in a typical segregated southern town. During the 1940s, society forced a life of hardship on minorities that made the African American community bond to become self-sufficient. "Service was as much a part of my upbringing as eating breakfast and going to school. It isn't something you do in your spare time. It was clear that it was the very purpose of life."

Marian watched her parents learning early the power of one individual to solve problems. Her father, Reverend Wright, established a haven called the Wright Home for the Aged that his wife operated after his death and until she died.

The teachers, preachers, and parents knew that respect, confidence, purpose, and faith are necessary for a worthwhile life. The elders made all the children feel important and encouraged them to believe that they could achieve whatever their minds could imagine. They buffered the children from the prejudice, fear, hatred, and injustice that are common in an oppressive society. Again, segregation forced Marian's father to turn a challenge into an opportunity to make a difference. When the teenagers had nowhere to go for recreation because they were denied use of the public park, he created a playground and canteen in the church's backyard.

Marian's socially conscious parents expected and received academic excellence from their five children. Even though her father died when she was a teenager, Marian fulfilled his expectations of her. Marian's high energy, combined with her intellect, propelled her to win scholarships to study in both America and Europe, and her quick mind and stamina led her to Yale Law School. With her law degree, she believed, she could work within the legal system to change laws to benefit all people.

Marian interned with the NAACP Legal Defense and Educational Fund in 1963. A year later, she went to Jackson, Mississippi, to establish voting rights for the African American citizens by preparing and winning civil rights cases. She fought for brave ordinary people who would register to vote, only to lose their jobs the next day. Oppressive, restrictive Mississippi was a pivotal point in Marian's life. During her four years there, she met her future husband and discovered the mission of her life.

After she returned to Washington in 1968, the same year Dr. King and Robert Kennedy were assassinated, the dismal existence of Mississippians haunted her. In 1973, a thought entered her heart and mind that prompted her to create the Children's Defense Fund to protect the interest of children. Lawyers, doctors, teachers, and plumbers have unions and lobbyists to speak on their behalf, yet the children had no one to take their concerns to Congress. Private donations support the Children's Defense Fund, and under Edelman's leadership the organization employs more than one hundred workers with a budget of $10 million. One idea + one person + one purpose = change. We all benefit, because, as Edelman says, "Investing in children is not a national luxury or choice. It's a national necessity ... we either pay up front, or we are going to pay a whole lot more later on."

DR. MARTIN LUTHER KING, JR.: COMMITTED TO JUSTICE

DOROTHY WINBUSH RILEY

Kwanzaa is a special time to remember the ancestors, the bridge builders, and the leaders. Nobel Peace Prize–winner Dr. Martin Luther King, Jr.'s, life is a prime illustration of the Nguzo Saba. We remember Dr. King, whose moral achievements and faith combined African American culture with a political agenda to gain universal human acceptance.

Dr. Martin Luther King, Jr., experienced humiliating prejudice growing up in Atlanta, Georgia, and knew firsthand the hard conditions of African Americans. Therefore, it was logical for him to respond when Rosa Parks refused to give up her seat in the front of the bus on December 1, 1955. Her simple refusal catapulted Dr. King into a position that fused his destiny with that of the African American people.

Dr. King realized that a new era had arrived and he mustered the courage to lead the cause for change. True leaders help people to change and they do the unexpected to challenge one's sense of purpose, belief, and values. He personally immersed himself in the struggle when he could have said no or claimed that he was the youngest minister in town. He stood his ground and reaped strength from his faith, his courage, and his values.

His vision stretched far beyond the limitations of segregation to what could or should be. He told the people that the system would not change unless they endured the ridicule of the racists, the cynicism of the frightened, and the selfishness of the politicians. Dr. King's upbringing, education, and travels increased his understanding that evil is not an ultimate reality. It is the misuse of power that will end once we stop indulging evil, believing evil, and fearing evil. He also knew that humans create suffering, but the will of the people can destroy it. The African American community decided they had suffered long enough under segregated laws and formed the Montgomery Improvement Association.

Like all great leaders, Dr. King bonded with the citizens of Montgomery and they elected him president of the Association. Dr. King recognized the need for a change, found the knowledge needed to accomplish the change, and dedicated himself to the struggle for change. He committed himself to action, which was not an announcement of fact, but an intention that determined the future standards of what was acceptable as solution. Dr. King and other leaders organized a bus boycott promising the citizens of Montgomery that the laws would change. In the next months, the bus company showed no consideration or courtesy to African Americans and Dr. King was arrested for the first time.

Yet, he believed that universal freedom, peace, and brotherhood could be achieved through non-violence, not by returning hate for hate. He based his thinking on Mohandas Gandhi's philosophy of *satyagraha*, or non-violent resistance to violence. Gandhi believed "Non-violence resistance is an all-sided sword. . . . It never rusts and cannot be stolen." Dr. King said in his book, *Stride Toward Freedom*, that "Nonviolence is a powerful and just weapon. It is a weapon unique in history which cuts without wounding. It is a sword that heals." In applying Gandhi's philosophy, Dr. King believed that if you controlled and managed your behavior, you could change your life. He knew that in our segregated country, African Americans don't control what happens, but they could master their reactions and responses. His followers realized that life is a reflection of their inner beings and that making internal adjustments will change one's life.

Dr. King transformed a broken-spirited, self-defeated community into a trained force of non-violent resisters that forced the oppressors to adjust. He took disenfranchised people who, for generations, had been psychologically, physically, and mentally abused, and united them into a powerful collective. His commitment to civil rights spread contagiously across the city while African Americans walked, carpooled, or rode bikes. Then the city leaders tried to outlaw carpools, but the Association forced them to present the case to the Supreme Court. After 382 days, the Court decreed that the laws were unconstitutional.

For the next twelve years of his life, Dr. King would not turn back from other fights for human and freedom rights. He received strength from his commitment despite the risk of death. The dangers did not sway him from his course, but made him "turn the other cheek" and persevere. His credibility and faith earned him universal respect that inspired people of all races.

Celebrating Kwanzaa is another opportunity to remember Dr. King's spirit, words, and hope for tomorrow. It doesn't take courage to live in the past, it takes courage to live today, and hope is the breeding ground of courage for the future. Dr. King's dreams, ideas, visions, and actions are legacies that enable African Americans to bear history. Remembering Dr. King strengthens us. We are reminded of this by the words of Benjamin Mays, who said, "Dr. King knew the meaning of suffering—house bombed, living day by day under the threat of death, maliciously accused of being a communist, falsely acused of being insecure, insincere, and seeking the limelight for his own glory, stabbed by a member of his own race, slugged in a hotel lobby, jailed thirty times." However, none of these incidents put evil thoughts of revenge or bitterness in his heart.

Our ancestors were challenged as they endured slavery, lived under Jim Crow laws, and fought against *Plessy vs. Ferguson.* Yet, we must keep them as part of our story and tell our children of the heroes who helped us survive. We must give the ancestors, the bridge builders, and the leaders the respect and space they are due. This does not mean reliving the past or being in a time warp. We must meet the challenge of today and speak in voices of love and harmony, decreeing prosperity and success. We are challenged to practice and apply the Nguzo Saba to protect each other and keep ourselves free of all addictions. As Dr. King said, "We must bear witness courageously and plan for today and tomorrow." Once we accept proudly our place in American history, our place today and our place in the future, we will embrace this land as our home. As we celebrate Kwanzaa, we honor Dr. King and vow that we will be self-determining: mentally, physically, spiritually, and economically.

CLARA HALE: DETERMINED TO LOVE

DOROTHY WINBUSH RILEY

People seek happiness and equate it with winning a million-dollar lottery. Others search for happiness as if they were buying a house. Many realize that to find happiness, they must find a purpose outside themselves. Clara Hale spent her life thinking of and doing for others. She knew that true happiness exists in giving, and she completely lost herself in her work with babies who were born drug addicted. Her simple goodness and clear conscience created Hale House, a haven for women and infants. She did what she had to do, always believing in the sacredness of human life. She had experienced prejudice and intolerance yet lived her life by treating the rich, the poor, the healthy, and the sick with the same spoon of love, tolerance, and respect.

Nia surfaces from opportunities, duties, and relationships with each other. When Clara's husband died in 1932, Clara bravely raised her three children alone and cared for the children of others, which allowed her to stay home and raise her children to be responsible, caring adults. Later she expanded her rainbow of love to care for wards of the court and then became a foster mother. Forty foster children, many of whom now have college degrees, received healing love and positive reinforcement from her.

Great opportunities come to everyone who recognizes that they are sometimes purposes, camouflaged. After more than thirty-five years as a caregiver, Clara had the opportunity to retire. Her retirement was as short as a firecracker's tip because her daughter, Lorraine, a physician, sent her a heroin-addicted young woman with a two-month-old baby. The grapevine spread the news that Clara opened her heart to addicted babies with no charge or obligation to the mothers. Small opportunities are often the beginning of great endeavors, new chances, a new beginning, a gift to do what we will with it.

In 1969, when Clara opened Hale House, she found a greater cause in something that was so much larger than herself. She was not seeking fame or material wealth; she started her work with little money and did not petition the government or private agencies for funds. Rather, she started with a sense of the urgency of the problem and a desire to help. Money for food, clothing, and other items came from her three children for almost two years. The aim of Hale House is survival: raising and saving drug-dependent children from birth until their mothers complete a drug rehabilitation program and can be reunited with them.

The most valuable people around us have lived to help others. They live in harmony with the universal consciousness and add years to their lives by doing something for others. Mother Hale (as she came to be called) did not wait; she acted in the present, and gave more than a thousand babies a chance at life. Now, in addition to drug addiction, HIV, the plague of the twentieth century, is creating more and more orphans daily, and referrals of HIV-infected babies to Hale House come from the police, churches, hospitals, and social service agencies. Just as addiction and HIV are color blind, Hale House takes children, regardless of their race, as well as their religion or gender.

Dr. Lorraine Hale was the stimulus for her mother's work when she sent the first homeless mother and baby to Clara. Today, she continues Clara Hale's legacy, helping others to a happier more purposeful life.

DESIGNED WITH A PURPOSE

EMMELINE KING

By nature humans are goal oriented and become what they think about. The principles of Kwanzaa play a key part in the life of Emmeline King. From her earliest memories, she has been a goal setter, using self-determination to achieve her desires and set goals in all the important areas of her life. She visualizes clearly what she wants; then works as though she had already achieved the goal. Emeline allowed the universal power to map out the road she would travel to success. The young designer accepts personal responsibility for her growth; she does not rely on others to make her successful. She did not put time limits on the actualization of her dream but kept it to herself, trusting in the Creator to make it real.

I practice the principles of Kwanzaa daily, from January to December, year in and year out. It is not a ritual that I observe the last week of December; the teachings are part of me. As an African American female I faced the challenge of succeeding against the odds in a male-dominated field to become a transportation designer and to work at Ford Motor Company. Whenever detours or roadblocks crossed my path, Kujichagulia propelled me over, around, or through the barriers to the road to success.

Every time I ride in my Thunderbird, I feel more than just the usual pride of a driver in a beautiful car. The shapes, colors, and creation of cars excite me, and I am now the lead interior designer on the new Mustang, with the goal of making the car attractive to both sexes. Since I was a kid, I loved to draw and my parents encouraged me to develop my Kuumba, which opened my mind to unlimited possibilities, so I was free to explore unknown territory and construct my own reality. My mother, a schoolteacher, taught me that I could do whatever I set out to do. She would say, "Some people just dream while others turn their dreams into reality." The Umoja of my family and their expectations prepared me for college. If they had not supported me, I don't know how I would have succeeded.

My early education did not provide training in transportation design. My school steered girls into secretarial or domestic-type careers, and the mere thought that I wanted to take automechanics or drafting was against the norm. At age eleven I discovered my Nia; I wanted to be a designer at Ford Motor Company with my mentor, my father. I was fortunate because my father nurtured my lifetime affair with cars, and his work as a plastic specialist was my license to automotive design. We spent time together attending auto shows, museums, local artists' studios, and Ford's annual open house. My father took me to his job, where I saw the design of a car from the idea to the model.

In 1981 I graduated with an industrial design degree. Even my father couldn't help me, since the auto industry was in the middle of a recession—no one was hiring. My Imani steered me to the Center of Creative Studies. A year later, I tried Ford again; the answer was still no. I decided I would have more clout with a second degree from Pasadena California's Design Center, from which I graduated in 1983 as the only female in my class of eighteen. Imani opened that locked door; Ford hired me right away.

My determination was ingrained: I would have tried again and again. I grew up with Ford products, and I believed I would work for the company. I'm currently the only African American female designer at Ford. Many times I felt like I was journeying alone through an uncharted test site. Then I changed my attitude to believe that I was a trailblazer, marking the path for any female to follow. In other words, I see my life as a bridge and my career is a freeway for others to cross.

EXCERPT FROM *AN AUTOBIOGRAPHY: BENJAMIN O. DAVIS, JR., AMERICAN*

BENJAMIN O. DAVIS, JR.

General Benjamin O. Davis, Jr., was a strategic thinker who clearly defined his goals early in his life. To reach his objective and take advantage of his potential and future opportunities, he knew certain things had to be in place and one of those was attending West Point Military Academy. This excerpt from his autobiography demonstrates that despite isolation, prejudice, and loneliness, General Benjamin O. Davis, Jr., could not fail because he had a vision with a goal to achieve.

Everyone in our family had been taught the value of a dollar, and the depression years made us even more careful in the handling of money. As children and teenagers, my sisters and I were always expected to turn in any extra change after a purchase, and we often joked about how the leftover nickels and pennies had to be returned to the "Colonel." But my father was so thrilled when he received my letter telling him I was going to be in West Point's class of 1936 that he sent me a check for $25, saying, "I am adding an extra five." He meant that I could spend that "extra five" without having to account for it.

With his letter came a few words of advice. Normally he was cautious in making suggestions to me or my sisters. He wanted us to learn how to think and make decisions for ourselves. At this point, however, he must have wanted to help guide me over the big changes I would have to make in entering the Academy.

Now just understand that I am very happy. I feel you have the makings of a good cadet and officer. Just have patience, concentrate all you have got and who knows you may lead your class, or certainly, at least make the Army Corp. of Engineers. If you do that you have the world waiting for you. Remember twelve

million black people will be pulling for you with all we have. . . .
I am indeed proud of you, am honored to be,

Your loving Dad

In climbing through the Army's ranks from 1898 to 1932, my father had overcome what seemed almost impossible odds. In spite of the attitudes of whites in the United States toward all people of color, he had managed to buck the system and accomplish his goals. He had made life easier for me. Now it was my turn to make things better for those who would come after me. I was determined to succeed. . . .

When the big day finally arrived, I was so excited that the train ride to West Point seemed to take forever. I marveled at the blue sky and the green forests, shimmering in the summer sunshine, that covered the domed hills of northern New York. The scenery was spectacular and I felt lucky to be alive and at the beginning of what promised to be the greatest adventure of my life so far. My admiration for West Point was unbounded. During my last hours on the train, I dreamed about the four wonderful years that lay ahead. I wondered about the new friends I would make and how I would adjust to taking orders and living the Academy motto, "Duty, Honor, Country." After four years of training, those of us who survived would all react to the same orders in the same way, think the same thoughts and dress the same way, but each of us would retain something unique toward improving the lot of our fellow soldiers. From the attrition statistics I had seen, I realized that many of us were destined to drop by the wayside. I was positive, however, that failure was not in the scheme of things, that I would perform at West Point exactly as I had performed in my life up to this time—with considerable routine and expected success. I had no way of anticipating how hard won that success would be.

No one spoke to me except in the line of duty . . . and they were going to enforce an old West Point tradition—

"silencing"—with the object of making my life so unhappy that I would resign.

I was to be silenced solely because cadets did not want blacks at West Point. Their only purpose was to freeze me out. What they did not realize was that I was stubborn enough to put up with their treatment to reach the goal I had come to attain.

HEAR THE VOICES:
QUOTATIONS TO INSPIRE NIA

"Your ancestors took the lash, the branding iron, humiliations and oppression because one day they believed you would come along to flesh out the dream."—Maya Angelou

"I am actually dying on my feet because I am giving every moment, almost night and day—every little crevice I can get into, every opportunity I can get to whisper into the ear of an upper official, I am trying to breathe my soul, a spiritual something into the needs of our people."—Mary McLeod Bethune

"You were born in this world with a duty, / decreed by your own destiny."—*Bhagavad Gita*

"Helping one another runs the gauntlet from birth to old age and has brought out the best in African American families throughout history."—Andrew Billingsley

"The only reason you were born was to be better than your parents and to make the world better for your children."—Drew Brown

"We create our own destiny by the way we do things. We have to take advantage of opportunities and be responsible for our choices."—Benjamin Carson

"Art is of great value to any people as a preserver of manners, customs—religious, political and social. It is a record of growth and development from generation to generation. No one will do this for us: we must ourselves develop the men and women who faithfully portray the inmost thoughts and feelings with all the fire and romance which lie dormant in our history."—Pauline Hopkins

"Service is the rent we pay for living. It is the very purpose of life and not something you do in your spare time."—Marian Wright Edelman

"The human race does command its own destiny and that destiny can eventually embrace the stars."—Lorraine Hansberry

"None of us is responsible for our birth. Our responsibility is the use we make of life."—Joshua Henry Jones

"Every man is born into the world to do something unique and something distinctive and if he or she does not do it, it will never be done."—Benjamin Mays

"The ability to conduct struggle is gained in struggle. The ability to score victories is a function of experience that you gain in struggle. Experience also means mistakes and failures. It is by learning from these that we are able to struggle in a better way."—Nelson Mandela

"We have to do whatever we have to do in order for there to be a new day. That means dealing with practical reality in a way that keeps you very close to the ground, always knowing what you have to deal with in every sense. . . . Maybe you propel your dreams two or three generations down the line."—Bernice Reagon

"We must hear the voices and have the dreams of those who came before us and we must keep them with us in a very real sense. This will keep us centered. This will help us to maintain our understanding of the job we must do.

And if we do the job we must do, then we will win."
—Sonia Sanchez

"What are you living for? What is your purpose, your passion, your plan? Once you answer these questions and commit yourself, no one can clip your wings."—Susan Taylor

"There is a Purpose that invades all his purposes and a Wisdom that invades all his wisdom."—Howard Thurman

TO REACH AND TO REMEMBER: FOLKTALES FOR NIA

SHANGO OBA

DOROTHY WINBUSH RILEY

Storytelling, the center of tribal life, told how things were or how they should be. The story gave a message that prompted discussions about the message while giving models of behavior that authenticated tribal heritage, celebrations, customs, rites, and beliefs. This fable, "Shango Oba," explains how "unplanned civilization" disrupts the orderly life of the villagers. It also illustrates the individual's role in the family and the community to initiate change while maintaining traditional values to create order, not chaos.

There was once a village called Shango Oba, where the people lived only to have feasts. For any reason, at any time of the day or night, the villagers celebrated one thing or another.

"The rain fed the river! We must celebrate!" said the villagers. "The sun has gathered up the rain! We must celebrate!" When a boy was born, Shango Oba celebrated. When a girl was born, Shango Oba celebrated. The day a child went to school, Shango Oba celebrated. When a child went to the city to attend the university, Shango Oba celebrated.

At the beginning of the planting season, after they planted the crops, the villagers feasted. Once the harvest season started, they planned a long festival. On any day of the year, the happy people found a reason to celebrate.

All the feasts were held on the ground called Oba Yumi Square; even the oldest memories said this was the place. The men killed goats, chickens, and cows, and the women cooked the meat, stew, fufu, and rice in a huge kettle in the middle of the square, while the children gathered firewood to keep the fire going. Everyone shared to make the festivities fun.

Once all the food was cooked, the Council of Elders selected four or five young men to divide the food fairly and equally among the villagers. Every man, woman, and child had a plate piled with fufu, rice, stew, and meat. The villagers of Shango Oba formed a circle, sitting, kneeling, or squatting on the ground in the square and eating happily.

One day, Jacob, the son of Chineke, returned from studying at a university in America. He arrived in the middle of a feast that was held simply because he was returning. Jacob was amazed to see the villagers sitting, kneeling, or squatting on the ground while they ate their food.

"My family, I mean no disrespect, but why are you eating your food on the ground?" Jacob asked.

"This is how we have always eaten when we have a feast. How would you expect us to eat: standing up or sitting in a tree?" asked a village elder.

"No," said Jacob, "Civilized people sit at a table!"

The village elder replied, "We are civilized, and if you feel we need a table, then go and get one for us."

Jacob left with four young men to get a table. After a week, the group returned carrying a table large enough for eight people. Of course, the villagers planned a feast to use the new table in a civilized manner. They cooked cows, chickens, and goats and prepared bowls of rice and fufu. After the men divided the food, everyone rushed to sit at the table, only to discover there was not enough room.

The elders gathered and said, "We have a problem. How can we decide who will sit at the table?"

One young man asked for permission to speak and said, "My fathers, let the young men eat at the table. It was a young man who brought it to us, and all others can eat sitting on the ground."

"No, no," cried the villagers of Shango Oba.

A young woman asked for permission to speak and said,

"The women cooked all the food; thus, it is only fair for us to rest and sit at the table while all others eat sitting on the ground."

No one liked that idea, so the elders had another conference. When they returned, Oba Yumi Square was full of pushing, yelling people who were fighting to get a place at the table. The elder shouted, "Stop, this instant! I cannot believe my eyes. What has happened to our senses? All those who are at the table, remain and eat. All others, eat wherever you are! The feast must continue!"

From that moment, the people forgot their purpose and thought only of who would sit at the table during the next feast. The next time, people rushed to sit at the table and stuck their noses in the air at anyone who was not at the table.

Chineke called his son to him and said, "Look what your civilization has brought us. Our people have forgotten the old ways and now want to sit at the table. We do nothing but fight about a place at the table, whereas before you brought this table to us, we were content to enjoy each other and our food."

Jacob said, "You are right, father. I brought the problem, and I will take care of it." Late that night, under a sickle shaped moon, Jacob chopped up the table with his ax. He took the wood and laid a small piece at the door of each house in the village. The next morning, he went to the Council of Elders and said, "Civilization is good, but it demands a table for each family. I have taken away the cause of your arguments because I want to see unity and harmony in Shango Oba."

The elder replied, "You are wise my son, and we should have removed the table ourselves. It is just as well, for now we shall have a feast to celebrate the end of the table." In this way, peace and harmony were restored to Shango Oba, and if you visit the village, they will probably have a feast just because you came.

HIGH JOHN DE CONQUER

ZORA NEALE HURSTON

High John de Conquer is a legendary black hero who came to America from Africa with a slave ship, riding the wind following the cries of kidnapped Africans. John is regarded as a prophet, and stories about him are found among East Africans, Haitians, Jamaicans, Puerto Ricans, and other Caribbean peoples. John was the trickster hero who triumphed on behalf of the people. He was the hope bringer who gave the people a purpose for struggling and living.

High John de Conquer came to be a man, and a mighty man at that. But he was not a natural man in the beginning. First off, he was a whisper, a will to hope, a wish to find something worthy of laughter and song. Then the whisper put on flesh. His footsteps sounded across the world in a low but musical rhythm as if the world he walked on was a singing-drum. The black folks had an irresistible impulse to laugh. High John de Conquer was a man in full, and had come to live and work on the plantations, and all the slave folks knew him in the flesh.

The sign of this man was a laugh, and his singing-symbol was a drumbeat. No parading drum-shout like soldiers out for the show. It did not call to the feet of those who were fixed to hear it. It was an inside thing to live by. It was sure to be heard when and where the work was the hardest, and the lot the most cruel. It helped the slaves endure. They knew that something better was coming. So they laughed in the face of things and said, "I'm so glad! Trouble don't last always.". . .

High John de Conquer was walking the plantation like a natural man. He was treading the sweat-flavored clods of the plantation, crushing out his drum tunes, and giving out secret laughter. He walked on the winds and moved fast.

Maybe he was in Texas when the lash fell on a slave in Alabama, but before the blood was dry on the back he was there. A faint pulsing of a drum like a goatskin stretched over a heart, that came nearer and nearer, then somebody in the saddened quarters would feel like laughing, and say, "Now, High John de Conquer, they couldn't get the best of him. That old John was a case!" Then everybody sat up and began to smile. Yes, yes, that was right. Old John, High John could beat the unbeatable. He was top-superior to the whole mess of sorrow. He could beat it all, and what made it so cool, finish it off with a laugh. So they pulled the covers over their souls and kept them from all hurt, harm and danger and made them a laugh and a song. Night time was a joke, because daybreak was on the way. Distance and the impossible had no power over High John de Conquer.

He had come from Africa. He came walking on the waves of sound. Then he put on flesh after he got here. The sea captains of ships knew that they brought slaves in their ships. They knew about those black bodies huddled down there in the middle passage, being hauled across the waters to helplessness. John de Conquer was walking the very winds that filled the sails of the ships. He followed over them like the albatross.

Old Massa met our hope-bringer all right, but when he met him, he was not going by his right name. He was traveling, and touristing around the plantations as the laugh-provoking Brer Rabbit ... playing his tricks of making a way out of no way. Hitting a straight lick with a crooked stick. Winning the jackpot with no other stakes but a laugh. Fighting a mighty battle without outside-showing force, and winning his war from within. Really winning in a permanent way, for he was winning with the soul of the black man whole and free. So, he could use it afterwards. For what shall it profit a man if he gain the whole world, and lose his own soul? You would have nothing but a cruel, vengeful grasping monster come to power. John de

Conquer was a bottom fish. He was deep. He had the wisdom tooth of the East in his head. Way over there, where the sun rises a day ahead of time, they say that Heaven arms with love and laughter those it does not wish to see destroyed. He who carries his heart in his sword must perish. So says the ultimate law. High John de Conquer knew a lot of things like that. He who wins from within is in the "Be" class. *Be* here when the ruthless man comes and *be* here when he is gone.

Moreover John knew that it is written where it cannot be erased, that nothing shall live on human flesh and prosper. Old Maker said that before He made any more sayings. Even a man-eating tiger and lion can teach a man that much. His flabby muscles and mangy hide can teach an emperor right from wrong. If the emperor would only listen. . . .

After a while freedom came. Therefore High John de Conquer has not walked the winds of America for seventy-five years now. His people had their freedom, their laugh and their song. They have traded it to the other Americans for things they could use like education and property, and acceptance. High John knew that was the way it would be, so he could retire with his secret smile into the soil of the South and wait.

The thousands upon thousands of humble people who still believe in him, that is, in the power of love and laughter to win by their subtle power, do John reverence by getting the root of the plant in which he had taken up his secret dwelling, and "dressing" it with perfume, and keeping it on their person or in their houses in a secret place. It is there to help them overcome things they feel that they would not beat otherwise, and to bring them the laugh of the day. John will never forsake the weak and the helpless, Nor fail to bring hope to the hopeless. That is what they believe, and so they do not worry. They go and they laugh and they sing. Things are bound to come out right tomorrow. . . .

So the brother in black offers to these United States the source of courage that endures, and laughter. If the news from overseas reads bad, and the nation inside seems like it is stuck in the Tar Baby, listen hard, and you will hear John de Conquer treading on his singing-drum. You will know then, no matter how bad things look now, it will be worse for those who seek to oppress us. . . . From his secret place, he is working for all Americans now. We are all his kins-folks. Just be sure our cause is right, and then we can lean back and say, "John de Conquer would know what to do in a case like this, and then he would finish it off with a laugh."

KILINDI THE HELPFUL

RETOLD BY DOROTHY WINBUSH RILEY

This folktale from Central Africa demonstrates how great rewards can grow out of small acts of kindness. Kilindi's nature caused him to show kindness and compassion to all living things, despite the ridicule or criticisms of others. The basic lesson of this folktale is that each individual is responsible for the well-being of the community, and the responsibility of caring starts with one person: you.

Kilindi the kind was the seventh son of his father, who was the chief of the village. His six brothers married beautiful women and thought of no one but themselves and their own pleasure. The hungry stayed hungry, the sick remained sick, and the poor became beggars unless Kilindi helped them.

His family resented him, but Kilindi's heart would not allow him to pass any living thing in distress, animal or human. From the time he learned to walk, Kilindi brought every outcast or endangered animal to his father's house.

The day came when all the village girls were married except Adamma (which means daughter of beauty), whose face was horribly scarred from acne and warts; Kilindi paid the bride price and became her husband. Adamma arrived at his house with her only companion, a dog, which the villagers accused of stealing their meat.

"Why would you marry such an ugly woman?" cried his father.

"You bring much shame on the family!" said his older brother.

"Why do you worry?" asked Kilindi. "She will live in my house, not yours, and what happens in my house is none of your business."

One day, as Kilindi walked home, he saw the villagers

with a hawk in a trap. The villagers accused the hawk of stealing chickens and were just about to kill it when Kilindi offered a fine rooster for the hawk's life.

"You must be out of your mind to take a hawk into your house," sneered his brother. "It will eat all your chickens!"

"Why do you worry?" asked Kilindi. "The hawk will live in my house, not yours, and what happens in my house is none of your business."

The next day, while Kilindi was walking through the forest near his house, he heard the clamor of hunters, who had cornered a snake and planned to beat him. Kilindi intervened and said, "Men, give me the life of this snake. Take my beads in exchange for the snake."

Bad news travels fast, and when Kilindi reached his house, his father and brothers were there to meet him. Before they could sneer and jeer at him for being soft-headed, he said, "Why do you worry? The snake will live in my house, not yours, and what happens in my house is none of your business."

Late that night Kilindi's wife told him she was mocked and teased wherever she walked in the village. Kilindi said, "I love this village, but I will move and start my own village very soon." After he sighed sadly, the snake hissed, "Kilindi, the kind one. My name is Ogbonnya [which means friends to his father]. You have broken the curse of the wizard in my village, and I am now a man. I had to crawl in the dust of the earth until someone showed kindness to a snake. My father is the king, and you must come with me. He will reward you for your mercy."

The moment the snake stopped speaking, his small reptilian head split open revealing a smooth brown face with arms stretching and ripping at the rest of the skin. Before Kilindi could move, the snake's skin lay on the ground and he handed the prince a loin cloth.

True to his word, the prince, dressed in royal loin cloth with omanda shells and beads around his neck, started out with Kilindi. Ogbonnya said, "Kilindi, listen to my words, If my father offers you a kingdom and ten thousand wives, just say no. If he offers you his royal rings, say no. Refuse all that gleams with gold and diamonds. You must say no to everything but his seventh offer: a bent iron ring."

The king welcomed his son as if he were the Prodigal Son. He honored Kilindi with a royal hut, and days of feasting and dancing followed. After seven days, Kilindi longed to return to his home and told the king. True to Ogbonnya's words, the king offered him ten thousand wives. Kilindi answered, "No, I have one wife, and she is enough. For where there are many wives, the soup is spoiled by much quarreling."

The king continued his offers until Kilindi accepted the bent iron ring. "You are very wise," beamed the king; "once you rub this ring, it will give you everything your thoughts desire. Guard it from jealousy and greed."

Kilindi returned home and rubbed the ring, thinking Adamma; then, every scar and wart on her face disappeared, and she was as beautiful as Kilindi was kind. Next, Kilindi went into the village, telling all who listened of his gift from the king. Then he rubbed the ring, thinking "this village can be beautiful"; instantly, the villagers set to work, and before nightfall, the village was like paradise. Everyone wanted to make Kilindi the king except his older brother, who became more jealously cruel when he saw that mercy was rewarded. He decided to get the bent iron ring from Kilindi. That evening, he asked Kilindi, "My brother, my youngest child is ill, can I take your ring to heal her?"

Kilindi gave him the ring, and he immediately left, rubbing it and thinking of gold and wealth for himself. When nothing happened, he became angry and decided to throw the ring into the river. The instant the ring touched the water, everything returned to the way it had been before Kilindi received it. The warts and scars on Adamma's face were more hideous than ever.

The hawk and the dog noticed Kilindi's brooding, and the dog said, "Come, brother hawk, we must find the ring. I followed Kilindi's brother to the river." The hawk hovered over the river until he spotted a fish with the ring around its mouth. Swooping down, he speared the fish and dropped it at the dog's feet. The dog pawed the ring from the fish's mouth and ran to Kilindi's house while the hawk flew overhead.

Together, the dog and the hawk found Kilindi with his hands cradling his head. The dog dropped the ring at Kilindi's feet, and without hesitation, Kilindi rubbed it, thinking of his wife; immediately, Adamma's scars and warts disappeared. He rubbed it again, and the village became even more beautiful than the villagers had made it. This time, the feeling in the village was unanimous; even Kilindi's brothers and father wanted him to be the king.

Kilindi and Adamma ruled for many decades and had sons and daughters to show their prosperity. Kilindi told all the villagers that they had the power of the ring in their thoughts of success, service, and kindness to all life, human and animal. And, he put the bent iron ring in a safe place, where people go to marvel at it even today.

GOLDEN GRAINS:
PROVERBS FOR NIA

Only the family knows the secret place in the house.
—Africa

A tree cannot stand without roots.—Africa

A good chief is like a food basket. He keeps the people together.—Africa

Brothers are like calabashes; they bump each other but do not break.—Buganda

The heart is a tree. It grows where it wants to.—Hausa

Father is a shady tree.—Kenya

We are people because of other people.—Lesotho

People are like plants; they bow down and rise up again.—Malagasy

A new brother is like a new house.—Nigeria

All authority is borrowed from God.—Swahili

A man's hands are his parents; they feed him.—Yoruba

The calves follow their mothers. The young plant grows up near the parent stem. The young antelope leaps where its mother has leaped.—Zulu

THOUGHTS FOR NIA

❖ Allow no one to control your dreams. Stay focused and never give up.

❖ Give a 110 percent effort and do your best the first time; you may not get a second chance. Never half do an assignment; it could come back to haunt you.

❖ Plan to succeed.

❖ Commit yourself to success. Develop a professional plan of the goals you want to achieve this year and five and ten years from now.

❖ Think about how you project yourself; it shows your self-esteem.

❖ Continue to learn; know current and future technologies. The more you desire to know, the more you'll grow.

❖ Set goals for yourself and don't give up when they don't materialize the first, second, or third time.

❖ Keep a positive outlook in every endeavor. Avoid *I can't*; it is habit forming.

❖ Believe in your dream, work for your dream, hold on to your dream, and you will achieve your dream.

❖ Use your determination to turn every negative situation into an opportunity.

CHAPTER SIX

PRINCIPLE 6

KUUMBA

SOUL OF THE NATION: THE MEANING OF KUUMBA

Creativity is the soul of the nation. It influences and shapes the mind and direction of the struggle for self-determination. It is concerned with the individual and collective ethos of the people. Without it, the whole of whatever we want to be cannot be realized. For when we speak of creativity of art, we are, in fact, speaking about the spiritual manifestations of the people, of their will to survive beyond the merely physical. We are speaking of ways of thinking, ways of styling the struggle, and ways of insuring that the victories gained in the area of politics and economics, will not be lost in the battle for the Soul.

—Larry Neal

We celebrate Kuumba, the sixth principle of Kwanzaa, on December 31, when family members and friends gather to light the second red candle. Once the black, green, and first red candles are relit, the events center on the principle that has a threefold purpose. First, Kuumba focuses on how we can use our talents, imagination, and creative skills to bring harmony and beauty to our communities. Second, Kuumba means honoring and remembering the ancestors whose legacy and gifts we use today. Third, Kuumba is the only principle that is celebrated by a feast (Karamu). Families may plan a simple Karamu involving the immediate family or an elaborate feast that involves the family and community.

The chief aspect of Kuumba is creativity, which is first spiritual and then physical; it is the visible appearance of invisible thoughts to build a new way of living. You are the creative force in your life. Only you can use your mind's divine power to create harmony, beauty, and rhythm wherever you find yourself. We all have innate abilities to make our communities better, and we display Kuumba in as many forms as there are snowflakes. Kuumba belongs to everyone, not just to artists, writers, composers, or inventors. When you see ordinary things in a unique way, find a new twist to an old task, or do the seemingly impossible, you use Kuumba. Creativity is an endless search for opportunities to spread order, beauty, and balance.

Whatever thoughts you believe create your reality, since the imagination is fed by faith and understanding. Visualize that you are in control of a bank, where your thoughts can deposit or withdraw peace, misery, fame, wealth, prosperity, success, poverty, harmony, despair, or love. The ability to operate this bank is dependent on you alone because you can only withdraw what you deposit. Most people never learn to control the power of their minds and continuously deposit and withdraw limitations. Kuumba is using the never-ending gift of imagination to fulfill your destiny and withdraw prosperity.

Achieving people practice Kuumba by enjoying the process of their work, rather than focusing solely on the end result. They are as tenacious as octopuses and do not give up or judge themselves too soon. Imagination drives achievers to overcome the impossible by stimulating hope and desire. This fantastic force is greater than any possession; it can ascend all hurdles and fulfill every desire.

Visualize pain or prosperity, fame or despair, health or sickness, and you have it. The internal voice of imagination is not based on humankind's limited knowledge, reality, facts, or vision. It has no form or shape; it is neither liquid nor solid. It can't be seen, felt, or captured, and it can't be special ordered or borrowed. Yet imagination spans the entire galaxy, covering all that exists and is to exist.

The stories, poetry, quotations, and proverbs in this chapter are a form of Kuumba. The personalities selected are also unique in the way they use the power of their minds to make a difference in the world. Whoopi Goldberg's Kuumba

"Headrest." Wood carving, Zaire, artist unknown. Photograph by Bill Sanders.

changed her world and the views of others. Margaret Walker Alexander writes about success and creativity. The excerpt from James Weldon Johnson's autobiography tells how he wrote the black national anthem, "Lift Every Voice and Sing." Maya Angelou has never been afraid to use her creativity from the time she shouldered responsibility for herself and her son to the present. Whatever job she accepted, no matter how menial, the gifted writer performed with imagination and dignity. Truly, her Kuumba carved her for greatness.

CIRCLE OF HOPE: POETRY FOR KUUMBA

SURVIVAL LESSON #1

ANEB KGOSITSILE

Choose a beautiful song
in the tradition
of our elder's faith.
Listen to it until
the tears come,
Stretch and
dance,
your body reflecting the centuries-old
  spiritual
of our people.
Bathe.
Feel the blessing of
cotton on your flesh,
Look for the sun,
Put one foot before the other,
Glory in each single step,
until the trudging becomes
a sprint!

THE MUSICIAN TALKS ABOUT "PROCESS"

(AFTER ANTHONY SPOONS POUGH)

BY RITA DOVE

I learned the spoons from
my grandfather, who was blind.
Every day he'd go into the woods
'cause that was his thing.
He met all kinds of creatures,
birds and squirrels,
and while he was feeding them
he'd play the spoons,
and after they finished
they'd stay and listen.

When I go into Philly
on a Saturday night,
I don't need nothing but
my spoons and the music.
Laid out on my knees
they look so quiet,
but when I pick them up
I can play to anything:
a dripping faucet,
a tambourine,
fish shining in a creek.

A funny thing:
when my grandfather died,
every creature sang.
And when the men went out
to get him, they kept singing.
They sang for two days,
all the birds, all the animals.
That's when I left the south.

FROM *THE BLUE MERIDIAN*

JEAN TOOMER

We are the new people.
Born of elevated rock and lifted branches.
Called Americans,
Not to mouth the label but to live the reality,
Not to stop anywhere, to respond to man,
to outgrow each wider limitation,
Growing towards the universal Human
   Being;
And we are the old people, witnesses
That behind us there extends
An unbroken chain of ancestors,
Ourselves linked with all who ever lived,
Joined with future generations
Of millions of fathers through as many years
We are the breathing receptacles,

There is greatness in the truth,
a dignity to satisfy our wish,
a solemn time to make us still,
a sorrow to fill our hearts,
A beauty and vision in the truth.

LIFE FOR MY CHILD IS SIMPLE AND GOOD

Gwendolyn Brooks

Life for my child is simple and good.
He knows his wish. Yes, but that is not all,
Because I know mine too.
And we both want joy of undeep and
    unabiding things,
Like kicking over a chair or throwing blocks
    out of a window
Or tipping over an icebox pan
Or snatching down curtains or fingering an
    electric outlet
Or a journey or a friend or an illegal kiss.
No. There is more to it than that.
It is that he has never been afraid
rather, he reaches out and lo the chair falls
    with a beautiful crash,
And the blocks fall, down on the people's
    heads,
And the water comes slooshing sloppily out
    across the floor
And so forth.
Not that success, for him, is infallible,
His lessons are legion.
But reaching is his rule.

DREAMERS FROM THE HEART: PEOPLE OF KUUMBA

WHOOPI GOLDBERG: HARVESTING THE IMAGINATION

DOROTHY WINBUSH RILEY

Imagination is the closest link to the soul and allows you to travel to any dimension or world. With imagination you can step outside and above limitations and transcend the physical world. Whoopi Goldberg used her fantasies to create a path to unlimited possibilities and choices; to prosperity, happiness, and success. She expanded the horizons of her mind to new territories and traveled beyond what she first thought possible.

To achieve success through this power is to live the dreams in your mind. Picture or feel yourself getting what you want, even down to the words you will say once the goal is achieved. Fantasize, then focus on simple steps to make the dream real. Put forth energy and action to take advantage of the opportunities that await. Begin as Whoopi Goldberg did and create facts from the fiction of your mind.

Whoopi Goldberg's imagination awakened her inner power and changed the conditions of her life. "A lot of people think the grass is greener on the other side. When I was a kid I used my imagination to make the grass whatever color I wanted it to be." Whoopi, a dimple-faced, bright-eyed, chocolate little girl, began performing at age eight and then dreamed of becoming an actress. Her instincts led her to the unchanging magic of words, and even as a child she wrote, produced, cast, and dramatized her own plays. Inspiration came from television and the live acting troupes that often visited her neighborhood. Goldberg watched the performances intently, conjuring up her own future.

She was never the typical teenager; instead of dancing

the Hully Gully or the Mashed Potato, she was enthralled with performing in the theater. "As a kid, I watched everything on TV, especially all the old black-and-white films on *The Million Dollar Movie*. What I saw gave me ideas about what I wanted to be—which was a lot of different people." Goldberg grew up in the Chelsea projects in New York, where poverty, racism, and sexism were unwelcome boarders. Nevertheless, she has great memories of a neighborhood surrounded by art, music, dance, and Broadway shows. And despite the bleakness of life in the projects, she constantly visualized a future in which she was accepted and recognized for her talent as an actress.

School provided little hope or recognition because Goldberg had dyslexia, a condition that makes reading tedious, if not nearly impossible. She had difficulty learning and performed poorly in her classes.

By the time Goldberg was twenty years old, she had dropped out of high school after giving birth to her only child. She knew that wishing was one thing, but doing something about it was another. So she packed up herself and her daughter and moved to San Diego, to train in improvisational theater. Even though she didn't fit the stereotype of an actress or have the money for professional training, she had God-given gifts: a flawless eye and ear for the details of character, a natural talent for mime, and a vivid imagination to be fine-tuned.

From 1974, Goldberg worked as a bank teller, bricklayer, mortuary beautician, and any other odd, menial job she could find to care for herself and her daughter. Often she relied on public assistance when she could not find work. Yet, welfare did not steal her drive or self-esteem; instead, it gave her insight into the conditions of a third of American women. With penetrating eyes, she studied her environment; observed life, on and off stage; and concentrated on the idiosyncrasies of society while adding to her character data bank.

Before any of her characters became authentic, Goldberg first had to see their facial expressions in her mind: the look of the eyes, the tone of the voice, the stance of the body, the movement of the hands. Using tremendous amounts of energy, time, and practice, she created each character, down to the last detail. By 1983, almost ten years after she had moved to California, she portrayed seventeen distinct characters, showcasing her comedic and acting abilities in a one-woman production, *The Spook Show.*

The Spook Show skyrocketed up the West Coast, across the ocean into Europe, and then home to New York. In a small off-Broadway theater, Mike Nichols watched fascinated as Goldberg's honey-velvet voice magically drew the audience into the world of her imagination and *The Spook Show.* Nichols moved the show to Broadway and produced it himself. A few months later the eagle soared, when Steven Spielberg cast Goldberg in *The Color Purple.*

Using her imagination, empathy, and warmth to portray diverse characters, Goldberg has the drive and confidence to try all areas of entertainment, from being a stand-up comic to an Oscar-winning actress. Intuitively, she uses her limitless, willing imagination to produce and direct events that completely transform lives. Goldberg is an inspiration to all who feel different and must find an audience for their unique kind of Kuumba. Imagination allows her to be recognized. Imagination causes her to be unique. Imagination makes her free. Imagination makes her soar. Goldberg says, "People have small minds. . . . I think of myself as an actor. I've said before, I can play a man—or a dog or a chair."

EXCERPT FROM
WILLING TO PAY THE PRICE

Margaret Walker Alexander

Here in America "Success" with a capital "S" is measured in materialistic terms of fame and fortune. An artist is not basically concerned with this kind of success. A creative worker dealing with the fiery lightning of imagination is interested in artistic accomplishment, and I have spent my life seeking this kind of fulfillment. As long as I live, this will be my quest; and, as such, the superficial trappings of success can have no real meaning for me. I do not really care what snide remarks my confreres make nor how scaring the words of caustic critics are. Life is too short for me to concern myself with anything but the work I must do before my day is done.

If there are any single factors which have blessed my life with the best, they are: intelligent parents who not only fired my ambition and demanded that I set my sights high and be judged by standards of excellence, but also insisted that I seek spiritual values and crave righteousness and integrity more than money; remarkable teachers in three of the nation's finest academic institutions; and lessons learned from bitter experience and from fellow writers. Linked with these factors has also been an indispensable element of luck and good fortune.

True, I have faced obstacles and have been forced to run every race with a handicap: I am of Africa born in America. All my life I have been poor in the goods of the world. I am a woman. And since birth I have been dogged with ill health. Yet each of these could have been worse. Despite these handicaps and race prejudice in America, which I discovered early and have lived with all my life, I was able to complete my education, attending some of the nation's finest institutions. Yes, my lot might have been worse; I have often heard poor whites speak of their lack of opportunity to get an education. As a woman I have known great personal freedom to do as I pleased and to further my career whether single or married. I have the complete fulfillment of being wife and mother and having a happy home.

Early in my life my parents instilled certain principles and beliefs in all their children, and these principles remain thoroughly ingrained in all of us. First, they provided us with a deeply religious background. For them the Protestant ethic was Puritan to the core, a stern moralistic code of duty and responsibility, and prayer was a daily occurrence in our home. We grew up in Sunday School and church, and I was amazed when I went away from home to discover that everybody did not go to church. We were taught that we were expected to achieve and that achievement must be one of excellence. However, we were taught not to expect excessive praise for a job well-done. . . .

I believe firmly in the goodness of the future, and that in the final analysis right will prevail—not through goodness and optimism, necessarily, but through stress and travail. I believe that man's destiny is a spiritual destiny and that God is not merely transcendent but also immanent, deeply involved in the affairs of men since men are made in his image, each with a spark of the divine and a human personality always maintaining that divine potential. Sometimes in America our future looks hopelessly dark, but against all evil this divinity and the human spirit or human personality will shine like a light.

EVERY MAN MUST DECIDE

HOWARD THURMAN

A major step to success is decision making. Theologian Howard Thurman describes the process each man and woman uses to decide on a course of action to fulfill his or her goals, dreams, and desires.

The ability to know what is the right thing to do in a given circumstance is a sheer gift of God. The element of gift is inherent in the process of decision. Perhaps gift is the wrong word; it is a quality of genius or immediate inspiration. The process is very simple and perhaps elemental. First, we weigh all the possible alternatives. We examine them carefully, weighing this and weighing that. There is always an abundance of advice available—some of it technical, some of it out of the full-orbed generosity of those who love us and wish us well. Each bit of it has to be weighed and measured in the light of the end sought. This means that the crucial consideration is to know what is the desirable end. What is it that I most want to see happen if the conditions were ideal or if my desire were completely fulfilled? Once this end is clearly visualized, then it is possible to have a sense of direction with reference to the decision that must be made. If it becomes clear that the ideal end cannot be realized, it follows that such a pursuit has to be relinquished. This relinquishment is always difficult because the mind, the spirit, the body desires are all focused upon the ideal end. Every person thinks that it is his peculiar destiny to have the ideal come true for him. The result is that, with one's mind, the ideal possibility is abandoned but emotionally it is difficult to give it up. Thus the conflict. The resources of one's personality cannot be marshaled. A man finds that he cannot work wholeheartedly for the achievable or possible end because he cannot give up the inner demands for the ideal end. Oftentimes precious months or years pass with no solution in evidence because there is ever the hope that the ideal end may, in some miraculous manner, come to pass. Then the time for action does come at last. There comes a moment when something has to be done; one can no longer postpone the decision—the definitive act resolves an otherwise intolerable situation. Once the decision is made, the die is cast. Is my decision right or wrong, wise or foolish? At the moment, I may be unable to answer the question. For what is right in the light of the present set of facts my not be able to stand under the scrutiny of unfolding days. My decision may have been largely influenced by my desires which were at work at the very center of my conscious processes. In the face of all the uncertainties that surround any decision, the wise man acts in the light of this best judgment illumined by the integrity of his profoundest spiritual insights. Then the rest is in the hands of the future and in the mind of God.

MAYA ANGELOU: THE RESILIENT SPIRIT

DOROTHY WINBUSH RILEY

One essential key to Kuumba is resilience, since no one reaps success overnight and no one lives without loss or disappointment. Successful people know that defeats are inspirations to try one more time. Resilience is the ability to climb more times than you slip or fall by discovering the faith, comfort, and inner power. It is recovering quickly from disruptions caused by change—change that you cannot control.

Climbing the golden altar means coming to grips with life's inevitable stresses. If you are in a state of inner calm, you regroup and start again each time you are knocked to the ground. Regardless of whether you receive pleasure or pain, sadness or happiness, poverty or wealth, hunger or plenty, you eventually feel confident and courageous enough to survive the risks of being human, the risks of success.

Trials are the natural rhythms of life and are necessary for growth; the weight and timing of them are no more than you can bear. Growth requires change, and change demands testing. Fortitude means to accept with dignity whatever disappointment change brings as if it was joyful good fortune. We accept our responsibility and then do what must be done. Endurance is viewing cruelty, envy, injustice, loneliness, poverty, and sickness calmly as part of life's cycle while reaching to the future and aiming to change strategies.

The ability to bounce back is to trust your convictions, talents, and inner voice with a belief that the answers to the puzzles of life are within. Kwanzaa affirms that mothers and fathers of previous generations transmitted African Americans' existence and persistence to the mothers and fathers of today. Pass it on.

Maya Angelou says, "To be successful is to be constant, to be patient and resilient—to accept things as they are. Resilience means . . . laying claim to your spirit."

On December 1, 1993, President Bill Clinton asked Angelou to create a poem for his inauguration. Although the time was short, she did so, and on January 20, 1994, the listening world heard "On the Pulse of the Morning."

Angelou's achievements demonstrated that her creative and physical powers determine her success or failure, while her spirit determines her creativity. She exudes wisdom learned from life's lessons, not in a classroom, combined with understanding gained from accepting adversity, poverty, wealth, and fame.

Angelou, a persevering woman with a firm faith in God, soars over the ignorance of racism and the stigma of sexism with their history of pain. She believes she is special; therefore, she triumphs over all obstacles, deadlines, and adversity. She used life's harsh lessons to strengthen her spirit and her faith as basic training for using her imagination to solve problems. Angelou's destiny prophesied greatness, and her preparation for it started in Arkansas. Angelou profited from the trials of her early years to enrich our lives with her stories and poetry. As a survivor, she bears witness to the lessons of history, accepting truth and moving on: "I speak to the black experience. . . . I am always talking about the human condition—about what we can endure, dream, fail at and still survive." The knowledge that she could live through traumatic childhood experiences, yet be true to herself, offered her seemingly divine protection against failure. She believed she would succeed whenever she tried to overcome obstacles.

Angelou lives creatively, generously, spiritually, and honorably because she loves and views hurts and disappointments courageously as a privilege to learn. Fortitude directed her purposefully, and each time she accepted change and acted with imagination, her view of the world changed. Angelou's most potent gift is an enthusiastic attitude that highlights the possibilities of hope. She is a self-created winner who molded herself and loves her creation. In traveling the world, Angelou learned French, Spanish, Italian, Arabic, and Fanti, a language of Ghana. From being

he Storyteller." Acrylic on canvas by Jamal Jones, 1993–94. Photograph by Bill Sanders.

a showgirl in Paris to working in civil rights, she carved out space for adventure. Each one pulled her in a different direction as she sought love, identity, and acceptance.

Her quest began an uncharted path careening through valleys, mountains, streams, floods, and all the unexpected bends, curves, and dips on the way. Intuitively, she knew how to change to meet the new circumstances without straying too far from the path. She chronicled life as an African American woman in her first book, *I Know Why the Caged Bird Sings,* and completes it in her fifth book, *All God's Children Need Traveling Shoes.* Today, she remains the resilient creator who says, "Whenever I get out of touch with my power, I think of our people, in their chains, having no names, not being able to move one inch without the license of someone who purportedly owned them. . . . I am overwhelmed by the grace and persistence of my people." Angelou translates experiences and the world sits at her feet, as she, like the griots of old, tells the stories of how we got over.

NO UNKNOWN WORDS:
QUOTATIONS TO INSPIRE KUUMBA

"A man who has no imagination has no wings."
—Muhammad Ali

"People create stories create people; or rather stories create people create stories."—Chinua Achebe

"What kind of people we become depends crucially on the stories we are nurtured on; which is why every sensible society takes pains to prepare its members for participation in its affairs by, among other things, teaching them the best and the most instructive forms of its inheritance stories . . . drawn from both the factual and the imaginative literature bequeathed by its ancestors: songs, poems, plays, epics, fables."—Chinweizu

"We are here children with the task of completing (one might say creating) ourselves."—William Cook

"Create and be true to yourself, and depend only on your own good taste."—Duke Ellington

"In the world through which I travel I am continuously creating myself."—Frantz Fanon

"The memories of our ancestors are traumatic. . . . I feel connected to the Africans who were brought here in chains and the generations of children that came after."—Laurence Fishburne

"Awake, awake, millions of voices are calling you! Your dead fathers speak to you from their graves."—Henry Highland Garnet

"Up, up you mighty race, you can accomplish what you will."—Marcus Garvey

"We must give our own story to the world."—Carter G. Woodson

"Potential powers of creativity are within us and we have the duty to work assiduously to discover those powers."—Martin Luther King, Jr.

"We must use time creatively and forever realize that the time is always right to do right."—Martin Luther King, Jr.

"May our ancestors rest knowing that their lives and experiences have not been in vain."—Jon Onye Lockard

"Our ancestors are an ever widening circle of hope."—Toni Morrison

"The traditional guidelines of our ancestors are the progressive directions and manifestations of our art today . . . a sacred living art that works toward promoting symbols and effects that are synonymous with spiritual progress . . . and blackness will be our accomplishment."—Ademola Olugebefola

"There are no unknown words, utterances, or sayings in new languages that have not already been said by the ancestors."—Senusret

"What God has intended for you goes far beyond anything you can imagine."—Oprah Winfrey

"We all have ability. The difference is how we use it." —Stevie Wonder

"A lot of living is done in the imagination."—Richard Wright

ACCOMPLISH WHAT YOU WILL: FOLKTALES FOR KUUMBA

EXCERPT FROM *THINGS FALL APART*

CHINUA ACHEBE

Kwanzaa is based on the harvest festivals of Africa. This excerpt by Chinua Achebe describes how the Nguzo Saba: unity, self-determination, collective work and responsibility, cooperative economics, creativy, and faith yield a bountiful harvest and a strong community. The Feast of the New Yam, like our Karamu, allowed the ancestors to plant seeds of hope in the future.

Yam, the king of crops, was a very exacting king. For three or four moons it demanded hard work and constant attention from cock-crow till the chickens went back to roost. The young tendrils were protected from earth-heat with rings of sisal leaves. As the rains became heavier the women planted maize, melons and beans between the yam mounds. The yams were then staked, first with little sticks and later with tall and big tree branches. The women weeded the farm three times at definite periods in the life of the yams, neither early nor late.

And now the rains had really come, so heavy and persistent that even the village rain-maker no longer claimed to be able to intervene. He could not stop the rain now, just as he would not attempt to start it at the heart of the dry season, without serious danger to his own health. The personal dynamism required to counter the forces of these extremes of weather would be far too great for the human frame.

And so nature was not interfered with in the middle of

the rainy season. Sometimes it poured down in such thick sheets of water that earth and sky seemed merged in one gray wetness. It was then uncertain whether the low rumbling of Amdiora's thunder came from above or below. At such times, in each of the countless thatched huts of Umofia, children sat around their mother's cooking fire telling stories, or with their father in his obi warming themselves from a log fire, roasting and eating maize. It was a brief resting period between the exacting and arduous planting season and the equally exacting but light-hearted month of harvest.

The Feast of the New Yam was approaching and Umofia was in a festival mood. It was an occasion for giving thanks to Ani, the earth goddess and source of all fertility. Ani played a greater part in the life of the people than any other deity. She was the ultimate judge of morality and conduct. And what was more, she was in close communication with the departed fathers of the clan whose bodies had been committed to earth.

The Feast of the New Yam was held each year before the harvests began, to honor the earth goddess and the ancestral spirits of the clan. New yams could not be eaten until some had first been offered to those powers. Men and women, young and old, looked forward to the New Yam Festival because it began the season of plenty—the new year. On the last night before the festival, yams of the old year were all disposed by those who still had them. The new year must begin with tasty fresh yams and not the shriveled and fibrous crop of the previous year. All cooking pots, calabashes and wooden bowls were thoroughly washed, especially the wooden mortar in which yam was pounded. Yam foo foo and vegetable soup was the chief food in the celebration. So much of it was cooked that, no matter how heavily the family ate or how many friends and relations they invited from neighboring villages, there was always a huge quantity of food left over at the end of the day.

The New Yam Festival was thus an occasion for joy throughout Umofia. And every man whose arm was strong, as the Ibo people say, was expected to invite large numbers of guests from far and wide.

SPIDER ANANSI STORIES

RETOLD BY DOROTHY WINBUSH RILEY

This myth is from the Ashanti people of Ghana, where the spider is called Anansi and is considered the cleverest of all the animals. When he appears in myths he is often the captain or the chief hand of God. In earlier times the griots recorded history through story-telling that communicated the values of the culture. Here Anansi uses a fertile imagination to get stories for humankind from the sky-god; in America we call them the Anansi stories.

Kwaku Anansi, the spider, approached Nyankonpon, the sky-god, to buy his stories. The sky-god replied, "What makes you think you can buy them?" The spider answered, "I know I shall because I am determined to have them."

Thereupon the sky-god said, "Great and powerful townsmen from Mali, Bekwai, Benin have come, but they couldn't buy them. Yet you, a mere man, think you can get my stories?"

"What do your stories cost? Name your price and I shall meet it!" said Anansi.

The sky-god answered, "They can be bought with Onini, the python; Osebo, the leopard; Mmoatia, the fairy; and Mmoboro, the hornets."

"Yes, I can get all of those things and when I do, will you give me your stories?" asked Anansi.

He immediately went home and discussed the situation with his wife, Aso. "How can we catch Onini, the python?"

Aso said, "Go into the bush and cut a branch of a palm tree and some stringcreeper. Bring them to the stream."

Later that day Anansi walked along the stream saying, "It's longer than he is, it's not so long as he; you lie, it's longer than he. It's longer than he is, it's not so long as he; you lie, it's longer than he."

The python, who was nearby, asked, "What are you talking about?"

Anansi acted surprised saying, "My wife, Aso, believes you are not as long as this palm branch. I believe you are the longest and strongest python in the bush."

Onini blushed at the compliment saying, "Bring it and measure me yourself." The python stretched himself out while Anansi laid the palms along his body. As the python lay basking in the compliment, Anansi took the rope creeper and tied Onini. "I shall take you to the sky-god and receive his stories in return."

After Anansi delivered the python, the sky-god said, "My hand has touched the snake, there remains what remains to be brought." He returned home and asked Aso how to catch hornets. "Find a gourd, then fill it with water."

Anansi found a gourd, and while walking through the bush he saw a swarm of hornets and sprinkled the water on them. He covered his head with a plantain leaf and sprinkled more water on the hornets. He called to the hornets, "Monstrous water is coming! You should crawl into this gourd or you will be washed away!" All the hornets disappeared inside the gourd and Anansi said, "I shall take you to the sky-god and receive his stories and fables in return." After Anansi delivered the hornets, the sky-god said, "My hand has touched the hornets, there remains what remains to be brought."

Again Anansi returned home and asked Aso how to catch Osebo, the leopard. "Go and dig a hole," said Aso.

"Say no more, my wife, I understand what I am to do." He left looking for the leopard's tracks. When he found them he dug a pit, covered it with banana and plantain leaves and returned home. The next day he went back and found a leopard staring from the hole. Anansi said, "Oh my poor leopard's child, I see you have stumbled and fallen into this pit. I would help you, but you may eat me once you are free."

The leopard replied, "I promise you I will do no such thing." Anansi cut two sticks and told the leopard to put his paws on them so he could lift him out of the pit. Once all four paws were tightly tied, Anansi lifted Osebo and took him to the sky-god. "My hand has touched the leopard, there remains what remains to be brought."

Next, Anansi took Akua, the flat-faced wooden doll and spread sticky tree sap over the doll's body. He took the pounded yams Aso had given him for lunch and placed them in the doll's hands. He tied string around Akua's waist and stood her at the bottom of the odum tree where the fairies play. Soon a fairy came and stumbled over Akua. She looked and then asked, "Akua, may I share your yams?" Anansi pulled the string and Akua's head nodded yes.

The fairy reached for the yams but her hand stuck fast to the sticky tree sap. She took her other hand and tried to push Akua. That hand stuck also. She took her right foot and then her left foot and tried to push Akua. Her feet stuck fast. When the fairy could no longer move Anansi stepped from behind the bush, tied her up and took her to the sky-god.

The sky-god called the council of elders to hear the matter and presented Onini, the python; Osebo, the leopard; Mmoatia, the fairy; and Mmoboro, the hornets. "Great kings and powerful warriors have come. They could not buy my stories, but Kwaku Anansi, the spider, has paid the price. We must sing his praise. Kwaku Anansi, I give you the sky-god's stories with my blessings so that our children and their children can tell the stories today and into times you will not see."

ON THE EVE OF KRINA

FROM THE EPIC *SUNDIATA*, AS RECITED BY GRIOT MAMDOU KOUYATE

The griot was the master of the spoken word and librarian of the people. The griot's job of telling and retelling stories is as ancient as Africa. All that was seen or heard—history, values, customs, disappointments and victories—was passed from one generation to another. Even in slavery, the griots preserved African culture by telling stories from memory. Many African American folktales were originally told by the African teachers: the griot. This excerpt from the story of Sundiata, king of Mali, reinforces his responsibility to act and to remember that he is following in the footsteps of his ancestors, who acted nobly and bravely before he was born.

The great battle was for the next day.

In the evening, to raise the men's spirits, Djata gave a great feast, for he was anxious that his men should wake up happy in the morning. Several oxen were slaughtered and that evening Balla Fasseke, in front of the whole army, called to mind the history of Old Mali. He praised Sundiata, seated amidst his lieutenants, in this manner:

"Now I address myself to you, Maghan Sundiata, I speak to you King of Mali, to whom dethroned monarchs flock. The time foretold to you by the plan is now coming. Sundiata, kingdoms and empires are in the likeness of man; like him they are born, they grow and disappear. Each sovereign embodies one moment of that life. Formerly the kings of Ghana extended their kingdom over all the lands inhabited by the black man, but the circle has closed and the Cisses of Wagadou are nothing more than petty princes in a desolate land. Today, another kingdom looms up, powerful, the kingdom of Sosso. Humbled kings have borne their tribute to Sosso. Soumaoro's arrogance knows no more bounds and his cruelty is equal to this ambition. But will Soumaoro dominate the world? Are we the griots of Mali, condemned to pass on to future generations the humiliations which the king of Sosso cares to inflict on our country? No, you may be glad children of the 'Bright Country,' for the kingship of Sosso is but the growth of yesterday, whereas that of Mali dates from the time of Bilal.

"Each kingdom has its childhood but Soumaoro wants to force the pace, and so Sosso will collapse under him like a horse worn out beneath its rider.

"You, Maghan, you are Mali. It has had a long and difficult childhood like you. Sixteen kings have preceded you on the throne of Niani, sixteen kings have reigned with varying fortunes, but from being village chiefs the Keitas have become tribal chiefs and then kings. Sixteen generations have consolidated their power. You are the outgrowth of Mali just as the silk-cotton tree is the growth of the earth, born of deep and mighty branches. To face the tempest the tree must have long roots and gnarled branches. Maghan Sundiata, has not the tree grown?

"I would have you know, son of Sogolon, that there is not room for two kings around the calabash of rice. When a new cock comes to the poultry run the old cock picks a quarrel with him and the docile hens wait to see of the new arrival asserts himself or yields. You have come too. Very well, then, assert yourself. Strength makes a law of its own self and power allows no division.

"But listen to what your ancestors did, so that you will know what you have to do.

"Bilal, the second of the name, conquered old Mali. Latal Kalabi conquered the country between the Niger and the Sankarani. By going to Mecca, Lahibatoul Kalabi, of illustrious memory, brought divine blessings upon Mali. Mamadi Kani made warriors out of hunters and bestowed armed strength upon Mali. His sons Bamari Tagnokelin, the vindictive king, terrorized Mali with his army, but Maghan Fon Fatta, also called Nare Maghan, to whom you owe your being, made peace prevail and happy mothers yielded Mali a populous youth.

"You are the son of Nare Maghan, but you are also the son of your mother Sogolon, the buffalo woman, before whom powerless sorcerers shrank in fear. You have the strength and majesty of the lion, you have the might of the buffalo.

"I have told you what future generations will learn about your ancestors, but what will we be able to relate to our sons so that your memory will stay alive, what will we have to teach our sons about you? What unprecedented exploits, what unheard of feats? By what distinguished actions will our sons be brought to regret not having lived in the time of Sundiata?

"Griots are men of the spoken word, and by the spoken word we give life to the gestures of kings. But words are nothing but words; power lies in deeds. Be a man of action; do not answer me any more with your mouth, but tomorrow, on the plain of Krina, show me what you would have me recount to coming generations. Tomorrow allow me to sing the 'Song of the Vultures' over the bodies of the thousands of Sossos whom you sword will have laid low before evening."

It was on the eve of Krina. In this way Balla Fasseke reminded Sundiata of the history of Mali so that in the morning, he would show himself worthy of his ancestors.

GIFTS OF GOD:
PROVERBS FOR KUUMBA

If you don't desire a thing, you'll never get it.—Africa

"I know, I know" surpasses everything.—Congo

Ancestors, ancestors guide me to whatever I'm looking for whatever it may be.—Ethiopia

Keep your counsel; the world knowing your plans will seek to destroy them.—Ghana

Jump at the sun; you may not land on the sun, but at least you'll be off the ground.—Traditional

You cannot improve on heaven's creation.—Mozambique

The path to your heart's desire is never overgrown. —Uganda

Planning is man's; doing is God's.—Yoruba

THOUGHTS FOR KUUMBA

❖ Use your imagination to create the world you desire.

❖ Follow your dreams; do not expect others to understand them.

❖ Learn from your neighborhood and the positive people surrounding you.

❖ Direct your energy to fulfill your desires.

❖ Allow no one to categorize you. Stereotypes are for boxes.

❖ Prepare yourself for the opportunities that you believe will come to you.

❖ Use your uniqueness, your differences, to showcase your ability.

❖ Give back to the community. There is something each of us can do to make the society better.

❖ Study the masters in the field you want to enter.

❖ Use your skills to create opportunities as you grow and the world changes.

CHAPTER SEVEN

PRINCIPLE 7

IMANI

TO REACH INSIDE OURSELVES: THE MEANING OF IMANI

> In African societies the spiritual universe is one
> with the physical, and these two intermingle and
> dovetail into each other so much that it is not
> easy, or even necessary, at times to draw the dis-
> tinction or separate them.
>
> —John Mbiti

On January 1, we celebrate, Imani, the seventh principle of Kwanzaa. The last red candle is lit and then all the other candles are lit in order. Imani, the last principle, represents our deep belief and link to the Creator that strengthens us to live righteous, value-filled lives. Imani is believing in all African people and gives us a sense of responsibility—to care for each other and to control our destiny.

This is the day that the zawadi (gifts) are given. All gifts should come from the heart and should be things that the people can make themselves to show our Kujichagulia, Ujima, Ujamaa, and Kuumba. This would be the perfect time to give someone a kinara, a mkeka, or a kikombe cha umoja. Any zawadi given to children are for accomplishments and goals met; thus, the children's zawadi should be educational and reinforce the Nguzo Saba.

We must remember that Imani is faith, and faith is a universal law of the mind, and what you believe, what you feel, what you attract, and what you imagine, you become. The mind gives what you desire; if you expect a prosperous harvest, you have one; Imani motivates you. When you reach your goal and are satisfied, the mind lulls you into apathy; when you believe you have more than you deserve, the mind sabotages your harvest. No matter who you are or what your circumstances, your harvest corresponds exactly to your faith.

Imani strengthens our trust in the ordinary with actions and behaviors that promote the teachings of the Creator. From life's experiences, we develop imagination, empathy, and compassion. We are able to think and imagine ourselves in the lives of others. Faith is using our talents, our genius, and our careers to network and strive to meet the needs of the poor and the suffering.

Imani is not an embankment against danger; it isn't sandbags against the rising Mississippi or a scud missile in the desert. It is eternal hope, assuring us that no matter where we travel on our road to success, we are never alone. Hope is believing that we are always in the process of becoming and that the job is as eternal as we are. Imani is the building blocks that shape our attitudes, behavior, ideas, and feelings as we travel from childhood curiosity into adult uncertainty. Faith gives structure and meaning to our lives, providing a deliberate, habitual, and immediate blueprint of how to act in certain situations. Imani is not necessarily knowing the ten thousand names of the Creator; it is the inner spirit that drives and pushes us forward through creative energy or power to go beyond our expectations. Diana Ross spoke for most believers when she said, "Failure was impossible because I made no space within to consider anything negative: I could only visualize success."

Imani charges African Americans to transcend and transform difficulties with thoughtful action. If we are to succeed, we must throw off the mental chains placed on us historically and become confident, positive, and poised to take our rightful place in the universal order. I once heard Debbie Turner, a former Miss America, speak at Windsor Village Church in Houston. She asked, "What report are we listening to? What messenger are we hearing? Whose dreams are we living?" As a people we must watch our thinking, our words, and our beliefs and not allow negatives to surround our consciousness and become real.

Imani-filled achievers believe they are a success, and their thoughts radiate hope, success, and expectancy. Picture a diamond mine with infinite resources available for everyone to take freely and use; some people enter with a wheelbarrow while others carry a thimble. Whether we participate in a life of poverty or abundance depends on what our minds are capable of believing. The only limitation to prosperity is the stoppers on your mind. It is your diamond mine, if you believe it is.

To know you are person with Imani, ask yourself, "Do I scamper in fear like a mouse when obstacles surface, or do I search within and deepen my inner trust that this, too, shall pass? An Imani-filled person receives wisdom in the bleakest, loneliest hour without speculation or doubt. Mary McLeod Bethune said, "I opened the doors of my school . . . with an enrollment of five little girls . . . whose parents paid me fifty cents' weekly tuition. . . . Though I hadn't a penny left, I considered cash money as the smallest part of my resources. I had faith in a living God, faith in myself, and a desire to serve."

Imani recalls our cultural and historical past, so we can focus our thoughts on making our future more glorious. It is the ultimate courage to work cooperatively and communally with love, strength, and inspiration, always seeking those things that are in harmony with life: health, prosperity, and happiness.

HOLD FAST TO FAITH:
POETRY FOR IMANI

HABARI GANI-KWANZAA!

DOROTHY WINBUSH RILEY

Saba Saba Saba
Seven Seven Seven
the mkeka
on the low table after
the harvest
of success after
reaping sowing
love stands
the kinara holding
our mishumaa saba.

Seven candle fires
illuminating the
success reaped
from the harvest of
love sowed
by the village
by the family
by you

EMOYENI, PLACE OF THE WINDS

HENRY DUMAS

we will climb the body of the hill
thru the bowing of the talking grass
up the footpath where the spirits pass

come
it is time to make the time
I see with my skin and hear with my tongue
emoyeni from the sky
emoyeni the tongue of many years passing
where the fingers from the earth rising
stroke all the singers passing passing
by the rumblings of the falling rock
down the valleys of the congo leaping
toward the body of the hill

breathe
it is time to make the time
it is my father singing
it is my mother at the river
it is the spear and the chain
it is your time to swallow the hill
breathe
emoyeni passing passing
behind the dust
emoyeni passing passing
behind the fear
emoyeni going going
I see the coming of the long green rain.

LIFT EVERY VOICE AND SING

JAMES WELDON JOHNSON

Lift every voice and sing,
Till earth and heaven ring,
Ring with the harmonies of Liberty;
Let our rejoicing rise,
High as the listening skies,
Let it resound low as the rolling seas.
Sing a song full of the faith that the dark past
   has taught us;
Sing a song full of the hope that the present
   has brought us.
Facing the rising sun of our new day begun,
Let us march on till victory is won.

Stony the road we trod,
Bitter the chastening rod,
Felt in the days when hope unborn had died;
Yet with a steady beat,
Have not our weary feet
Come to the place for which our fathers
   sighed?
We have come over a way that with tears has
   been watered,
We have come, treading our path through
   the blood of the slaughtered;
Out from the gloomy past,
'Til now we stand at last
Where the white gleam of our bright star is
   cast.

God of our weary years,
God of our silent tears,

Thou who has brought us thus far on the
   way;
Thou who has by Thy might
Led us into the light,
Keep us forever in the path, we pray.
Lest our feet stray from the places, Our God,
   where we met Thee,
Lest, our hearts drunk with the wine of the
   world, we forget Thee;
Shadowed beneath Thy hand,
May we forever stand,
True to our God,
True to our native land.

"Lift Every Voice and Sing," also known as "The Harp," by Augusta Savage, 1939. Collection of American Literature, Beinecke Rare Book and Manuscript Library, Yale University. Photograph by Carl Van Vechten.

EACH GENERATION MUST DISCOVER ITS MISSION

(for Frantz Fanon)

ANEB KGOSITSILE

Can't you see the distance is long
and the search prolonged anguish?
It may be you will not see the Dawn
and the first sunlight of the Day.
What do you say to this possibility?
Can you say, "Yes, that is possible!"
And struggle on in the dark?
Can you accept the questions unanswered,
your mouth frozen as you shape the words?
Perhaps you, in this time, have no words to
    utter,
only the deep groan of longing
pouring out of the heart,
flowing like a blood river.

THE CIRCLE OF FAITH

TIAUDRA RILEY

I
have faith in you
because I trust you. I trust you
because I like you. I like you because I
understand you. I understand you because I
care for you. I care for you because I am a part
of you. I am a part of you because I depend on
you. I depend on you because I am honest with
you. I am honest with you because I can talk to
you. I can talk to you because I am for you. I
am for you because I need you. I need you
because I love you. I love you because I
believe in you. I believe in you
because I have faith in
you. . . .

ASPIRE TO BE: PEOPLE OF IMANI

DIANA ROSS: IMANI AND DESIRE

DOROTHY WINBUSH RILEY

When true faith exists in the heart, all dreams and desires are heard and given by the Highest Power. One thing everyone seeks is happiness; it is supreme goal of all ambition, work, dreams, and desires. Diana Foss discovered that happiness stems from a quality within, from the way she thought of life, from her faith and beliefs. She learned that fame and wealth meant nothing without faith and inner contentment. After understanding and applying this basic principle, she reaped fame, with a family to keep her centered and full of purpose. Through Imani, Diana Ross found the courage to be herself and create roles for millions to follow.

From her earliest moments Diana Ross was drawn to the spotlight, knowing intuitively that destiny had a role for her. Belief in self begins at home, where the seeds of Ross's future success were planted by family members who encouraged her to sing whenever they gathered. Diana always believed she was special: "I think I always sang. I must have come out of the womb that way. . . . I knew that with music, I had something of my own and it would last me a lifetime if I so desired."

Ross's loving, nurturing family allowed her to blossom into a world-class entertainer. There was no money for singing lessons to fuel her dreams, but Ross received basic values from her parents. "We may not have had a lot of money, and every moment was not great, but I was brought up to have ideals, to believe that anything was possible and that hard work was part of that."

Once you put a desire into the universe, the circumstances, the people, and the things necessary to fulfill it materialize. Divine order placed Ross's home near the infant Motown Record company; to make her entrance easier, she knew Smokey Robinson's niece. She watched as the different groups worked, rehearsed, and recorded their dreams. Ross said, "Singing became my life. I lived, ate, drank, and breathed it. It was all that I cared about. I had a dream and I was completely determined to make it real."

Ross's passionate desires turned her ideas into dreams; by her midteens, she knew that singing was her passport to universal promises. In those adolescent years, she began weaving the tapestry of her life with Mary Wilson and Florence Ballard, and together, as the Supremes, the three of them would set a new standard of entertainment. During the 1960s, images of elegantly dressed African American women were not the norm until the television debut of the Supremes on October 10, 1965. The appearance of these elegantly dressed young women changed the ambitions of women of all colors. In 1959, Diana Ross hung around the new Motown studios hoping to be discovered. A decade later, as a solo artist, she was scaling every entertainment platform: nightclub circuit, concert tours, film and television actress. Her evolution into a dynamic entertainer, business woman, and successful parent is evidence that prosperity comes from hopes and desires hinged to hard work and preparation.

Belief in self is gained from daily experiences and efforts. Diana Ross released all negatives from her past and is not bound by the sexist, stereotyped views about women. Her mother showed her that a woman could mother and still have a career. We must remember, that with Kuumba and Imani, our expectations empower and free our individual belief in the possible.

EXCERPT FROM *ALONG THIS WAY*

JAMES WELDON JOHNSON

This excerpt from James Weldon Johnson's autobiography describes how his Kuumba and Imani produced "Lift Every Voice and Sing." Once the idea took form, he and his brother combined their talents to create our anthem. They wrote this legacy for the children, who revived it and passed it from generation to generation. In this manner Kwanzaa will be passed to future generations.

When I got back to Jacksonville I found that my artistic ideas and plans were undergoing a revolution. Frankly, I was floundering badly: the things I had been trying to do seemed vapid and nonessential, and the thing I felt a yearning to do was so nebulous that I couldn't take hold of it or even make it out. In this state, satisfactory expression first came through writing a short dialect poem. I was at Mr. McBeatah's house talking about school matters; then about books and literature. He read me a long poem he had written on Lincoln. . . .

A group of young men decided to hold on February 12, a celebration of Lincoln's birthday. I was put down for an address, which I began preparing; but I wanted to do something else also. My thoughts began buzzing round a central idea of writing a poem on Lincoln, but I couldn't net them. So I gave up the project as beyond me; at any rate, beyond me to carry out in so short a time; and my poem on Lincoln is still to be written. My central idea, however, took on another form. I talked over with my brother the thought I had in mind, and we planned to write a song to be sung as part of the exercises. We planned, better still, to have it sung by schoolchildren—a chorus of five hundred voices.

I got my first line—Lift ev'ry voice and sing. Not a startling line; but I worked along grinding out the next five.

When, near the end of the first stanza, there came to me the lines:

> Sing a song full of the faith that the dark past has
>   taught us
> Sing a song full of the hope that the present has
>   brought us.

The spirit of the poem had taken hold of me. I finished the stanza and turned it over to Rosamond.

In composing the other two stanzas I did not use pen and paper. While my brother worked at his musical setting I paced back and forth on the front porch, repeating the lines over and over to myself, going through all of the agony and ecstasy of creating. As I worked through the opening and middle lines of the last stanza:

> God of our weary years,
> God of our silent tears.
> Thou who hast brought us thus far on our way,
> Thou who hast by Thy might
> Let us into the light
> Keep us forever in the path, we pray:
> Lest our feet stray from the places, our God where
>   we met Thee,
> Lest, our heart drunk with the wine of the world,
>   we forget
> Thee.

I could not keep back the tears, and made no effort to do so. I was experiencing the transports of the poet's ecstasy. Feverish ecstasy was followed by the contentment—that sense of serene joy—which makes artistic creation the most complete of all human experiences. . . .

As soon as Rosamond had finished his noble setting of the poem he sent a copy of the manuscript to our publishers in New York, requesting them to have a sufficient number of mimeographed copies made for the use of the chorus. The song was taught to the children and sung very effectively at the celebration; and my brother and I went on with other work. After we permanently moved away from Jacksonville, both the song and the occasion passed out of our minds. But the schoolchildren of Jacksonville kept singing the song; some of them went off to other schools and kept singing it; some of them became teachers and taught it to their pupils. Within that time the publishers had recopyrighted it and issued it in several arrangements. Later it was adopted by the National Association for the Advancement of Colored People, and is now quite generally used throughout the country. The publishers consider it a valuable piece of property; however, in traveling around I have commonly found printed or typed copies of the words pasted in the backs of hymnals and the songbooks used in Sunday schools, Y.M.C.A.s, and similar institutions; and I think that is the method by which it gets its widest circulation. Recently, I spoke for the summer labor school at Bryn Mawr College and was surprised to hear it fervently sung by the white students there and to see it in their mimeographed folio of songs.

Nothing that I have done has paid me back so fully in satisfaction as being the past creator of this song. I am always thrilled deeply when I hear it sung by Negro children. I am lifted up by their voices, and I am also carried back and enabled to live again the exquisite emotions I felt at the birth of the song. My brother and I, in talking, have often marveled at the results that have followed what we considered an incidental effort, an effort made under stress and with no intention other than to meet the needs of a particular moment. The only comment we can make is that we wrote better than we knew.

THE HIGHEST POWER

SUSAN L. TAYLOR (FROM *IN THE SPIRIT*)

This excerpt from Susan Taylor's odyssey describes the universal source of success and happiness, the Highest Power. It is available to each person who allows him or herself to love and believe.

There is a force that supports all existence. It is the energy that governs every aspect of the universe and orders every cell in every living thing. It is unfailing, always at work. It is our source and our substance, an unlimited power that we call by many names: Yahweh, Jehovah, Allah, Divine Intelligence, Spirit, God.

Most of us agree that there is a Highest Power. We testify to that truth. But to experience the inner peace we are seeking, we must do more than speak and sing its name to the heavens. We must keep the awareness that the Power lives within us. It's difficult to sustain trust in the unseen when we're taught to believe only in what is visible. So we put our faith in the material world, when the greatest power is in the nonvisible spiritual world.

We all want material things, and we work hard to get them. But we surrender the very freedom we are seeking when we believe possessions will make us happy, secure or content. We will always hunger for more when we look to the material world to sustain us. We can see the result of this misplaced faith all around us. It fuels most of the pain and suffering of the world. Even the wealthiest people don't feel they have enough money. Most want more, and some use any means to get it. They create wars, foul the environment, hook children on drugs, market cancer-causing foods, close factories and ship jobs off shore where even poorer people can be exploited—all to make more money.

When we believe that money gives us our essential power, we let down our moral guard and give up our humanity. We no longer concern ourselves with preserving and enhancing life, so our divinity is stifled and demeaned. When we believe our power is in the material world, we never feel quite strong enough or confident enough or attractive enough to live fully and freely. We always feel that something is lacking, that we should have more. We will violate ourselves trying to boost our self-image so that people will admire us more.

We all want people to like and admire us, but when we need their confirmation or adulation, we don't live our lives on our own terms. We are focused outward, intent on surrounding ourselves with the trappings they undoubtedly admire. We were not created to please people. We were created to please God, to recognize the Highest Power in ourselves and make it manifest in our daily lives.

The Highest Power is love and it protects us and all of creation. Love is the very nature of the energy we call God. It is the force that orders this universe and is greater than we can fully comprehend. It choreographs the movements of the more than 200 billion stars, including our sun, hurtling through space—all spinning, spiraling, whirling and revolving in billions of galaxies like the one we live in. Imagine such a power, ordering planets and comets and moons through eons, in a perfect cosmic dance. Our African ancestors discovered the laws of life thousands of years ago. They understood that the same power that governs the cosmos and protects the lilies of the fields sustains us, too.

Love yourself as a beautiful and necessary light that was created by God. Remember that the Highest Power is alive within you. It is alive as you. You are human and divine. As is true of the universe, nothing about you is haphazard or accidental. Know that the channels for your existence were put into place in the very beginning. You were created on purpose, with a purpose. You are exactly who and where you need to be, with all the power you need to take your next steps forward. Accept yourself as you are, and make any changes *in* your life based on your discoveries of what is best for you, what nourishes you and celebrates God through you.

Lift up your faith in yourself and in the miracle that is your being. You never doubt that tomorrow the sun will rise. Have faith that you, too, are an important part of creation. You, too, are protected by love. Don't put faith in transitory things. They are here today and gone tomorrow. Put your faith in God, the unseen source of all goodness. Make a ritual of spending quiet time to focus inward so that you can experience God, the Highest Power, the source of wisdom and strength in you awaiting you at the center of your being.

WISDOM TO UNDERSTAND ONESELF: QUOTATIONS TO INSPIRE IMANI

"Faith is to believe what we do not see, and the reward of this faith is to see what we believe."—St. Augustine

"A believer is an optimist in tomorrow."—Duke Ellington

"As I reflect down the vistas of the past, as I think about all the problems and all the experiences I have had; without faith in God, a faith in prayer and a disposition of loyalty to God, I don't know what I would have done."—Rev. C. L. Franklin

"Hold fast to faith. Desert not the ranks, but as brave soldiers march on to victory. I am happy and shall remain so as long as you keep the flag flying."—Marcus Garvey

"Before the ship of your life reaches its last harbor, there will be long drawn-out storms, howling and jostling winds, and tempestuous seas that make the heart stand still. If you do not have a deep and patient faith in God, you will be powerless to face the delay, disappointment and vicissitudes that suddenly come."—Martin Luther King, Jr.

"Lift up! and read the sky/written in the tongues of your ancestors./ It is yours, claim it."—Henry Dumas

"Do I believe I am blessed? Of course, I do! In the first place, my mother told me so, many times, and when she did it always quietly, confidently . . . I knew that anything she told me was true."—Duke Ellington

"Cause and effect are in fact joined and if you build a sufficient cause then not all the talk or all the tears in God's creation can prevent the effect from presenting itself one morning as the now ripened fruit of your labors." —William Grier and Price Cobb

"Desire is the germ of the mind. There is no creation without it."—Zora Neale Hurston

"We believed—because we were young—and had nothing as yet to risk."—Paule Marshall

"Find the good. It's all around you. Find it, showcase it, and you'll start believing it."—Jesse Owens

"The more you believe in yourself, the more you can develop an internal power source, out of which comes the strength to choose a positive outlook on life."—Diana Ross

"Whatever I believed, I did; and whatever I did, I did with my whole heart and mind as far as possible to do so— and thus I gained in intensity of experience what may have taken a less intense person a much longer time."—Jean Toomer

"Your belief combined with your willingness to fulfill your dreams is what makes success possible."—Oprah Winfrey

"We live by faith in others, but most of all we must live by faith in ourselves—faith to believe that we can develop into useful men and women."—Benjamin Mays

STRENGTH TO ENDURE: FOLKTALES FOR IMANI

THE MULE OF FAITH

DOROTHY WINBUSH RILEY

The Mule of Faith is an illustration of the power of the mind and the law of prosperity. Many of us rush around trying to find success by ourselves and in our own way, with one idea and one vision of material evidence. This story shows that with patience, we demonstrate faith. It reminds us that blessings always existed and will continue to exist and that we only need believe.

Solmon Kirks lived in Kansas with his wife, Louise, and their seven children. No matter what he did, no matter where he looked, he could not find work or earn enough money to care for his family. Many days he loaded his mule and hired himself out to his neighbors. Occasionally he earned a dollar for the whole day's labor, but more often he was given food or other goods.

One Monday, Solmon told Louise he'd decided to move to Kansas City, hoping he'd be successful in finding steady work. Before the smiling sun opened the day, he loaded his mule with a quilt and a pick ax; then he promised his wife he would return as soon as he found success. Solmon walked until the winking and blinking stars made his eyes heavy. He saw an underground cave and figured it would make a good place to rest. He unrolled the quilt; then stopped when he heard an owl hooting. He searched and then saw a one-winged great horned-bill owl with its beak opened wide, perched on a stone ledge. Solmon watched as the owl's beak drew gnats, moths, spiders, and other insects like a magnet draws iron. Once it was filled, the owl shut its beak tight as a vault, swallowed his food, and opened its beak again. Solmon watched this process until his eyes could no longer stay open. He finally went to sleep thinking: *I will have all that my family needs: clothes, food, education. The Creator will provide.* While he slept, a voice said to him, *"Go home Solmon. If the Highest Power provides for the great horned-bill owl with one wing, surely he will provide for you. Trust, Solmon. Have faith, Solmon. Go home, Solmon; your success is waiting there."* Solmon returned home before dawn and found Louise and the children working in their garden.

Louise asked, "Did you find success so soon?"

"No," answered Solmon.

Louise said, "Solmon, you know, faith is like planting this garden. The children and I work on it every day, yet we never know what we are going to harvest. We plant seeds, but we don't know if they are good seeds or bad; we weed; we fertilize; we pray that the rabbits won't destroy our seedlings; we pray for rain. Sometimes we get too much, and the rains flood our crops away, and often we don't receive enough rain. But we don't stop, Solmon, we keep planting, and each day we come to work in our garden controlling the things that we can."

Solmon responded, "I know that now; I let fear enter my mind. I know now that everything will be all right." He joined his family in weeding the garden.

When the sun was directly overhead, two men stopped and asked Solmon, "Do you have a horse or mule we can buy?"

Solmon answered, "I may have a mule you can rent. How much are you offering?"

The taller man said, "We don't want to rent him, but we'll buy him for this gold piece, which is more than he's worth. With it, you can buy another mule and anything else you want."

The strangers left, pulling the mule behind them. They

walked about two miles into a forested area, where they met a third man who had been guarding a silver-coated chest that had been buried during the Civil War. The tallest man placed saddlebags across the mule, and the shortest man took three cotton sacks out, and they divided the treasure of gold, coins, silver, necklaces, rings, and brooches. The tallest man placed the sacks in the saddlebags while the middle man placed radishes, dandelion leaves, and carrots on top of them.

As they were leaving, the short man noticed the silver chest and said. "I'll take this home with me."

The tallest man interrupted him, "No, I'm the one that dug the chest out of the ground; it should go home with me."

The middle-sized man shouted, "I'm the one who guarded the chest while you two found this mule; it should go with me."

The three men screamed, cursed, and hit each other with rocks and knives. Before the sun sank behind the trees, they had destroyed each other. The mule patiently waited for someone to lead him from the cave. But not one of the men moved.

The mule ate the remaining vegetables and then headed straight out of the cave. The banana-shaped moon slipped behind the clouds as he trotted into Solmon's yard. "Hee, haw, hee, haw," he brayed. Solmon opened the door, smiled, and called his wife.

His wife said, "Those saddlebags are bulging with enough vegetables to feed our children for weeks!" Solmon said, "I have faith that the Highest Power provides for us and all the beasts on the earth. I had to be reminded last night when I watched a great horned-bill owl. He had one wing, but enough sense to find a safe cave so he wouldn't be eaten by larger animals. Miraculously, the cave was filled with insects of every kind, and he ate until he was satisfied. Once in a while he would let out a loud hoot, praising the blessings he received. I returned home believing that I could work right here on our land and harvest enough food to feed my family and still have some to sell."

At that moment, his wife's hand touched the treasure. She jerked and pulled out an emerald ring. She called, "Solmon, wait; there is something else here!" They spilled the gold, coins, silver, necklaces, rings, and brooches on the floor. All Solmon could think was, *He who provides for the owl provides for me.*

RISE AND FLY

DOROTHY WINBUSH RILEY

I heard many accounts of flying Africans and slaves when I was a child. I believed people could fly through magic and fantasy; superpower appealed to my imagination and I remember wishing I could fly away. This story originated in Africa and was changed to suit the circumstances of American slavery. Whenever a slave disappeared from the fields during the day or vanished under the blanket of night, the people said he "just up and flew away." The story reminds us of the suffering that our people endured during slavery; the joy of those who escaped; and the power of Imani for those who survived slavery. It is a reminder that no situation is worse than slavery and all obstacles facing African Americans today must be overcome by applying the principles of Kwanzaa. Our ancestors bore the lash of slavery while they imagined freedom. They had faith to believe it would happen—if not for themselves, then for us, their children.

"Grandpa! Grandpa! Come quick, I see a man flying over the piney woods!"

"That can't be, you must be dreaming, Martay!"

"No, I saw him with my own eyes. He was flying like an eagle with wings. Grandpa! Come quick or you will miss him!"

The two rushed across the meadow to a tiny hill where they could see the man disappearing into the horizon.

"I heard a story right before Emancipation about some Ibos who flew back to Africa. But this is the first time I have witnessed it."

"Grandpa, please tell me the story."

"I don't recall much and the only part I remember is the Ibos were on a ship that docked in the Carolinas. They joined hands, shackles and all and rose into the air when they learned they were slaves for life. People say they flew back to Africa."

"Why didn't the others fly back instead of staying here in slavery?" asked Martay.

"There was so much pain, sickness and death on the ships that it imprisoned their power. It broke their spirits and they plain forgot how to fly. Let's talk to Brother Kabumba and tell him of the miracle we saw. He is one whose mind can journey backward and tell the story."

This is the story that he told my grandpa and me. In times long past people lived in crowded cities where evil spread like the kudzu vine and goodness vanished from the land. Many hoarded wealth while poverty was an unwelcome guest living with the people. Then men stole and were executed. They armed themselves to kill any witnesses who could testify against them in times long past when goodness vanished from the lands. Lies were common as kernels of corn in a field and speaking evil of others was sport. Abusive words and rumors sparked hatred and fear. Disrespect for life caused wars to destroy the towns in times long past when goodness vanished from the lands. The bite of the jackal consumed humankind. Unjustly, men and women were thrown into prisons for no reason and often released for the same. Bitterness flowed and animosity reigned; brother toward brother, sister toward sister, child toward parent in times long past when goodness vanished from the lands.

The kings and queens knew of Africa and sent ships to steal her wealth. When the plunderers arrived they found that the people were the wealth. They snatched thousands of Africans—the healers, the wizards, the singers, the dancers, the craftsmen, the weavers, the builders, the hunters, the planters, the leaders, the women and the children—from their tribal circle of love to be slaves. The captives carried no material possessions, but each had special talents and powers to make the tribe prosper. These skills helped to build America into a strong country.

Nevertheless, the Africans kept their powers secret and

revealed them to help each other survive plantation life. The healers searched the woods for medicinal roots and plants to cure pains and sorrows. The hunters and planters provided food so no one slept on an empty stomach. The wizards taught the secret calls and the power to move with the wind far above the earth. They communicated the magic, in their heads, to others like them by practicing speaking with their eyes.

One ancient seer was Amunra. He answered only to Amunra, although seven planters tried to change his name. He was tall and strong, with arms that stretched five feet and he ran as if his feet were winged meteors lifting him into the sky. Amunra watched as his night-shaded people labored in back-breaking, dream-draining eighteen-hour days in the fields. The females hoed and chopped the cotton with their babies on their backs. The males worked until they dropped from the scorching sun. Then a rumor flying through the plantation crept as quietly as breath into the ears of the slaves. The planter was broke. He didn't have a penny to his name. He planned to sell them to regain his wealth and sell them without their families. He was going to separate the babies from their mothers; the husbands from their wives; the brothers from their sisters. They were his property to sell to the highest bidder. Amunra knew the rumor was true and called a meeting down in the holler.

Before anyone arrived he picked certain plants and gave one to each as they entered the meeting ground. "You must leave now, before it's too late! Go, as I have taught you the power of our ancestors. Focus your mind and you can rise above this. Focus your mind and stay united. Focus your mind and go! Remember the star! Follow the star until you land on freedom. Now, rise and fly! Rise and fly!" He spoke the chant of the wizard and the captives; healers, wizards and carvers joined hands and rose into the air. They felt the magic mystery of freedom calling as Amunra chanted the magic words: *Om Om Kumbaya . . . Maat! Freedom Kumbaya! Kumbaya . . . Maat! Freedom Om Om Kumbaya!* The ancestors' words were a ticket to freedom as they too chanted and disappeared above the trees. They flew like proud eagles against the magnificent sky high above the plantation, away from the sorrow, away from the land of the slave, away to freedom.

Amunra returned to the plantation. The next day he gave the signal for a second group to meet in the holler. "The rumor is true and you must leave now, before it's too late! Go, as I have taught you the power of our ancestors. Focus your mind and you can rise above this. Focus your mind and stay united. Focus your mind and go! Remember the star, follow the star until you land on freedom." Again he spoke the chant of the wizard and the captives; healers and carvers joined hands and rose into the air. They too felt the power of self-determination calling as Amunra chanted the magic words: *Om Om Kumbaya . . . Maat! Freedom Kumbaya! Kumbaya . . . Maat! Freedom Om Om Kumbaya!*

Amunra repeated this process until there were less than two hundred slaves left on the plantation. He knew it was time to go when the overseer started missing the workers and asked, "Where is everybody? Don't tell me they are in the fields because I checked. People are disappearing like nobody's business and we can't find them even with the hounds. Somebody better tell me what is going on here! Don't just look at me like you don't know what I'm talking about! You might be the next one we sell into Mississippi! All of you, get back to work before I take this whip to your backs!" No one moved as the sound of chirping crickets boomed through the air. Their cutting eyes looked through the overseer to the woods.

Amunra knew it was time for him to leave with the next group. It would be too dangerous to save everyone. Many could not fly while others could fly and chose to stay in slavery. His eyes watered as he wished he could teach everyone to rise and fly. Amunra gave the secret sign to the last group. Those who understood went to the holler in the woods.

He looked at the people who could not fly and uttered these soft words of good-bye that the wind carried to their ears: "I must leave you but I will never be far away. Look for me in your thoughts. Find me in your determination. Carry me in your hearts. I must leave but I will return." He turned and walked into the woods.

The overseer returned to see him walking into a tree and started riding his horse to catch Amunra. He called, "Hey, you there! Where are you going? Come back here! I said come back here!" He whipped the horse and raced off toward the woods. By the time he reached the holler all he could hear was the fading chant: *Om Om . . . Maat! Freedom Kumbaya! Kumbaya . . . Maat! Freedom Om Om Kumbaya!*

The children of the ones who could not fly told their children as I am telling you. Those that could not fly began to run and they headed north to Canada and freedom. Nevertheless, when Emancipation came their children returned to the South and started schools to teach the ones that were left behind.

"But Grandpa, that was a long, long time ago. How did the man we saw fly?" asked Martay.

Grandpa looked at Brother Kabumba, who answered, "Every person can rise and fly if they set their mind to it. You must fly over situations that would bury your will and your dreams. What you saw is an omen, Martay, because one day, you too shall fly and be a legend for our people."

THE FIRE ON THE MOUNTAIN

RETOLD BY DOROTHY WINBUSH RILEY

This story is based on an Ethiopian folktale, "Fire on the Mountain," by Harold Courlander and reflects the country's history and culture. It also shows that self-determination may include risk, but passionate belief in the universal laws can overcome negative conditions. Zere received strength to endure when he focused his vision for twelve hours, demonstrating the law of ever-present abundance.

In the olden time a young man named Zere came to Addis Ababa from the country of Gurage. After he settled, he became the servant of a rich merchant, Tariku Taharka, who had more money than he could count. Tariku owned everything that money could buy and more land than the eyes could see. Despite his great wealth, he bored easily when there was nothing new to entertain him. Then he spent five days traveling across his land.

Once, while returning, night captured Tariku's band, and they camped near a plateau with cutting winds racing around it. Even though Tariku wore layers and layers of clothing, he called Zere to add more wood to the fire. After Zere finished, Tariku asked, thinking aloud, "How much cold can a man actually stand? I wonder if it is possible for a man to stand on the highest peak, Mount Selassie, where the temperature drops far below zero, for an entire night without blankets or clothing and still live?"

"I don't know," Zere answered, "But it sounds foolish to me. He could lose his life, and what would he gain?"

"Yes, it would be foolish for a man to stand in freezing weather all night if he had nothing to gain. It does not matter because I would bet that no man can do it."

"I believe a strong man can endure," Zere replied, "but

as for me, it doesn't matter, since I have nothing to gain and nothing to bet."

"If you actually believe that you can stand on the rocks on Mount Selassie for an entire night without food or water or clothing or blankets or fire and live, then I will give you ten acres of good farmland, a house fit for a merchant, and enough cattle to feed your village," responded Tariku.

Zere thought his ears were playing tricks on him. "Do you really mean this?" he asked.

"My word is my honor," Tariku replied.

"Then tomorrow night I will do it," Zere said, "and afterward I will own land and be independent."

Despite his bold words, Zere worried as he slept because the mountain wind shot killing icy pellets across the peak. The next morning, he visited an elderly wise man from his tribe and told him of the bet. The old man listened quietly until Zere finished and then said, "If you believe you can do this, I will help you. Directly across the valley from Mount Selassie is another high peak. Tomorrow evening I will build a fire there; you will be able to see it from where you stand on Mount Selassie. Watch the light from my fire all night long. Do not close your eyes or let sleep creep up on you. Think of warmth and think of me, your tribesman, sitting there tending the fire for you. If you do this, you will survive, no matter how bitter the wind."

Zere thanked him and returned to Tariku's house. In the afternoon, Tariku sent him and several servants to the top of Mount Selassie. As the day slipped beneath the horizon, Zere undressed and stood in the damp, biting wind that was sweeping across the plateau. He searched across the valley, until he saw his friend's fire, shining like a comet frozen in space.

The cold wind passed through his skin and seemed to freeze the marrow in his bones. It numbed his body until he thought he would never feel warm again. The spot he stood on felt like a snowbank. Nevertheless, Zere wiped those thoughts from his mind and focused his eyes on the glowing flame several miles away while he pictured his friend tending the fire. As night crept by, blankets of fog whirling and winding like a snake blotted out the light. Then Zere felt the cold cut to his heart, and his body shook with sneezes and shivers. Yet, he stood there, and when dawn arrived, he dressed and returned to the city.

Tariku was surprised to see Zere and questioned his servants thoroughly. Finally he said to Zere, "You are a strong fellow. How did you manage to survive the cold night? I could name men who had clothing and cover, yet they did not survive the freezing cold of Mount Selassie."

"It was difficult, but I watched the light from a fire across the valley," Zere replied.

"What!" Fire? Light? Then you lose the bet."

"The fire could not warm me; it was miles away on another mountain. I could not touch it. It was far across the valley!"

"I won't give you the land," Tariku said. "You didn't fulfill the conditions. You are still my servant, and I owe you nothing. The fire saved you!"

Zere went to his friend and told him what had happened. His friend advised Zere to file a complaint with the judge. Zere told the judge, who went to hear Tariku and the servants tell their story. The judge agreed with the merchant and later told Zere, "You lost because you did not follow the condition that you must be without fire."

Again Zere went to his tribesman, who told him. "It is not your destiny to be a servant. Don't give up hope because even for a judge, wisdom does not come overnight."

The old man went to Hakim, a man he served when he was young. He told Hakim every detail of the bet between Tariku and Zere and asked if something could be done. Seven days later, Hakim invited many people to a feast at his house. He invited Tariku and the judge who had ruled against Zere. On the day of the feast, the guests came dressed to show their wealth with strings of servants trailing them. Tariku brought twenty servants and four drummers to announce his entrance.

The guests sat on soft rugs laid out for them and talked. They smelled wonderful odors of things to eat from the kitchen: roast goat, roast corn, durram pancakes called injera, and many tantalizing sauces. Time passed, and the aromas stirred more hunger in the stomachs of the guests. Hours passed, and the food was not served. They knew the food was there because the smells drifted from the kitchen. Evening came, and still no food was served. The guests began to whisper that it was very strange that the honorable Hakim had not served food. Finally, a guest asked, "Hakim, why do you invite us to a feast and then serve us nothing? What have we done to offend you?"

"Why, can't you smell the food?" Hakim asked with surprise.

"Of course, we can, but smelling is not eating; there's no pleasure or reward in it!"

"Tell me my friends, is there warmth in a fire so far away that it can hardly be seen?" Hakim asked. "If Zere can be warmed by a fire he watched while standing on Mount Selassie, then you can be fed by the smells coming from my kitchen."

All the guests agreed with Hakim; even the judge saw his mistake. Tariku was embarrassed and shamed. Nevertheless, he publicly thanked Hakim and announced that Zere was then and there the owner of the land, the house, and the cattle.

Then the honorable Hakim ordered the food brought in, and the feast began.

OTHER PEOPLE'S WISDOM: PROVERBS FOR IMANI

God gave us the seed of every plant, but we must sow it.—Africa

The true believer begins with herself.—Berber

God gives you gifts. Do not forget where he took you from.—Burundi

God does not sleep.—Congo

Wisdom is like mushrooms; it comes up late in the season.—Malawi

God gives nothing to those who keep their arms closed.—Mali

What you have seen, you know. What you have not seen, you must believe.—Namibia

When God shuts a door for us, he will open another door.—Swahili

Other people's wisdom often prevents a chief from becoming a fool.—Yoruba

THOUGHTS FOR IMANI

❖ Believe in the universal laws and practice them daily.

❖ Recognize the Highest Power and manifest it daily in your life.

❖ Practice loving—giving love, accepting love, and expecting love.

❖ Accept yourself as you are and live life on your own terms.

❖ Maintain your morality and humanity.

❖ Overcome obstacles with faith, courage, endurance, and persistence.

❖ Honor, revere, and respect the Divine in yourself. Remember to be nice and expect the best for yourself.

❖ Speak words with feeling, life, and meaning to experience the desires of your mind. Your words give body to your thoughts.

❖ Use your imagination to project and clothe your ideas in reality.

❖ Imagine a successful, prosperous harvest for yourself. You are what you imagine yourself to be.

CHAPTER EIGHT

KWANZAA'S KARAMU

CELEBRATE THE JOURNEY

I shall dance at the Karamu after the candles are lit on the sixth day of Kwanzaa. The perfumed air surrounds the feast, and the drums move my feet as I circle among the elders, recalling memories of the ancestors from the illusion of time. My heart remembers the wondrous words that weave a tapestry of the journey across barriers to fulfill our destiny.

—Dorothy Winbush Riley

There is only one feast day in Kwanzaa, and anticipation of it is a golden thread woven into the tapestry of human existence, to unite friends and family members on the sixth day at the Karamu feast. During the feast, we share the fruits of our labors, wealth and security, with others, while celebrating the journey.

The Karamu is like a family reunion that bonds young and old through music, dance, memories, and love. The location of the Karamu varies as much as the people who celebrate it. At large gatherings specific greeters welcome guests and set the tone for the evening in the African tradition by saying "Habari Gani." The guests respond with "Kuumba," which is the day of the feast. After a number of guests arrive, a sing-along may be started to cement further the feeling of unity among the guests.

The festivity of the sixth day highlights an opportunity to create order, beauty, and balance. Some celebrants incorporate the red, black, and green colors that reflect our African heritage into their decor, while others simply display the seven symbols. Many hosts and hostesses prepare a program with the seven principles printed on it to organize and keep the activities flowing. A typical program can be simple or elaborate, according to the style of the host or hostess. The festivities can be divided into six main parts, and each part may take several minutes or an hour, depending on the size of the gathering and the feelings of the guests. The six main parts are as follows:

- Libation to ancestors
- Rejoicing through expressions of poetry, song, dance, and music and eating
  - Reflections: reassessment and commitment
  - Teachings from the Nguzo Saba
  - Libation to posterity
  - Farewell statement

The following is a sample program that contains all the elements that can be adapted for any Karamu.

KWANZAA CELEBRATION
HOME OF _____
THE KARAMU FEAST
December 31, _____

Kukaribisha (welcoming statement)
- Opening remarks
- Tamshi la tambiko: libation to the ancestors
- Reflection and meaning of Kuumba
- Reflection and meaning of the Karamu feast
- Lighting the candles

Kukumbuka (reflecting and remembering)
- Story by a man
- Song or dance by a woman
- Poem or story by a child
- Kutoa majin: Calling the names of the ancestors

Kuchunguza tena na (reassessment and recommitment)
- Historical point of view
- Pledges and commitment to the future

Kushangilia (rejoicing)
- Tamshi la tambiko: libation to posterity
- Kikombe cha umoja: unity cup
- Kutoa majin: Calling the names of the ancestors
- Feasting and entertainment

Tamshi la tuanonana (farewell statement)

Kukaribisha (welcoming statement)

This statement is usually given by the oldest person present or the head of the house. If a younger person gives the welcome, he or she first asks the elders for permission to speak. All the guests gather reverently around a low table that holds the seven symbols of Kwanzaa for the libation to the ancestors. This libation causes us to remember the achievements of all those who have gone before us, just as in ancient African societies. It opens the Karamu when a small portion of the libation is poured on the floor in the directions of the four winds to honor and remember the ancestors.

Children are important to the Karamu, and after the libation, they light the second red candle for Kuumba. Other children or guests relight the Umoja (black candle) and the first red and three green candles, and the speaker reflects on what Kuumba means.

Kukumbuka (remembering)

During this part of the evening, we honor and remember the ancestors and those who have lived and applied the Nguzo Saba with songs, poetry, literature, or music. Guests or family members recite a poem, relate a historical incident, or retell stories of the ancestors.

Kutoa majin is the calling of names of family members, ancestors, and African-descended heroes to invite their presence. As the proverb says, *As long as someone is here to speak your name, you exist.* We first call forth beings of the past—leaders and teachers who left us a place on Earth to harvest our success. Next, we call out the names of those who are living now—our partners, friends, family members, and co-workers. Finally, we call on the nameless, faceless, formless children of the future. We ask a moment of silence for them because they have not been named, but we feel their presence. We feel their light because the work of freedom, dignity, and prosperity must continue, and we leave a legacy of triumph for them.

Kuchunguza tena na (reassessment and recommitment)

A member of the family or a friend may speak to the meaning of Kwanzaa and Nguzo Saba for him or her by sharing a historical piece. A guest may give a short speech. (No matter how important the guest is, the speech and presentation should be short; this is an occasion for dancing, remembering, and eating.)

Kushangilia (rejoicing and praising through songs or poetry)

The gathering may sing selected songs, such as "Lift Every Voice and Sing," or other songs that signify the victory that African Americans have won in the past three hundred years.

Just as with the first libation to the ancestors, the final libation is performed and the libation statement is read by an elder, a designated guest, or the head of the house. In tamshi la tambiko, the libation to posterity, the kikombe cha umoja is used to signify unity. The following is one example of a libation statement, but celebrants can always write their own.

> To all who came before us: the elders and the ancestors. To all who will come after us: the unborn babies and the children. We honor them and their creative minds that flow from the Highest

Power. We practice the universal laws to ensure our survival, triumph, and prosperity. At this time, we allow the divine power to come forth and guide our people to the success, prosperity, justice, and dignity that is our promise. Today we accept all truth and our inheritance from the Creator.

After the libation statement is given, the speaker holds the kikombe cha umoja with both hands, drinks from it, and leads the gathering in a call to unity by shouting "Harambee!" seven times. Next, the kikombe cha umoja is passed to the family members and guests, who sip from it as a sign of unity. The last few ounces of the libation are poured into the cup of the host or hostess, who sips from the cup and then hands it to the oldest person in the group. The elder again asks the ancestors to share in the festivities and, in return, to bless all the people present, as well as their relatives and friends who are not at the gathering, and returns the kikombe cha umoja to the table.

Ngoma, drumbeats or other forms of music, are essential to African life, so next, a drummer performs or African-style recordings are played. Once the music starts, the Karamu begins.

After the feast, which is accompanied by music and other cultural expressions, the farewell statement is given. The following is one example of a farewell statement, but celebrants may choose to modify it or write their own.

Tamshi la tutaonana (farewell statement)

Have faith in tomorrow; enjoy today as you learn that all existence rests in a circle of love. Strive for an understanding heart filled with sympathy and hopefulness toward others. Dare to dream, dare to think, and dare to act as power flows from your mind. Expect new revelations of truth as your thoughts build and create wherever you are and whatever you desire. Understand that you are not the first to suffer, love, or prosper and that life, despite changes, is always a measure of the legacy our ancestors left. Accept the lessons and experiences of the past, taking the best from all that has occurred, and press boldly into the future, moving closer and closer to your goal. Understand connections; we are all mutually dependent, and the circle of love must not be broken. Look to the future as if it were already here; use hindsight and foresight to expect a prosperous harvest.

Live the universal laws as the Nguzo Saba—Umoja, Kujichagulia, Ujima, Ujamaa, Nia, Kuumba, and Imani—demonstrate them. Follow in the path of wisdom and seek virtue with your every word, act, and gesture.

May our children walk like us, talk like us, and work like us in balance and harmony with nature and each other, spreading honor in all that they do. May we enter the new year with the seeds of prosperity planted in our minds, radiating harmony, peace, and abundance wherever we go. May we travel in safety and security to meet again at the end of the new year to share in a harvest of success.

Harambee! Harambee! Harambee! Harambee! Harambee! Harambee! Harambee!

THE RILEY FAMILY'S KARAMU BRUNCH

Once I began to celebrate Kwanzaa, my attitude about the new year changed as I focused my children on our history and their roles in choosing their future. I wanted my children to see that the grades they received in school were as important as was Booker T. Washington working as a janitor, sweeping the room at Hampton, as a test for his entrance to the Institute. I knew that Kwanzaa would be the ritual to bring us closer as a family working for each other's benefit. After talking about Kwanzaa to my students, observing the seven principles, and attending elaborate and beautiful Karamu feasts given by friends, I created my own version of the Karamu to suit my family, time, and money.

On New Year's Eve, my four children and I attended midnight church services. After hearing a great sermon, singing, and rejoicing, we returned home about 3 A.M., too energized to sleep and hungry enough to eat a turkey. In 1983, I started our tradition, and we prepared a Karamu brunch. We gathered in the kitchen and began preparations by talking and laughing in the new year. Since I was a single mother raising four children, each child was already responsible for cooking a meal one day a week. During the brunch preparations, each one contributed his or her specialty, from the oldest, Schiavi, who made a quiche, to the youngest, Tiaudra, who stirred the grits and cut up food.

The first brunch was just for our little nuclear family, and we did not have a program. We poured an orange juice libation and proceeded to tell stories and sing songs related to African American history. It was quite informal and fun. I enjoyed this early Karamu because it freed me to attend some of the larger, more elaborate feasts planned by my friends in the evening.

Welcoming the new year is a joyful time, and by the time of our second Karamu brunch, we understood the importance and seriousness of the Nguzo Saba and invited our friends and relatives to join us and share the love in our family. Nieces and nephews came with other members of the family, who brought pineapple upside-down cake and fried chicken, and Tiaudra cooked her special fried green tomatoes. My oldest son, Ted, planned a program similar to the one suggested in Chapter One.

During the ritual part of the ceremony, Ted offered the orange-juice libation to the ancestors, and Tiaudra offered the libation to posterity; we did not use a unity cup, but each person had a glass. Then, Tiaudra sang and played the piano; my son, Robert, entertained us with stories; and I presented the historical connection. We did not have any elaborate entertainment, but we had a lot of conversation and expressed a great deal of love while discussing the Nguzo Saba. The children committed themselves to going to college, so they could be useful and helpful to themselves, to me, and to the community. I believe that our Kwanzaa celebrations reinforced my children's sense of purpose and encouraged them to become the successful adults they are today.

FRANK AND BEVERLY WALKER'S KARAMU DINNER

This account describes the experiences of Frank and Beverly Walker, of San Diego, in celebrating Kwanzaa, especially Kuumba, as told by Frank Walker.

Most families do not plan an elaborate feast, but create a special intimate dinner for the Karamu to celebrate Kuumba. For the first six years of our marriage, we saved my wife's salary, so we would be able to open our own business. I made a kinara from driftwood, and Beverly bought the seven candles. We had no children yet, but many friends joined us in the celebration. As the years passed, we added three ears of corn to represent our children. Beverly made the mkeka from African materials she had bought at a fabric store. We also encourage our children to make zawadi for members of the family. One year, my youngest daughter made an address book with an African design on the cover. My sons are artists and combine their talents to create individual pictures for family members. Our children are familiar with the principles and the symbols of Kwanzaa because they celebrate them in school.

In our family, we follow a program, but during our first Kwanzaa, we combined the libations and performed only one because we were just learning about the holiday and did not understand the significance of the second libation. A huge goblet that belonged to my father served as our kikombe cha umoja, and we all drank from it. As the years passed, we prospered, and our family feast grew to include other family members and friends, who provide entertainment and the essential elements of a Karamu.

During the Karamu, we always play music, from the

Motown sound to the jazz greats and African singers. This background music, together with our African sculptures and mkeka covered with the symbols of Kwanzaa, create a special ambience that bonds our family and guests. Once we light the candles, they remain lit throughout the evening. After I, as the head of the house, give the farewell statement, we discard the burned-down candles and replace them with seven new candles. We display our mishumaa saba and kinara throughout the year to remind us to continue to work hard and purposely in preparation for the next Kwanzaa.

DIANE AND CORDELL HALL'S KARAMU FEAST

This account of the Diane and Cordell Hall's celebration of Kwanzaa and their Karamu feast is related by Diane Hall.

I had attended several Kwanzaa celebrations, but the one that inspired me was at a meeting of the Detroit Board of Education in 1989, where we received programs that explained the principles and meaning of Kwanzaa. I knew that this celebration would be a unifying force and, I hoped, would become a tradition with my family and extended family.

For our first Kwanzaa, I made invitations and sent them to family members and friends, asking them to come prepared to share in the entertainment or presentations and to wear red, black, and green clothes or African garments. I purchased the kinara and the seven candles and then created a mkeka from fabric my aunt brought from Sierra Leone. During the week, we lit the candles for each day and discussed what each principle meant to us as a family.

On December 31, we gathered at the Karamu, and as people entered, my son gave each a program explaining Kwanzaa and listing the seven principles. Several guests brought food, and I prepared Jollof rice.

My husband, Cordell, directs the formal ceremony. Everyone quietly gathers in front of the fireplace, where I have placed a table with the seven symbols on it. Cordell begins the ritual by reading selections from both the Koran and the Bible. He then gives the tamshi la tambiko. He recognizes the elders who are present and pours a small portion of the libation (fruit juice) on the floor in four directions: east, south, north, and west. We raise the unity cup with joined hands: I hold one side, and Cordell holds the other. We do not pass the libation cup around to guests; rather, our children give each guest a glass while we stand holding the kikombe cha umoja. I call for the eldest person to lead the group in a call to unity by shouting "Harambee!" seven times.

Cordell and I have a combination of seven sons. The oldest boy, Cordy, organizes the next part of the ritual. The youngest boy, Clifton, lights the candles when directed by his brother. Then each boy shares one of the Nguzo Saba and tells how it applies to him or to our blended family. The ceremony ends with Cordy inviting guests to share their knowledge. Since I plan the activities, someone always reads a poem or reflects on how the values of Kwanzaa have helped him or her.

Then the feasting begins. I play the music of Olatunji, Duke Ellington, or Wynton Marsalis while we share a harvest of love. Once we have eaten, the entertainment, which can range from recitations of the works of writers, songs, and authentic African dances, begins. At the end, either Cordell or I give the farewell statement.

Each of our Kwanzaa celebrations has been different. In 1990, we planned a huge feast; in 1991, we invited only

"At the Karamu." Acrylic on canvas by Jamal Jones, 1993–94. Photograph by Bill Sanders.

family members. In 1992, I was nine months' pregnant with Paul, so we lit our candles and celebrated with our sons. A year later, the baby joined us at our 1993 Kwanzaa and played his drums to entertain us. In 1994, we invited family members and friends, who enjoy the opportunity to share the beautiful celebration of Kwanzaa. Our blended family will always observe this holiday because it spotlights the purpose of life and gives us direction with a historical structure. We must live together in this world as brothers and sisters, and, for me, Kwanzaa is in my heart.

KARAMU MENUS

The Riley Family's Karamu Brunch

Fried Chicken

Soufflé Omelet with Shrimp Salad

Salmon Croquettes

Robert's Home Fries   Fried Green Tomatoes

Corn Fritters   French Toast

Breakfast Grits

Schiavi's Quiche

Odessa's Candied Yams

Banana Nut Bread

Broiled Peaches

Biscuits

Pound Cake

Chilled Coconut Milk and Pineapple Drink

Frank and Beverly Walker's Karamu Dinner

Seafood Gumbo

Chicken and Dumplings

Black-eyed Peas and Rice

Judy's Succotash

Ambrosia

Pineapple Upside-down Cake

Banana Pudding

Iced Mint Tea

Diane and Cordell Hall's Karamu Feast

Deviled Crabmeat

Sujah Diane   Jollof Rice

Smoked Turkey

Corn Bread Oyster Dressing

Baked Ham

Chicken Yassa

Red Beans and Rice   Stewed Okra

Corn Pudding   Mixed Greens   Corn on the Cob

Macaroni and Cheese

Potato Salad   Avocado and Cabbage Salad

Sweet Potato Pie   Merdey Kerney's Fruit Cake

Grandma's Peach Cobbler

Ginger Beer   Lemonade

KARAMU RECIPES

ENTREES AND SIDE DISHES

Sujah Diane's Jollof Rice

Serves 8
Cooking time: 30 minutes

Diane Hall gave me the recipe for Jollof rice, her favorite main dish at her family's Kwanzaa feast. It is believed that this dish originally came from the Wolof people of Gambia. Every cook has a favorite way of preparing this dish of meats, vegetables, and rice cooked in one pot. Diane's recipe is delicious and you can add other meats and vegetables if you desire.

2- to 3-pound chicken, cut into 8 serving pieces

2 pounds lean boneless beef, cut into half-inch cubes

4 tablespoons flour

Freshly ground pepper

6 tablespoons peanut oil

1 cup finely chopped onions

3 medium-size firm red tomatoes, peeled, seeded, and diced
   (or 1 cup drained canned tomatoes)

¼ cup tomato paste

1 tablespoon finely chopped garlic

1 fresh hot chili pepper, about 3 inches long, stemmed,
   seeded, and finely chopped

1 medium-size bay leaf

2 stalks celery, finely chopped

1 8-ounce package frozen peas

6 medium carrots, scraped and cut in rounds

1 8-ounce package frozen or ½ pound fresh green beans,
   chopped

1 lb. chopped cauliflower (about 1 small head)

1 lb. chopped cabbage (about 1 small head)

1 pound fresh or 1 8-ounce package frozen spinach

¼ cup coarsely chopped parsley

2 cups chicken or beef broth

2 cups water

½ pound lean boneless smoked ham, diced

1½ cups cooked long-grain white rice

1. Pat the chicken and beef dry. Mix the flour with black pepper and dredge the pieces of chicken and beef with it.

2. Place 3 tablespoons of the oil in a 3- to 4-quart casserole until a light haze forms at medium heat.

3. Brown the chicken and beef separately and add the remaining oil as necessary.

4. Set the chicken and beef aside.

5. Leave enough oil to coat the pan and pour out the rest. Add the onions and cook until browned.

6. Add the tomatoes, tomato paste, garlic, chili pepper, bay leaf, and vegetables.

7. Raise the heat to high and cook until most of the liquid in the pan has evaporated and the mixture is thick enough to hold its shape.

8. Stir in the broth and water.

9. Add the beef, chicken, and diced ham to the casserole.

10. Stir to mix all the ingredients.

11. Bring to a boil.

12. Reduce the heat to low and simmer partially covered for about 30 minutes.

13. Serve over piles of steaming rice; add salt to taste.

Fried Chicken

Serves 8–12

Cooking time: 30 minutes (5 to 7 minutes per skillet)

Fried chicken is a traditional African American dish that you find from Maine to New Mexico in a country breakfast or as a main dish. Growing up in Detroit meant that we had chicken every Sunday. My mother roasted, baked, and stewed chickens, but the best taste was her crispy fried chicken. When I first married, my husband and I searched the city for a cast-iron skillet, which is what I still use today.

Vegetable oil for frying

2 (2–3 pound) frying chickens, trimmed and skinned, each cut into 8 pieces

Salt to taste (approximately 1 teaspoon)

Ground black pepper to taste (approximately 1 teaspoon)

2 cups all-purpose flour

2 teaspoons paprika

1. Pour the oil in a heavy skillet and heat to 375 degrees.

2. Lay the chicken pieces on a plate and sprinkle with salt and pepper.

3. Stir the flour and paprika together in a bowl.

4. Coat each piece of chicken with the flour and paprika.

5. Place the pieces of chicken in the skillet, making sure they do not touch each other.

6. Fry the chicken pieces 5–7 minutes until golden brown on one side and use tongs or a fork to turn them to cook on the other side.

7. Remove each piece and drain on paper towels.

8. Serve hot.

Roast Turkey

Serves 14–16
Cooking time: 4 hours

I learned to cook turkey in a brown paper bag in 1978 from Mrs. Lemke, a teacher at Durfee Middle School, when we prepared a meal in school for the students. She used a plain brown paper grocery bag. Now I cook my turkeys that way, and they are mouth-watering good.

1 14–16 pound turkey

1 large onion, whole

2 apples, quartered

3 stalks celery, sliced lengthwise

½ teaspoon salt

½ teaspoon ground black pepper

1. Preheat the oven to 450 degrees.
2. Remove the giblets and neck from the cavity of the turkey.
3. Place the turkey under cold running water and rinse it, inside and out.
4. Place the onion, apples, and celery in the cavity.
5. Rub the outside of the turkey with the salt and pepper.
6. Place the turkey in a brown paper grocery bag and tuck the ends of the bag under it.
7. Place the bag in the oven and roast the turkey for about 4 hours. (Look at the cooking time on the wrapper of your turkey, if you buy a frozen turkey.)
8. Remove the bag from the oven. The turkey will be golden brown.
9. Allow the turkey to cool before you serve. (The slices are filled with the natural juices of the bird.)

Oyster and Corn Bread Dressing

Serves 12
Cooking time: 30–40 minutes

Most folks call it stuffing, but in my family, we always asked for dressing. Dressings may contain sausage, sage, rice, and mixtures of other family favorites. No matter what we put in our dressing, the base is always corn bread. Fresh oysters add a special taste and are optional in this recipe.

4 stalks celery, chopped

2 medium green bell peppers, cored, seeded, sliced, and
diced

8 cups corn bread, crumbled

3 cloves garlic, minced

2 onions, chopped or diced

1 8-ounce package of onion soup mix

2 cans cream of mushroom soup

Drippings from the roast turkey

Salt to taste

Ground black pepper to taste

Optional oysters

1. Mix the celery, bell pepper, cooked corn bread, garlic, and onions in a large mixing bowl.

2. Add the onion soup mix, mushroom soup, drippings from the turkey, salt, pepper, and optional oysters and mix until they are evenly distributed.

3. Place the dressing in the neck and interior of the turkey and roast the turkey.

4. Bake the remainder of the stuffing in a baking pan for 30–40 minutes.

Salmon Croquettes

Serves 8
Cooking time: 10 minutes

The best salmon croquettes I ever tasted were made by my mother's second cousin, who always used fresh salmon. My daughters and I use
salmon from a can—juice and all.

2 cans or 2 pounds pink salmon

1 medium onion, finely chopped

4 eggs, lightly beaten

½ cup yellow cornmeal

Salt and ground black pepper to taste

Vegetable oil

1. Remove all the bones and skin of the salmon and place
in a shallow bowl.
2. Stir the salmon with a fork.
3. Add the onion, eggs, cornmeal, salt, and pepper to the
salmon and mix.
4. Shape the mixture into cakes or ovals.
5. Heat the oil in the skillet and add the cakes.
6. Cook for 10 minutes or until brown on both sides.

Chicken and Dumplings

Serves 8
Cooking time: 1 hour

This is a favorite family recipe that my son, Ted, requests whenever he comes home. I learned from my mother, who made the lightest dumplings I have ever tasted.

> 2 teaspoons paprika
>
> $\frac{1}{2}$ teaspoon salt
>
> $\frac{1}{2}$ teaspoon ground black pepper, or to taste
>
> 1 tablespoon vegetable oil
>
> 1 3–4 pound chicken, cut into 8 pieces
>
> 2 celery stalks, cut into 2-inch pieces
>
> 2 carrots, cut into 2-inch pieces
>
> 1 medium green pepper, sliced and diced
>
> 1 medium Bermuda onion, quartered
>
> 4 cups canned chicken broth

1. Combine the paprika, salt, and pepper in a small bowl.

2. Wash the chicken pieces and pat them dry; then roll each piece in the paprika mixture.

3. Preheat oil in a large iron skillet and cook the chicken until browned (no more than 10 minutes).

4. Place the chicken in a Dutch oven or a large covered pot. Add the vegetables and broth and bring to a boil.

5. Lower the heat and cook the chicken for about 45 minutes. Remove the chicken from the broth.

DUMPLINGS

> 1 cup unbleached all-purpose flour
>
> 1$\frac{1}{2}$ teaspoons baking powder

2 tablespoons fresh parsley

2 tablespoons solid vegetable shortening

⅓ cup milk

Chopped fresh parsley for garnish

1. Mix the flour, baking powder, and parsley.

2. Using your fingers or two knives, cut in the shortening until the flour mixture is coarse and crumbly.

3. Add the milk gradually, just enough to moisten.

4. Knead the dough into a ball and cut into 12 balls.

5. Bring the broth to a boil, then drop the dumplings in it, one at a time.

6. Cover and simmer for about 15 minutes until the dumplings are puffy.

7. Remove the dumplings from the broth and serve hot, garnished with fresh parsley.

Seafood Gumbo

Serves 8 to 10
Cooking time: 25 minutes

I learned to love okra by eating it in my mother's gumbos. Gumbo is from the Bantu name for okra—*guingombo, tchingombo,* or *kingombo.* My friends who live in Louisiana and around the Gulf add shrimp, oysters, and crabmeat which were plentiful in their areas. The secret to a good gumbo is to prepare it in advance and let all the seasonings soak in overnight.

½ pound kielbasa or Cajun sausage, cut into 1-inch rounds

½ cup of olive oil

2 cups diced onions

1 cup chopped red bell pepper

1 cup chopped green bell pepper

1 cup grated celery

6 cloves garlic, minced

3 cups drained whole tomatoes

¼ teaspoon cayenne pepper

½ teaspoon salt

½ teaspoon ground black pepper

2 bay leaves

1½ pounds large shrimp, cleaned and deveined

1 pound sea scallops

1 pound cooked lobster meat

½ pound crabmeat

2 tablespoons fresh parsley

5 cups chicken broth

1 pound okra, cut into rounds

Cooked rice for eight people

1. Combine all the ingredients except the okra in a large heavy cooking pot and bring to a boil.

2. Lower the heat, add the okra, and simmer for 15 minutes.

3. Remove from the heat and cool.

4. Refrigerate the gumbo overnight.

5. The next day reheat, but don't boil, the mixture.

6. Remove the bay leaves and serve over rice.

Baked Ham

Serves: 20 to 24
Cooking time: 1½ hours

A baked ham is a delight at any celebration, and the glaze gives it a special taste. I received this recipe from Gloria Green Jones of Homer, Louisiana, and it is delicious.

20 whole cloves

⅔ cup (packed) dark brown sugar

3 5½-ounce cans pineapple chunks in their own juices

1 cup honey

1 cup red wine

1 precooked 12–14 pound bone-in ham

1. Preheat the oven to 350 degrees.

2. Prepare a marinade of ⅓ cup dark brown sugar, pineapple chunks and juice, honey, and wine. Heat the mixture in a saucepan over low heat.

3. Use a sharp knife to score the ham in a diamond pattern.

4. Insert the cloves at the crossed point of each diamond and spread ⅓ cup of brown sugar over the ham.

5. Place the ham on a rack in a shallow baking pan and bake for 30 minutes.

6. Remove the ham, baste thoroughly with the marinade, and return it to the oven.

7. Continue to bake, basting frequently, for another hour, or until a meat thermometer reads 120 degrees.

Crab Cakes

Serves 8 (large crab cakes)
Cooking time: 15 minutes

My oldest brother, Jack, moved to Alexandria, Virginia, with his family. When I visit them, I eat the best crab cakes. This is their recipe, which is simple and good.

1 pound fresh or frozen lump crabmeat

1 cup fresh soft bread crumbs or saltine cracker crumbs

2 eggs, lightly beaten

4 tablespoons mayonnaise

½ cup onions, finely diced

2 tablespoons unsalted butter

Salt and ground black pepper to taste

2 teaspoons fresh parsley, chopped

Flour for coating

Hot sauce to taste

2 tablespoons olive oil or vegetable oil for frying

1. Mix the crabmeat, bread crumbs, eggs, mayonnaise, onion, salt, pepper, and parsley in a mixing bowl.

2. Shape the mixture into 8 large patties or 2 dozen small cakes.

3. Sprinkle with flour.

4. Fry the cakes slowly on both sides in 1½ inches of hot vegetable oil for 5–7 minutes each side, or until golden brown.

5. Serve with hot sauce.

Deviled Crabmeat

Serves: 6–8
Preparation time: 1 hour to chill

This appetizer can be made ahead and refrigerated. It can be served on crackers or vegetables, and adds a special touch to the Karamu table.

1 pound fresh lump crabmeat

½ cup red bell pepper, finely minced

½ cup onion, finely minced

½ cup mayonnaise

1 teaspoon prepared mustard

1 teaspoon fresh lemon juice

Hot sauce to taste

1. Mix all the ingredients except the hot sauce in a bowl.
2. Cover and chill for 1 hour.
3. Serve chilled on crackers, celery sticks, or with other vegetables.
4. The hot sauce is optional and can be used as a condiment to taste.

Schiavi's Quiche

Serves 8
Cooking time: 30–40 minutes

This is a family favorite. Schiavi prepares it using many variations of meats and vegetables, depending on what is in the refrigerator. The bacon should be cooked crisply then broken into pieces. I have also prepared it without fresh bacon by using a cup of bacon bits. It is just as delicious.

4 tablespoons olive oil

2 cups of the following mixture: mushrooms, crisp cooked
   bacon, chopped onions, and green and red peppers

4 eggs

2 cups milk

2 teaspoons chopped parsley

1 teaspoon celery salt

Ground black pepper

2 cups grated Swiss, cheddar, or Monterey Jack cheese

2 prepared pie crusts

1. Preheat the oven to 375 degrees.
2. Heat the oil in a frying pan.
3. Sauté the mushrooms, ham, bacon, onions, and green and red peppers for 5 minutes.
4. Beat the eggs in a bowl and add the milk, parsley, celery salt, pepper, and cheese.
5. Mix well, then add the sautéed vegetables from the pan.
6. Pour into pie shells and bake for 30 minutes, or until a knife inserted in the middle comes out clean.

Chicken Yassa

Serves 12
Cooking time: 30 minutes

This recipe from Senegal is great on any holiday. It is simple and reminds us of our ancestors.

2 frying chickens (2½-3 pounds each) cut into 8 pieces

2 cups lemon juice, strained

6 large Bermuda onions, finely chopped

4 tablespoons fresh hot chiles, finely chopped

10 teaspoons peanut oil

1½ cups water

1 chile, pricked with a fork

1 teaspoon ground ginger

Salt and ground black pepper to taste

1. Mix the lemon juice, onions, half the chopped chiles, ginger, salt, pepper, and 6 tablespoons of the peanut oil to create a marinade.

2. Place the chicken in a large bowl and cover it with the marinade. Refrigerate for at least 2 hours.

3. Remove the chicken from the marinade, place it in a shallow baking dish, and broil until lightly browned (save the marinade).

4. Remove the onions from the marinade with a slotted spoon and cook them in the remaining 4 teaspoons of oil in a Dutch oven for about 5 minutes, or until soft; do not brown.

5. Add the marinade, chicken, water, and the rest of the chopped chiles.

6. Stir and simmer for about 20 minutes, or until the chicken is well cooked.

7. Serve over steaming hot rice.

Vegetables

Stewed Okra

Serves 8
Cooking time: 25 minutes

Okra was introduced to America by the slaves, and for many years was grown and eaten only by them. Today okra is used to thicken dishes, and this stew perfectly highlights the taste of the vegetable.

2 pounds fresh okra

2 tablespoons butter

2 cups onions, finely chopped

2 teaspoons hot chiles, finely chopped

8 medium-size firm red tomatoes peeled, seeded, and diced

   (or 3 cups canned chopped tomatoes, drained)

2 tablespoons garlic, finely chopped

2 teaspoons salt

½ teaspoon freshly ground black pepper

1. Wash the okra under cold water and scrape the skin softly with a sharp knife.
2. Cut the tops off the okra.
3. Melt the butter over moderate heat in a heavy 10–12-inch skillet.
4. Add the onions, stir, and cook for 5 minutes; do not brown.
5. Add the chiles, tomatoes, and garlic; stir; and cook, covered, for 5 minutes.
6. Add the okra, salt, and pepper.
7. Reduce the heat to low and cover tightly.
8. Simmer for 15 minutes, or until the okra is tender.

Red Beans and Rice

Serves 12
Cooking time: 1 hour

This recipe is from the Caribbean and is prepared differently by different islanders and by African Americans. I have tasted great dishes all the way from the islands to New York, but the best versions were in New Orleans. I don't cook with measuring spoons and this recipe from John Pinderhughes's *Family of the Spirit Cookbook* is almost exactly what I do when I cook red beans and rice.

1 pound dried kidney beans

1 teaspoon salt

2 quarts water

1 large Bermuda onion, chopped

1 small green pepper, diced

1 bay leaf

1 teaspoon thyme

5 tablespoons lard or bacon fat

Ground black pepper to taste

1 pound Creole sausage or spicy sausage

½ pound smoked ham, cubed

3 cloves garlic, minced

2 tablespoons chopped parsley

4 cups cooked long-grain white rice

1. Put the beans in a colander and wash under cold running water.

2. Place the beans in a heavy sauce pan and add salt, water, and the onion.

3. Bring to a boil over high heat, then reduce and simmer for about 30 minutes, or until the beans are tender.

4. Add the green pepper, bay leaf, thyme, lard or bacon fat, black pepper, sausage, and ham.

5. Add more water if necessary.

6. Cook for 30 minutes more, or until the beans are soft and the mixture is creamy.

7. Add the garlic and parsley.

8. Turn off the heat and cover until cool.

9. Serve the cooked beans over hot rice.

Mixed Greens

Serves 8
Cooking time: 2 hours

West Africans and African Americans eat cooked greens in great quantities in dishes with meat and peppers. When I was a child my mother had her own garden from which we ate fresh greens almost every day in the summer. This recipe can be cooked with all the different greens listed or just some of them and it is still healthy and good. I usually mix turnips, mustards, and kale, but cook my collards alone. Fresh onions, tomatoes, and peppers are always on the table and we season to suit our individual tastes. Once in a while my mother added ham hocks, salt pork, and ham bones to the pot, making the greens really delicious. I cook with just one of the meats in my greens.

8 pounds mixed mustard, collard, kale, and turnip greens

2 large ham hocks *or* 2 pounds of meaty ham bones *or* ½ pound salt pork

12 cups water

Hot sauce, peppers, and onion slices (optional to satisfy individual tastes)

1. Put the meat in a large boiling pot and cover with boiling water and bring to a boil.
2. Pick through the greens and remove any brown leaves.
3. Wash the greens well and drain.
4. Cut or tear the greens into small pieces.
5. Place the greens in the pot with the meat and reduce the heat to low.
6. Cook for about 2 hours, or until tender.

Corn on the Cob

Serves 12
Cooking time: 10 minutes

Corn is an important symbol of Kwanzaa and adds beautiful color to the Karamu table, whether a feast, a dinner party or a simple brunch. Corn can be boiled, fried, and is delicious roasted.

**12 ears of corn, shucked and cleaned of all silk, or enough
corn to serve the number of guests invited
Salt, butter, and freshly ground black pepper to taste**

1. Bring a large pot of water to a boil over high heat.
2. Place the corn in boiling water.
3. Boil for 5 minutes.
4. Serve hot with the salt, butter, and ground pepper available for individual tastes.

Odessa's Candied Yams

Serves 8–10
Cooking time: 25 minutes

In Africa there are fifty-nine varieties of yellowy white-fleshed yams, but only five of them are eaten. There is no similarity between the yams found in Africa and what we call yams, because the yams here are really sweet potatoes. Candying the potatoes is one way to eat them. They can also be baked, fried, or eaten raw.

6 medium yams

1 teaspoon nutmeg

1 teaspoon cinnamon

1 cup water

1 cup sugar

8 tablespoons butter, salted or unsalted

2 teaspoons vanilla extract

1. Peel the yams and slice them lengthwise.
2. Place the yams in a large pot, cover with water, and bring to a boil.
3. Drain half the water and place the yams and remaining water in a large skillet or pan.
4. Sprinkle with half the nutmeg, cinnamon, and sugar.
5. Bring to a boil and cook for approximately 3 minutes.
6. Add the remaining nutmeg, cinnamon, sugar, and the vanilla extract.
7. Spoon the mixture over all the yams and allow to simmer slowly for 15 minutes until the yams have absorbed all the syrup.
8. Remove from the heat until ready to serve.

Judy Griffie's Succotash

Serves 8
Cooking time: 1 hour and 10 minutes

This dish is a Kwanzaa favorite, although it was originally a Native American dish. It includes many traditional African American foods that add color to the Karamu.

> **4 medium onions, chopped**
> **3 cups fresh corn kernels, taken from the cob (or frozen kernels)**
> **2 tablespoons vegetable oil**
> **8 ripe tomatoes, skinned, seeded, and chopped**
> **1 pound fresh okra, sliced**
> **Salt and freshly ground black pepper to taste**
> **½ cup water, or enough to cover the okra and tomatoes.**

1. Saute the onions and corn kernels in the vegetable oil in a heavy saucepan.
2. Add the tomatoes and okra. Cover with water.
3. Season with salt and pepper to taste.
4. Simmer for one hour, adding more water if necessary.

Black-eyed Peas and Rice
(Hopping John)

Serves 8
Cooking time: 40 minutes

My Arkansas mother could cook the rice and peas together without the rice ending up on the bottom of the pot. I have never been able to cook like her; therefore, I use the simpler method of cooking the peas and rice separately.

> **1 pound dried black-eyed peas, rinsed and all the stones**
>   **picked out**
> **½ pound salt pork**
> **1 Bermuda onion, quartered**
> **3 cloves garlic, minced**
> **2 quarts water**
> **1½ teaspoons salt**
> **4 cups cooked long-grain rice**

1. Let the peas stand for four hours or overnight.
2. Fry the salt pork until it is crisp, pour off excess fat.
3. Combine the black-eyed peas, garlic, onion, and salt pork in a 5 quart Dutch oven and bring to a boil for about a ½ hour.
4. Season with salt to taste.
5. Serve the peas over cooked rice.

Corn Fritters

Serves 8–12 (makes about 40 fritters)
Cooking time: 3 minutes per fritter

Corn fritters are little crunchy corn cakes that are perfect for brunch or dinner.

Vegetable oil for deep frying

2 cups flour

2 teaspoons baking powder

4 cups corn kernels (from the cob or frozen)

4 eggs, separated

1 cup heavy cream

2 teaspoons melted butter

1. Heat the oil in a heavy skillet at 375 degrees.

2. Combine the egg yolks and cream and beat in a medium-size mixing bowl.

3. Add the flour, salt, baking powder, and melted butter.

4. Beat the egg whites until stiff and fold in to the mixture.

5. Add the corn and stir until evenly distributed.

6. Drop spoonfuls of the batter into the skillet.

7. Fry each fritter for about three minutes or until golden brown.

8. Serve hot.

Corn Pudding

Serves 10

Cooking time: 35 minutes (or until the mixture is a golden brown)

I first tasted corn pudding while visiting my in-laws in Kentucky. Since then this custard-like pudding has accompanied many of my Sunday dinners.

4 cups corn, freshly cut from the cob

½ cup sugar

1 teaspoon salt

Ground black pepper to taste

4 eggs lightly beaten

2 cups milk

½ teaspoon baking powder

8 tablespoons butter

1. Preheat the oven to 350 degrees.

2. Combine the corn, sugar, salt, and pepper in a large mixing bowl.

3. Stir in the eggs, milk, and baking powder and mix well.

4. Pour into an 8 x 8-inch baking dish and dot the top with the butter.

5. Bake for 30 minutes or until golden brown.

Robert's Home Fries

Serves 6–8
Cooking time: 30 minutes

Home fries are better than French fries and are perfect for serving at breakfast. They are an African American creation that stretched a meal and filled everyone's stomach.

6 large potatoes, peeled, washed, and cut into quarters

2 tablespoons vegetable oil

4 tablespoons olive oil

1 large Bermuda onion, sliced thinly

1–2 teaspoons salt

1 teaspoon ground black pepper

2 cloves garlic, chopped

1 teaspoon paprika

½ cup red bell peppers, diced

½ cup green bell peppers, diced

1. Combine the oils and heat in a cast-iron skillet.
2. Add the potatoes and cover.
3. Fry gently over medium heat until the potatoes are soft.
4. Remove the cover and add the onion, salt, pepper, garlic, paprika, and peppers.
5. Turn the potatoes and mix well.
6. Allow the bottom layer to brown; then turn and allow the top layer to brown.
7. Cook until all the potatoes are brown and crisp.

Fried Green Tomatoes

Serves 8
Cooking time: 2–3 minutes

Fried green tomatoes are an African American tradition because tomatoes were so easily grown and available. We had a garden and my children's joy was watching the tomatoes until a green one was big enough
to fry. This is one of the first dishes I taught my children to cook.

4 large green tomatoes, sliced into ½-inch slices

Salt and ground black pepper to taste

1 cup cornmeal

½ cup vegetable oil

1. Sprinkle the tomatoes with salt and pepper.
2. Dredge each slice in cornmeal.
3. Heat the vegetable oil in a frying pan.
4. Brown the tomato slices on both sides,
5. Remove to a platter and drain on paper towels.

SALADS

Avocado and Cabbage Salad

Serves 8 to 10
Preparation time: 20 minutes

This salad is simple to prepare and is delicious when made with black-skinned Hass avocados.

4 cups finely shredded green or red cabbage

½ cup finely chopped onion

2 apples, cored and chopped, or 2 carrots, scraped and grated

2 ripe avocados, peeled, stoned, and diced

⅔ cup roasted peanuts, coarsely chopped

Favorite salad dressing

Fresh mint

1. Mix the cabbage, onion, apples or carrots, and avocado with the salad dressing.
2. Place in a serving dish.
3. Chop the fresh mint and sprinkle over the salad.
4. Sprinkle roasted peanuts over the salad.

Soufflé Omelet with Shrimp Salad

Serves: 6
Cooking time: 90 minutes

This recipe is a meal within itself and has nutrients from every food group. It is the centerpiece at a brunch because of the colorful foods it combines. The cooking time includes time needed to prepare the mayonnaise dressing.

¾ cup skim milk

12 eggs, separated

3 tablespoons brandy

6 teaspoons unsalted butter

1. Beat the milk, egg yolks, and brandy together.
2. Beat egg whites until stiff but not dry.
3. Stir ⅓ of the egg whites into the yolk mixture.
4. Gently fold the remainder of the whites into the yolk mixture.
5. Preheat a 9-inch frying pan over medium heat.
6. Melt the butter add the batter, and cover.
7. Make sure the heat penetrates the crust formed to ensure that the mixture is cooked.
8. After 5 minutes, remove the cover and transfer the pan to the broiler.
9. Broil for 3 minutes until the omelet is golden.

Shrimp Salad with Mayonnaise Dressing

3 egg yolks

1 tablespoon Dijon mustard

2 tablespoons white wine vinegar or lemon juice,

  plus 1 teaspoon lemon juice

½ cup safflower oil

¼ cup plus 1 tablespoon Neufchâtel

Salt and ground black pepper to taste

1 scallion, chopped

1 pound medium-size shrimp, fresh or frozen, peeled

⅛ teaspoon dill weed

1 sprig fresh parsley or dill for garnish

1. Place egg yolks and mustard in a blender or stir until well blended.

2. Slowly add 2 tablespoons wine vinegar or lemon juice and continue to blend.

3. Add oil slowly and continue blending until it flows into the mixture.

4. Mix in ¼ cup of the cheese.

5. Season to taste with salt and pepper.

6. Take two tablespoons of the mayonnaise and blend with the remaining cheese. (Save the remainder of the mayonnaise for serving with the salad.)

7. Mince the scallion.

8. Add the remaining salad ingredients.

9. Fold in the precooked shrimp.

10. Chill for 1 hour before serving.

11. Garnish with a sprig of parsley or dill.

Potato Salad

Serves 12–14
Cooking time: 30 minutes

Every family has its potato salad recipe. This one is a combination of different recipes I have gathered from aunts, uncles, friends, and my mother. This is a basic recipe, and you may add other vegetables to it.

4 pounds white potatoes, peeled and diced

1 medium red onion, minced

3 large celery ribs, minced

½ cup red bell pepper, minced

½ cup green bell pepper, minced

2 cups mayonnaise

5 tablespoons prepared mustard

10 hard-boiled eggs, peeled and quartered

4 tablespoons sweet pickle relish

Salt and ground black pepper to taste

1. Cover the potatoes with water and boil in a large heavy pot.
2. Cook until soft, about 20 minutes.
3. Drain the potatoes and cool.
4. Combine the onion, celery ribs, red bell pepper, green bell pepper, and eggs.
5. Add the drained diced potatoes to the vegetables.
6. Add the pickle relish and the mayonnaise and mix until the potatoes are covered.
7. Add the salt and pepper and mix the salad well.
8. Cover and refrigerate before serving.

BREADS AND CEREALS

French Toast

Serves 8
Cooking time: 15 minutes

One of the easiest dishes to teach a child is French toast because children really believe they are cooking when they mix the ingredients. At our house we didn't use a recipe; however, this one is adapted from John Pinderhughes's *Family of the Spirit Cookbook* and uses the same basic ingredients we used.

2 cups half and half or evaporated milk

8 eggs, lightly beaten

1/4 teaspoon cinnamon

1/4 teaspoon nutmeg

2 teaspoons vanilla extract

16 thick slices bread

1 stick butter

Confectioner's sugar

1/2 cup chopped pecans

Maple syrup

1. In a mixing bowl, mix the half and half or evaporated milk, eggs, cinnamon, nutmeg, and vanilla extract.
2. Heat the butter in a frying pan.
3. Dip the slices of bread in the mixture, covering both sides.
4. Brown the slices two at a time, adding more butter as needed.
5. Sprinkle with confectioner's sugar and chopped pecans and cover with maple syrup.

Basic Cass Tech Biscuits

Serves 8
Cooking time: 15 minutes

I learned this recipe from Mrs. Litwin, my home economics teacher in high school.

2 cups of unbleached flour all purpose flour

½ teaspoon baking powder

1 teaspoon sugar

½ teaspoon salt

5 tablespoons unsalted butter, cold

¾ cup half and half

1. Preheat the oven to 450 degrees.
2. Mix the flour, baking powder, sugar, and salt in a large mixing bowl.
3. Cut the butter into small pieces and add it to the dry ingredients.
4. Stir in the half and half until the dry mixture forms a ball.
5. Place the ball of dough on a lightly floured surface.
6. Knead the dough for about one minute and then pat it into a ¾-inch-high circle.
7. Cut biscuits from the dough with a 2–3-inch cookie cutter.
8. Arrange the biscuits on a greased baking sheet and cook for 15 minutes, or until golden brown.
9. Place the biscuits on a wire rack to cool before serving.

Dorothy Mae's Corn Bread

Serves 8
Cooking time: 25–30 minutes

I learned to make corn bread by watching my mother, who never mea-sured the ingredients. She just put a pinch of this and a cup of that, and the corn bread was always crunchy and good. I still make cornbread without measuring, but I checked with my friends to get these measure-ments.

2 cups yellow or white cornmeal, stone ground

1 cup unbleached all-purpose flour

1 teaspoon baking powder

¼ teaspoon salt

2 cups buttermilk

2 eggs, lightly beaten

1 tablespoon sugar

½ cup unsalted butter, melted

1. Preheat the oven to 350 degrees.
2. Mix the dry ingredients.
3. Add the buttermilk, eggs, and butter.
4. Pour into well-greased 9- or 10-inch round pan or an 8-inch square pan.
5. Bake 20 or 25 minutes until golden brown.

Breakfast Grits

Serves 6–8
Cooking time: 20 minutes

Grits are another form of dried corn that the Native Americans introduced to the settlers. No southern breakfast is complete without a dish of hominy grits.

5 cups water

1 cup grits

2 tablespoons butter

1 teaspoon salt

1 teaspoon ground black pepper

1. Place the water in a large pot and bring to a boil.
2. Stir the grits in slowly.
3. Bring to a boil, lower the heat, and simmer uncovered for 20 minutes.
4. When the grits have thickened, remove the pot from the heat.
5. Stir in the butter.
6. Add salt and pepper to taste.

Banana Nut Bread

Serves 6–8 (makes 2 loaves)
Cooking time: 1 hour

Apples, zucchini, or other fruits or vegetables can be substituted for the bananas in this recipe.

2½ sticks unsalted butter, soft

4 cups all-purpose flour

1½ teaspoons baking powder

1 teaspoon ground nutmeg

½ teaspoon salt

5 large bananas, ripe

2 teaspoons vanilla extract

1 cup sugar

3 large eggs

½ cup raisins

1 cup chopped pecans

1. Preheat the oven to 350 degrees.
2. Sift the flour, baking powder, nutmeg, and salt in a bowl.
3. Mash the bananas until smooth and add the vanilla extract.
4. In a mixing bowl, cream the butter and sugar, add the eggs, and blend well.
5. Add the dry ingredients to the butter mixture; then add the bananas, raisins, and pecans until they are well blended.
6. Butter and flour two 9 × 5 × 3-inch loaf pans.
7. Divide the mixture in half and spoon into each loaf pan.
8. Bake 1 hour, or until golden brown.
9. Cool before removing from the loaf pans.

DESSERTS

Merdey Kerney's Fruit Nut Cake

Serves 25 (makes 3 loaves)
Cooking time: 60 minutes

Merdey gave me this easy and delicious recipe in 1969. I like cherries and nuts, but you may prefer to add pineapples, dates, and other dried fruits. After baking the cakes, I often sprinkle them with rum and get a taste that is fit for a queen.

1 cup granulated sugar

1 cup dark brown sugar

1 cup unsalted butter

8 eggs, separated, at room temperature

4 cups flour

8 cups glazed pineapple, about 3 pounds

8 cups glazed cherries

8 cups pecans (about 2 pounds)

2 tablespoons vanilla extract

½ teaspoon almond extract

Grated rind and juice of 1 lemon

Pinch of salt

1½ teaspoons baking powder

5 tablespoons heavy cream

1. Preheat the oven to 325 degrees. Butter three 9 × 5 × 3-inch loaf pans.

2. Combine the glazed pineapples, glazed cherries, and pecans in a large mixing bowl.

3. Mix in 1 cup of flour.

4. Combine the egg yolks and both sugars in a second

mixing bowl. Beat in the butter, cream, and vanilla and almond extracts.

5. Add the remainder of the flour and baking powder to the batter and stir.

6. Beat the egg whites in a separate bowl. Fold a quarter of the whites into the batter, mix, and then fold in the remainder.

7. Add the batter to the fruit mixture in the first bowl and mix well.

8. Spoon the mixture into the 3 loaf pans, cover with aluminum foil, and bake for 40 minutes.

9. Remove the foil and bake for an additional 20 minutes, or until the centers are firm.

10. Remove the loaves from the pans when cool and wrap tightly in plastic wrap until ready to serve.

Basic Pie Crust

Serves 8
Cooking time: dependent on pie or cobbler

I learned the secret of this recipe in high school: Use ice-cold water to mix the flour and shortening.

2 cups unbleached all-purpose flour

½ teaspoon salt

½ cup solid vegetable shortening (or lard), cold

2–4 tablespoons water, ice cold

1. Mix the flour and salt in a large mixing bowl.
2. Cut the shortening or lard into the mixture using a pastry cutter.
3. Add a tablespoon of water at a time and mix until the dough forms a ball.
4. Place the ball of dough on a lightly floured surface.
5. Roll out the dough until it is about 10 inches round and ⅛-inch thick. (For cobblers, I like a thicker crust, about ¼-inch thick.)
6. Fit into a 9-inch pie pan without stretching it.
7. Bake according to recipe instructions.

Sweet Potato Pie

Serves 8
Cooking time: about 30 minutes

I started making sweet potato pies when I was 12 years old and added all the spices that I saw my mother put in her pies. I have been making the pies this way since then, and they are rich and creamy. This recipe makes two pies; double or triple it for additional ones.

4–5 medium-size sweet potatoes, peeled, boiled, and mashed

1 cup granulated sugar

1 teaspoon cinnamon

1 teaspoon nutmeg

1 teaspoon allspice

1 teaspoon pure vanilla extract

1½ cup evaporated milk

5 large eggs

2 9-inch pie shells, unbaked (see Basic Pie Crust)

1. Preheat the oven to 325 degrees.

2. Combine the sugar, cinnamon, nutmeg, and allspice in a large bowl.

3. Stir in the sweet potatoes.

4. Add the vanilla, evaporated milk, and eggs.

5. Using a hand mixer or rotary mixer, beat until the mixture is smooth.

6. Pour the mixture into the uncooked pie shells.

7. Bake until a knife inserted in the filling comes out clean.

Grandma's Peach Cobbler

Serves 12
Cooking time: 30 minutes

Cakes are not my specialty, but I have always been able to make pies and cobblers, and I am teaching my youngest daughter, Tiaudra, to make this one now. The secret to a good cobbler is the rich crust that cradles the peaches.

3 29-ounce cans cling peaches, halved, quartered, sliced (or 10–15 medium-size ripe peaches, peeled, pitted, and sliced)

1½ cups sugar

2 sticks unsalted butter

2 tablespoons cinnamon

2 tablespoons nutmeg

2 unbaked pie shells, ¼-inch thick (see Basic Pie Crust)

1. Preheat the oven to 375 degrees.
2. Combine peaches (fresh or canned), water, sugar, cinnamon, and nutmeg in a mixing bowl.
3. Cut the butter and dot the peaches with it.
4. Cover the bottom of a 1½-quart deep dish baking dish with 1 pie shell.
5. Trim the edges of the dough and place them in the peaches.
6. Cover the entire top of the peaches with the second pie shell.
7. Bake 30 minutes, or until the crust is golden brown.
8. Serve in small bowls, plain or topped with vanilla ice cream or whipped cream.

Pound Cake

Serves 10
Cooking time: 1 hour

I am not a cake baker and so I leave cake baking to those who can. My daughter Schiavi is the cake maker in our family and does an excellent job. This is her recipe. Many cooks use loaf pans, but Schiavi uses a round pan.

> **4 cups cake flour**
>
> **½ teaspoon salt**
>
> **¼ teaspoon baking powder**
>
> **1 pound unsalted butter at room temperature**
>
> **4 cups granulated sugar**
>
> **8 large eggs**
>
> **2 teaspoons vanilla extract**
>
> **1¼ cups sour cream**

1. Preheat the oven to 350 degrees.
2. Butter and flour a baking pan.
3. Cream the butter and sugar in a large mixing bowl.
4. Beat the eggs for two minutes.
5. Add ⅓ of the eggs and ⅓ of the flour to the butter and sugar.
6. Mix thoroughly with an electric mixer.
7. Repeat this procedure until the other ⅔ of the eggs and the flour are added and mixed thoroughly.
8. Add the vanilla, sour cream, salt, and baking powder and mix well.
9. Pour into a 10-by-3-inch-round baking pan and bake for 1 hour, or until golden brown.
10. Cool on a wire rack before serving.

Banana Pudding with Meringue Topping

Serves 8
Cooking time: 30 minutes

Puddings, like those of rice or corn, were often made from leftovers. Banana pudding is made with cookies. If you wish, you can make a pound cake (see Pound Cake recipe) and layer it with the banana pudding. This recipe calls for a meringue topping, although many people top the pudding with whipped cream. Use whichever topping you prefer.

8 ripe bananas, sliced in rounds ¼-inch thick

4 yolks of large eggs, at room temperature

4 cups milk, heated

1 12-ounce box vanilla wafers

1 teaspoon vanilla extract

1 cup granulated sugar

½ cup light cream

1. Preheat the oven to 350 degrees.
2. Combine the the milk, sugar, egg yolks, and vanilla in a mixing bowl and stir.
3. Pour the milk and cream into a saucepan or double boiler and heat until hot but not boiling.
4. Pour the milk mixture into the egg mixture.
5. Stir the mixture until it thickens and coats the spoon.
6. Spread a layer of the vanilla wafers over the bottom of a 9 × 14-inch baking dish.
7. Add a layer of cut bananas.
8. Pour half the pudding mixture over the bananas.
9. Continue to alternate the layers of vanilla wafers, bananas, and pudding mixture.

10. Top with the meringue and bake until the meringue is golden brown, about 5–10 minutes.

11. Refrigerate the pudding for an hour before serving.

Meringue

4 whites of large eggs, at room temperature
⅛ teaspoon cream of tartar
½ cup granulated sugar

1. Pour the egg whites into a medium-size mixing bowl.

2. Beat the egg whites with a portable hand mixer at medium speed until they are foamy.

3. Add the cream or tartar, increase the speed to high, and beat until peaks are formed.

4. Add the sugar and beat until the meringue is stiff.

5. Spread over the pudding.

Broiled Peaches

Serves 8
Cooking time: 10 minutes

When I was growing up on the east side of Detroit, practically every backyard had a peach tree or two. We ate fresh peaches walking to school. They were on every menu, in cobblers and in this simple recipe for broiled peaches from Jessica Harris's *The Welcome Table*, which is just like the one my mother used.

8 large freestone peaches, firm

2 29-ounce cans cling peach halves

3 tablespoons unsalted butter

3 tablespoons light brown sugar

1 teaspoon ground cinnamon

1 teaspoon ground nutmeg

½ teaspoon ground cloves

1. Cut the fresh peaches in halves.
2. Lay the halves, open side up, in a broiler-proof baking dish.
3. Place a small dot of butter in each peach half.
4. Mix the sugar and all the spices and sprinkle a bit on each peach half.
5. Place the baking dish under a broiler and broil until the peaches are lightly browned.

Pineapple Upside-Down Cake

Serves 8
Cooking time: 35 minutes

This is a family favorite and a beautiful addition to any table. I have tasted pear, peach, and apricot upside-down cakes, but pineapple is my favorite and the only one I make.

1 No. 2 can sliced pineapple

½ cup salted butter

3 tablespoons large pecans, whole

1 cup cake flour, sifted

⅛ teaspoon salt

1 teaspoon baking powder

1 cup granulated sugar

1 cup brown sugar

4 large eggs, separated

6 tablespoons pineapple juice

1. Preheat the oven to 375 degrees.
2. Melt the butter in a large 10 x 12-inch baking pan.
3. Spread the brown sugar evenly in the pan and place the pineapple slices over it.
4. Fill in all the spaces with the pecans.
5. Mix the flour, baking powder, and salt.
6. Beat the egg yolks. Add the granulated sugar gradually, then add the pineapple juice and flour.
7. Beat the egg whites until stiff and fold into the mixture.
8. Pour the batter over the pineapple slices and bake for 30–35 minutes. The cake should be browned and pulling away from the edges of the pan.
9. Cool and turn upside down onto a cake plate.

BEVERAGES

Chilled Coconut Milk and Pineapple Drink

Serves 12 cups
Preparation time: 2 hours

Coconuts are the fruit of the tropical palm tree. They are available year round, but are best in the fall and winter months when the juices don't ferment as quickly. This recipe combines coconuts with pineapples, which are best when picked in the spring. For this reason, I use canned fruits when I can't find them fresh. This cold drink is good any time of the year, especially during Kwanzaa.

> **8 cups coconut milk, made from 2 cups coarsely chopped
>   fresh coconut and 2 cups hot water**
> **10 cups chopped fresh pineapple**
> **8 tablespoons sugar**
> **Almond extract (optional)**

1. Combine the coconut milk, pineapple, and sugar in an electric blender.

2. Blend at high speed for 2 minutes, or until the mixture is pureed.

3. Pour the mixture into a sieve over a bowl to extract all the juice.

4. Discard the pulp.

5. Taste and add more sugar and almond extract, if desired.

6. Cover tightly and refrigerate for 2 hours.

Minted Iced Tea

Serves 10–12
Preparation time: 10 minutes

The best place to drink iced tea is in the Deep South where it is served as freely as water is served in most other states. You make a strong pitcher of hot tea, add ice to cool it, and mix in lots of sugar to suit your taste.

10 bags orange pekoe tea

2 quarts boiling water

10 sprigs fresh mint

Cold water to weaken, if necessary

Granulated sugar to taste

1. Place the teabags in a large pot, add the water, and bring to a boil.

2. Break 5 sprigs of mint in half and add to the boiling water.

3. Remove the pot from the heat and let the mixture steep for 20 minutes.

4. Add the remaining 5 sprigs of mint and allow to cool.

5. Place ice in tall glasses and pour in the tea.

6. Sweeten to taste and add cold water to weaken, if necessary.

Ginger Beer

Serves 10–12
Preparation time: 30 minutes

West Africans make ginger beer as easily as we make lemonade. This is one version of the drink; others add fruit or yeast. This recipe is from *A West African Cook Book* by Ellen Gibson Wilson.

½ pound fresh ginger root, peeled and grated or thinly sliced
2 quarts boiling water
Juice of 2 lemons (or ½ cup lemon juice)
2 cups sugar, or to taste
6 whole cloves or a stick of cinnamon (optional)
Ice cubes

1. Boil 1 quart of water, the cloves or cinnamon, and ginger *for 20 minutes.*
2. Stir in the lemon juice and sugar and cool.
3. Strain the mixture and add the remaining water and ice cubes.
4. Serve cold.

GLOSSARY AND PRONUNCIATION KEY

bendara (behn-DEH-rah): the red, black, and green flag of African Americans, created by Marcus Garvey

Fu Fu (Foo-Foo): A dish that accompanies many stews and meats made by pounding yams, cassava, cocayam, or plantain

Habari gani (hah-BAH-ree GAH-nee): Kwanzaa greeting in Swahili, meaning "What's up?"

Harambee! (Hah-rahm-BEH): the call to unity and collective work. It is always said in sets of seven to honor and recall the seven principles of Kwanzaa

Imani (ee-MAH-nee): faith, the seventh principle of Kwanzaa, meaning belief in self and our leaders and teachers

Karamu (kah-RAH-moo): the Kuumba feast held on the sixth day of Kwanzaa, December 31

kikombe cha umoja (kee-KOM-beh-chah oo-MOH-jah): the unity cup, one of the symbols of Kwanzaa

kinara (kee-NAH-rah): the candle holder, one of the symbols of Kwanzaa

Kuchunguza tena na kutoa shadi tena (koo-choon-goo-zah tay-nuh koo-toe-ah shah-dee tay-nah): reassessment and recommitment

Kujichagulia: (koo-ji-chah-goo-LEE-ah): self-determination, the second principle of Kwanzaa, meaning acting and speaking for oneself

Kukaribisha: the welcoming statement said at the beginning of the Karamu feast on the sixth day of Kwanzaa

Kukumbuka: (koo-KOOM-bu-KAH): remembering

Kushangilia: (koo-SHAN-gee-la): rejoicing and praising through group songs or poetry

Kutoa majin (koo-Toe-ah MAY-jeen): calling the names of family ancestors and African-descended heroes

Kuumba (koo-OOM-bah): creativity, the sixth principle of Kwanzaa, meaning using one's talents and creativity to think of new ways to do things and solve problems

Kwanzaa (KWAHN-zah): the African American holiday celebrated from December 26 through January 1. It is from the Swahili phrase "ya kwanza," which means first fruits

mazao (mah-ZAH-oh): the fruits, nuts, and vegetables that represent the work of the people, one of the symbols of Kwanzaa

mishumaa saba (mee-shoo-MAH SAH-bah): the seven candles (three green, one black, and three red), one of the symbols of Kwanzaa

muhindi (moo-HIN-dee): the corn representing the children in the family, one of the symbols of Kwanzaa

Nguzo Saba (nn-GOO-zoh SAH-bah): The Swahili term for the seven principles of Kwanzaa

Nia (NEE-ah): purpose, the fourth principle of Kwanzaa, meaning having a purpose for doing what you do

Swahili (swah-HEE-lee): a language of East Africa that is also called Kiswahili

tambiko (tam-BEE-koh): the libation, which is usually water or fruit juice (the essence of life), performed at the beginning and end of the Karamu feast on the sixth day of Kwanzaa

Tamshi la tambiko (tam-SHEE-la tam-BEE-koh): libation statement or toast to the ancestors and to posterity, said at the beginning and end of the Karamu feast, respectively, on the sixth day of Kwanzaa

Tamshi la tutaonana (tam-SHEE-la TOOT-ah-ona-na): farewell statement, said at the close of the Karamu feast

Ujamaa (oo-jah-MAH): businesses, the fourth principle of Kwanzaa, meaning that we support each other in our businesses

Ujima (oo-JEE-mah): working together, the third principle of Kwanzaa, meaning that we work together to achieve our goals

Umoja (oo-MOH-ja): unity, the first principle of Kwanzaa, meaning that we stay together under all circumstances

zawadi (zah-WAH-dee): gifts, representing commitment or promises kept, one of the symbols of Kwanzaa

CONTRIBUTORS

CHINUA ACHEBE is an internationally known Nigerian-born novelist and poet, who also works as a journalist, publisher, and teacher. He is best known for his novels *Things Fall Apart, No Longer at Ease, Arrow of God,* and *Anthills of the Savannahs.*

JAMES AGGREY (1872–1927) was the first African to receive a Ph.D. from Columbia. He was a famous orator who organized the first African American credit union in America. He founded Achimata College in Ghana and later worked at Livingstone College in North Carolina. He is buried on the campus of Livingstone.

MARGARET WALKER ALEXANDER was born in Birmingham, Alabama, in 1915, and graduated from Northwestern University in 1935. Her first book of poems, *For My People,* was published in 1942. She is a griot who grew up in a family of talkers that focused on African American history. She worked on the Federal Writer's Project that included Richard Wright in 1937, and went on to earn her Ph.D from the University of Iowa. She lives in Jacksonville, Mississippi, where she is the director of the Institute for the Study of the History, Life, and Culture of Black People at Jackson State University.

SAMI BENTIL is a fine artist and poet from Ghana, who lives in Texas, where he continues to work in all mediums.

ANDREW BILLINGSLEY is professor and chair of the Department of Family Studies at the University of Maryland. He is a leading scholar on the African American experience and the author of *Climbing Jacob's Ladder* and *Black Families in White America,* among other works.

WILLIAM STANLEY BRAITHWAITE (1898–1962) was born in Boston. He received the Spingarn Award for his poetry in 1918. He received many honorary degrees during his career and taught literature at Atlanta University until 1945.

GWENDOLYN BROOKS, a native of Topeka, Kansas, won the American Academy of Arts and Letters Award and a Guggenheim Fellowship in 1947. Three years later, she won the Pulitzer Prize for poetry for her collection *Annie Allen.* Her first book of poetry, *A Street in Bronzeville,* was published in 1945 and is still a favorite of young readers and teachers. She is also the author of many children's books. She lives in the heart of Chicago where she continues to write and mentor aspiring poets and writers as the Poet Laureate of Illinois.

DONALD CALLOWAY, a native of Detroit, is a multitalented media artist who creates memorable paintings and drawings in oils, watercolor, and pastels, as well as sculpture. This self-taught artist further perfected his talents while attending Wayne State University and the Center for Creative Studies in Detroit, Michigan. He has received local, national, and international acclaim. Calloway created the line drawings that introduce each chapter of this book.

ELIZABETH CATLETT is an internationally known painter, sculptor, and printmaker who was born in Washington, D.C. She is known for art that preserves African American cultural traditions. She became a citizen of Mexico in 1962, so she could continue her political activism.

RITA DOVE received the 1987 Pulitzer Prize for her book of poems, *Thomas and Beulah*. She is the poet laureate of the United States and has published both poetry and short stories.

HENRY DUMAS was born in Sweet Home, Arkansas, in 1934 and moved to New York, where he was killed by a subway policeman in Harlem in 1964. His *Ark of Bones and Other Stories, Rope of Wind, Jonah and the Green Stone*, and *Knees of a Natural Man: Selected Poems of Henry Dumas* were all published after his death.

JAMES A. EMANUEL was born in 1921 in Nebraska. He earned a Ph.D. from Columbia University and taught English at The City College of New York. He is also a writer, poet, critic, teacher, and editor. He now lives in Paris.

MARI EVANS is a poet, writer, and editor who lives in Indianapolis, Indiana. Her work appears in numerous anthologies and periodicals. Her poetry collections include *I Am a Black Woman, Nightstar*, and *A Dark and Splendid Mass*.

NIKKI GIOVANNI is a professor, poet, and writer from Knoxville, Tennessee, who has authored more than eight books. She is currently professor of English at Virginia Polytechnic University in Blacksburg, Virginia.

LORNA GOODISON, born in Kingston, Jamaica, has worked as an art teacher, advertising copywriter, and scriptwriter, and is an internationally known poet. Her published books of poetry are *Tamarand Season, I Am Becoming My Mother,* and *Heartease.* She has also published a book of short stories, *Baby Mother and the King of Swords.*

SERENA GORDON was born in London and her writing is included in *Daughters of the Dust,* international collection of writing by women of color.

JUDY BOSWELL GRIFFIE, a former teacher, writer, and poet from Kansas City, Kansas, now works for the Chrysler Corporation as a writer.

ROBERT HAYDEN (1913–1980) was born in Detroit, where he also published his first book of poetry, *Heart-shape in the Dust.* He was a professor of writing at Fisk University from 1946–1968 and received many awards and prizes. He returned to Michigan to work at the University of Michigan, where, during his graduate student days, he had been forced to live in segregated housing. In 1976, Hayden became the first African American to serve as Poetry Consultant at the Library of Congress.

ZORA NEALE HURSTON, who was born in 1881 in Eatonville, Florida, pioneered anthropological research in the South and the Caribbean to preserve African American culture. She was associated with the Harlem Renaissance of the 1920s, which also included such writers as Arna Bontemps, Langston Hughes, Claude McKay, Countee Cullen, James Weldon Johnson, and Jean Toomer. Before her death in 1960, she published seven books, three novels, two works of folklore, and an autobiography.

JAMES WELDON JOHNSON, born in Jacksonville, Florida, in 1871, was a man of many accomplishments: attorney, writer, poet, songwriter, professor, American Consul in Venezuela and Nicaragua, and a founder and secretary of the NAACP. He is remembered and honored for writing the words to "Lift Every Voice and Sing." He died in 1938.

JAMAL JONES, a native of Chattanooga, Tennessee, is a self-taught artist, who is nationally known for his bright, vibrant colors and pictures filled with exact details. Jones works in all mediums: oils, pastels, acrylics, and pen and ink. The drawings in this book are from a series and are done in colorful acrylic.

ANEB KGOSITSILE (Gloria House) taught humanities at Wayne State University in Detroit and has been active in political and cultural organizations in the African American community. Her political concerns led her to relocate her present home in South Africa.

JULIUS NYERERE, born in 1922, is the former president of Tanzania who stepped down in 1985. During his twenty-four years as president, he introduced free and universal education and raised the standard of living of the people.

SHIRLEY WOODSON REID is a multitalented artist who works in all mediums. She was a professor of art at Eastern Michigan University and is currently the director of art for the Detroit Public Schools. Her work is found in national collections and anthologies and is part of the collection of the Detroit Institute of Arts.

TIAUDRA RILEY, a student at Spelman College in Atlanta, was born in Detroit. She will graduate in 1997 with a degree in psychology and a minor in English. She has been writing short stories and poetry since she was seven years old.

BILL SANDERS is a native of Memphis, Tennessee, who carried a camera with him from elementary school. He was inspired to pursue photography as a profession after taking one class at a community college in Detroit. From that stimulus in 1976, he worked persistently to earn a master of fine arts degree from Wayne State University in 1987. His works are in the collections of the Detroit Institute of Arts, Los Angeles African American Museum, and other major institutions and corporations. He photographed many of the works illustrated in this book.

AUGUSTA SAVAGE, born in Florida in 1900, began her art career by modeling clay figures when she was six years old. She studied at the Tallahassee Normal School (Florida A & M) and in France. She started an art school in New York and won grants to provide free art classes to children.

HOWARD THURMAN, the distinguished theologian, poet, and mystic, lived from 1900 to 1981. He was the dean of Morehouse College,

Howard University, and Boston College. He founded the Church for the Fellowship of All People in San Francisco and wrote more than twenty books.

JEAN TOOMER, a metaphysician, poet, and short story writer, was born in Washington, D.C., in 1894 and died in 1967. A major figure of the Harlem Renaissance of the 1920s, he is known for the work *Cane*, a collection of poems and short stories.

BIBLIOGRAPHY

"A Galaxy of Expectations: Astronaut Mae Jemison." *Sisters*, Spring 1989.

Abraham, Roger D., ed. *Afro-American Folktales*. New York: Pantheon, 1985.

Achebe, Chinua. *Things Fall Apart*. New York: Fawcett Crest, 1958.

Anderson, Chris. "Meet Oprah Winfrey." *Good Housekeeping*, August 1986, pp. 37–39.

Angelou, Maya. *The Heart of a Woman*. New York: Bantam Books, 1982.

"An Intimate Talk with Oprah Winfrey." *Essence*, August 1987.

Anyasodo, Umunnakwe. *Ebolachi: Have You Survived the Night?* Detroit: self-published, 1975.

Awiatka, Marilou. *Selu: Seeking the Corn Mother's Wisdom*. Golden, Colorado: Fulcrum Publishing, 1993.

Baldwin, James, *No Name in the Street*. New York: Dial, 1972.

Ball, Millie. "Ad Whiz Was on Her Way with Her First SBA Loan." *New Orleans Times-Picayune*, April 30, 1977.

Bethune, Mary McLeod, "My Last Will and Testament." *Ebony*, August 1955.

Billingsley, Andrew. *Climbing Jacob's Ladder*. New York: Simon & Schuster, 1992.

Bly, Nellie. *Oprah! Up Close and Down Home*. New York: Zebra, 1993.

Brewer, J. Mason. *American Negro Folklore*. Chapel Hill: University of North Carolina Press, 1988.

Brooks, Gwendolyn. *Family Picture*. Detroit: Broadside Press, 1975.

———. *Blacks*. Chicago: Third World Press, 1991.

Busby, Margaret. *Daughters of the Dust*. New York: Pantheon, 1992.

Casey, Kathryn. "The Mystery of Oprah and Millions of Other Women." *Ladies' Home Journal*, November 1992, pp. 269–72.

Chapelle, Tony. "The Reigning Queen of TV Talk: Oprah." *Black Collegian*, 21: November–December 1990, p. 14.

Cleage, Pearl. "Diana: Down to Earth." *Essence*, October 1989, pp. 71–73.

Collins, Marva. *Choosing to Succeed* (pamphlet). General Foods, 1986.

Courlander, Harold, and Wolfe Lesnau. *The Fire on The Mountain*. New York: Holt, Rinehart & Winston, 1950.

Current Biography. New York: H. N. Wilson, 1989–1994.

Davis, Benjamin O. *An Autobiography: Benjamin O. Davis, Jr., American*. Washington, D.C.: Smithsonian Institution Press, 1991.

Douglass, Frederick. *North Star* (editorial), December 3, 1847.

Dove, Rita. "The Musician Talks about 'Process.'" *Chelsea* 49, 1990.

Du Bois, W. E. B. *An ABC of Color: Selections from Over a Half-Century of the Writings of W. E. B. Du Bois.* New York: Seven Seas Press, 1946.

Dudley, Percy. "Entrepreneur Urges Women to Take Control of Their Lives." *Atlanta Constitution*, September 24, 1987.

Dudley Hair Products Company Newsletter, Spring 1994.

Dumas, Henry. *Play Ebony, Play Ivory*, edited by Eugene Redmond. New York: Random House, 1974.

Edelman, Marian Wright. *The Measure of Our Success: A Letter to My Children and Yours.* Boston: Beacon Press, 1992.

Fitzgerald, Sharon. "Catalyst Camille." *American Visions.* December–January 1995, pp. 20–23.

Frankie, Richie L. "Proctor Takes a Gamble and Hits the Jackpot." *Working Woman*, August 1979, p. 19.

Fraser, George. *Success Runs in Our Race.* New York: William Morrow, 1994.

Friere, Paulo. "Pedagogy of the Oppressed."

Gaston, Arthur G. *The Successful Way of A. G. Gaston.* Baton Rouge, Louisiana: Southern University Press, 1968.

Giovanni, Nikki. *Cotton Candy on a Rainy Day.* New York: William Morrow/Quill, 1978.

Goldberg, Whoopi. "My Role Models." *Cosmopolitan*, April 1992, p. 228.
———. *Entertainment Weekly 1992 Year End Special*, p. 25.

Goodison, Lorna. *Heartease.* London: The New Beacon Press, 1992.

Gordy, Berry. *To Be Loved: The Music, the Magic, the Memories of Motown.* New York: Warner Books, 1994.

Haley, Alex, and Malcolm X. *Autobiography of Malcolm X.* New York: Grove Press, 1965.

Harris, Jessica. B. *The Welcome Table: African American Heritage Cooking.* New York: Simon & Schuster, 1995.

Harrison, Barbara. "The Importance of Being Oprah." *The New York Times Magazine* 138, June 11, 1989, p. 28.

Hayden, Robert. *Selected Poems by Robert Hayden.* October House, 1966.

Holmes, Ernest. *The Science of Mind.* New York: G. P. Putnam's Sons, 1938.

Howard, Jeff. "The Third Movement: Developing Black Children for the 21st Century." *The State of Black America.* New York: National Urban League, Inc., January 1993.

Johnson, James Weldon. *Along This Way.* New York: Viking Press, 1961. First published in 1933.

Johnson, Marta C. "Upward with Worldly Lessons." *Greensboro News and Record,* January 28, 1991, p. 8.

Jordan, Michael. *Rare Air: Michael on Michael.* San Francisco: Collins Publishers, 1993.

Kage, Elizabeth. "The Face of Success." *Working Woman,* October 1993, p. 53.

Karenga, Maulena. *Kwanzaa: Origins, Concepts, Practices.* Los Angeles: Kwaida Publications, 1977.

Kerlins, Robert. *Negro Poets and their Poetry,* 3rd ed. New York: Associated Publishers, 1935.

Kerman, Cynthia, and Richard Eldridge. *The Lives of Jean Toomer: A Hunger for Wholeness.* Baton Rouge: Louisiana State University Press, 1987.

Kgositsile, Aneb. *blood river.* Detroit: Broadside Press, 1983.

Killens, John O. *An ABC of Color: Selections from Over a Half-Century of the Writings of W. E. B. Du Bois.* New York: Seven Seas Press, 1946.

Kimbro, Dennis. *Think and Grow Rich: A Black Choice.* New York: Fawcett Crest, 1991.

King, Martin Luther, Jr. "Facing the Challenge of a New Age." *Phylon,* vol. 28, April 1957, pp. 24–26.

Kluger, Richard. *Simple Justice.* New York: Random House, 1977.

Madhabuti, Haki. *Kwanzaa: A Progressive and Uplifting African American Holiday.* Chicago: Third World Press, 1972.

Malcolm X. *Malcolm X Speaks: Selected Speeches and Statements.* New York: Merit, 1965.

Malveaux, Julienne. "Maxine Waters: Woman of the House." *Ladies' Home Journal,* August 1992, p. 35.

Mays, Benjamin. "What Man Lives By." *Best Black Sermons,* edited by William M. Philpot. Valley Forge, PA: Judson Press, 1972.

McClester, Cedric. *Kwanzaa: Everything You Wanted to Know But Didn't Know Where to Ask.* New York: Gumbs and Thomas, 1990.

Mixon, Veronica. "An Author's Best Ally: Black Agents Break Through." *Emerge,* April 1993, pp. 53–54.

Niane, D. T. *Sundiata as Recited by Griot Mamdou Kouyate,* translated from the French by G. D. Pickett. London: Longman Group, 1965.

"1988 Essence Awards." *Essence,* October 1988, pp. 59–60.

Nyerere, Julius. *Freedom and Socialism: A Selection from Writings and Speeches, 1965–1967.* New York: Oxford University Press, 1968.

——. *Ujamaa!* United Kingdom: Oxford University Press, 1968.

Olson, Lynn. "Jeff Howard's Third Movement." *Education Week,* December 8, 1993, pp. 18–23.

Pinderhughes, John. *Family of the Spirit Cookbook*. New York: Simon & Schuster, 1990.

Puckett, Newbill Niles. "Race, Pride, and Folklore." *Opportunity*, 1926.

Randolph, Laura B. "The Whoopi Nobody Knows." *Ebony*, March 1991, pp. 110–12, 114–16.

Rensin, David. "Whoopi Goldberg, the US Interview." *US*, October 1992, p. 67–72.

Robeson, Paul. *Here I Stand*. Othello Associates (self-published), 1958.

Ross, Diana. *Secrets of a Sparrow*. New York: Villard Books, 1993.

Rowan, Carl. *Dream Makers: The World of Justice Thurgood Marshall*. Boston: Little, Brown and Company, 1993.

Smith, Edwin. *Aggrey of Africa*. New York: Doubleday Doran, 1929.

"Space Is Her Destination." *Ebony*, October 1987, pp. 93–98.

Stewart, Julia. *African Names*. New York: Carol Publishing, 1994.

Taylor, Susan L. *In the Spirit*. New York: HarperCollins, 1994.

———. "Your Spiritual Armor." *Essence*, March 1993.

Tomkins, Calvin. "Profiles: A Sense of Urgency." *The New Yorker*, March 1989, pp. 48–74.

Walker, Alice. *Revolutionary Petunias*. New York: Harcourt Brace, 1971.

Washington, Booker T. *Up from Slavery*. New York: A. L. Burt, 1901.

Washington, James, ed. *Testament of Hope: the Essential Writings of Martin Luther King, Jr*. New York: Harper & Row, 1969.

Williams, Chancellor. *The Destruction of Black Civilization: Great Issues of a Race from 4000 B.C. to A.D. 2000* Chicago: Third World Press, 1976.

Wilson. Ellen Gibson. *A West African Cook Book*. Philadelphia: J. B. Lippincott, 1971.

Winfrey, Oprah. "Wind Beneath My Wings." *Essence*, June 1989, pp. 46–48.

Woods, Sylvia, and Christopher Styler. *Sylvia's Soul Food*. New York: Hearst Books, 1992.

COPYRIGHT
ACKNOWLEDGMENTS

INDEX